C000015499

Foundations in Accountancy / ACCA

Financial Accounting (FFA/FA)

Welcome to BPP Learning Media's Practice & Revision Kit for FFA/FA. In this Practice & Revision Kit, which has been reviewed by the **ACCA examining team**, we:

- Include **Do you know?** Checklists to test your knowledge and understanding of topics

- Provide you with **two** mock exams including the Specimen Exam

- Provide the **ACCA's exam answers** to the Specimen Exam as an additional revision aid

FOR EXAMS FROM 1 SEPTEMBER 2018 TO 31 AUGUST 2019

BPP LEARNING MEDIA

First edition May 2011
Seventh edition February 2018

ISBN 9781 5097 1755 2
Previous ISBN 9781 5097 1138 3
e-ISBN 9781 5097 1904 4

British Library Cataloguing-in-Publication Data
A catalogue record for this book
is available from the British Library

Published by

BPP Learning Media Ltd
BPP House, Aldine Place
London W12 8AA

www.bpp.com/learningmedia

Printed in the United Kingdom

Your learning materials, published by BPP Learning Media Ltd, are
printed on paper sourced from sustainable, managed forests.

We are grateful to the Association of Chartered Certified Accountants
for permission to reproduce past examination questions. The
suggested solutions in the practice answer bank have been prepared
by BPP Learning Media Ltd, except where otherwise stated.

BPP Learning Media is grateful to the IASB for permission to
reproduce extracts from the International Financial Reporting
Standards including all International Accounting Standards, SIC and
IFRIC Interpretations (the Standards). The Standards together with
their accompanying documents are issued by:

The International Accounting Standards Board (IASB) 30 Cannon
Street, London, EC4M 6XH, United Kingdom. Email: info@ifrs.org
Web: www.ifrs.org

Contents

Page

Finding questions

    Question index v

Helping you with your revision.. viii

    Using your BPP Practice & Revision Kit... ix

    Passing the FFA/FA exam x

    Approach to examining the syllabus x

    Tackling Multiple Choice Questions... xi

    Using your BPP products.. xii

Questions and answers

    Questions 3

    Answers 177

Exam practice

    Mock exam 1 – ACCA Specimen Exam

       ●   Questions.. 245

       ●   Answers... 259

    ACCA's exam answers to Specimen Exam 267

    Mock exam 2

       ●   Questions.. 275

       ●   Answers... 289

Review form

Contents

Question index

	Marks	Time allocation Mins	Page Question	Page Answer
Part A: The context and purpose of financial reporting				
The context and purpose of financial reporting				
Questions 1.1 to 1.14	28	34	5	177
Part B: The qualitative characteristics of financial information				
The qualitative characteristics of financial information				
Questions 2.1 to 2.13	26	31	11	178
Part C: The use of double entry and accounting systems				
Double entry bookkeeping				
Questions 3.1 to 3.19	38	46	17	179
Questions 4.1 to 4.18	36	43	20	180
Part D: Recording transactions and events				
Sales tax				
Questions 5.1 to 5.8	16	19	27	182
Inventory				
Questions 6.1 to 6.19	38	46	28	183
Tangible non-current assets				
Questions 7.1 to 7.19	38	46	34	186
Questions 8.1 to 8.20	40	48	39	188
Intangible non-current assets				
Questions 9.1 to 9.12	24	34	43	190
Accruals and prepayments				
Questions 10.1 to 10.15	30	36	46	191
Receivables and payables				
Questions 11.1 to 11.20	40	48	50	194
Provisions and contingencies				
Questions 12.1 to 12.13	26	31	54	196
Capital structure and finance costs				
Questions 13.1 to 13.14	28	34	58	197

	Marks	Time allocation Mins	Page Question	Page Answer
Part E: Preparing a trial balance				
15 mark question: trial balance				
Question 14.1	15	18	65	199
Control accounts				
Questions 15.1 to 15.19	38	53	66	200
Bank reconciliations				
Questions 16.1 to 16.15	30	36	72	203
Correction of errors				
Questions 17.1 to 17.18	36	44	76	204
Suspense accounts				
Questions 18.1 to 18.11	22	27	80	206
Part F: Preparing basic financial statements				
15 mark questions: preparing basic financial statements				
Questions 19.1 to 19.7	105	126	87	207
Incomplete records				
Questions 20.1 to 20.16	32	38	97	213
Company financial statements				
Questions 21.1 to 21.10	20	24	101	215
Disclosure notes				
Questions 22.1 to 22.9	18	22	103	216
Events after the reporting period				
Questions 23.1 to 23.9	18	22	105	216
Statements of cash flows				
Questions 24.1 to 24.21	42	51	108	217
Part G: Preparing simple consolidated financial statements				
15 mark questions: preparing simple consolidated financial statements				
Questions 25.1 to 25.4	60	72	117	218
Consolidated financial statements				
Questions 26.1 to 26.27	54	65	124	221

	Marks	Time allocation Mins	Page Question	Page Answer
Part H: Interpretation of financial statements				
15 mark question: interpretation of financial statements				
Question 27.1	15	18	135	225
Interpretation of financial statements				
Questions 28.1 to 28.11	22	26	136	225
Mixed banks				
Mixed bank 1: Questions 29.1 to 29.19	38	46	138	226
Mixed bank 2: Questions 30.1 to 30.20	40	48	143	228
Mixed bank 3: Questions 31.1 to 31.19	38	46	149	230
Mixed bank 4: Questions 32.1 to 32.17	34	43	155	232
Mixed bank 5: Questions 33.1 to 33.20	40	48	160	234
Mixed bank 6: Questions 34.1 to 34.18	36	41	165	236
Mixed bank 7: Questions 35.1 to 35.18	36	43	170	238
Mock exams				
Mock exam 1 (ACCA Specimen Exam)	100	120	245	259
Mock exam 2	100	120	275	289

BPP Learning Media – ACCA Approved Content Provider

As an ACCA **Approved Content Provider**, BPP Learning Media gives you the **opportunity** to use revision materials reviewed by the ACCA examining team. By incorporating the ACCA examining team's comments and suggestions regarding the depth and breadth of syllabus coverage, the BPP Learning Media Practice & Revision Kit provides excellent, **ACCA-approved** support for your revision.

These materials are reviewed by the ACCA examining team. The objective of the review is to ensure that the material properly covers the syllabus and study guide outcomes, used by the examining team in setting the exams, in the appropriate breadth and depth. The review does not ensure that every eventuality, combination or application of examinable topics is addressed by the ACCA Approved Content. Nor does the review comprise a detailed technical check of the content as the Approved Content Provider has its own quality assurance processes in place in this respect.

Selecting questions

We provide signposts to help you plan your revision, including a full **question index**.

Attempting mock exams

There are two mock exams that provide practice at coping with the pressures of the exam day. We strongly recommend that you attempt them under exam conditions. **Mock exam 1** is the ACCA Specimen Exam. **Mock exam 2** reflects the question styles and syllabus coverage of the exam.

Using your BPP Practice & Revision Kit

Aim of this Practice & Revision Kit

To provide the practice to help you succeed in the examination for *FFA/FA Financial Accounting.*

To pass the examination you need a thorough understanding in all areas covered by the syllabus and teaching guide.

Recommended approach

- Make sure you are able to answer questions on **everything** specified by the syllabus and teaching guide. You cannot make any assumptions about what questions may come up in your exam. The examining team aims to discourage 'question spotting'.

- Learning is an **active** process. Use the **DO YOU KNOW?** Checklists to test your knowledge and understanding of the topics covered in *FFA/FA Financial Accounting* by filling in the blank spaces. Then check your answers against the **DID YOU KNOW?** Checklists. Do not attempt any questions if you are unable to fill in any of the blanks – go back to your **BPP Interactive Text** and revise first.

- When you are revising a topic, think about the mistakes that you know that you should avoid by writing down **POSSIBLE PITFALLS** at the end of each **DO YOU KNOW?** Checklist.

- Once you have completed the checklists successfully, you should attempt the questions on that topic. All sections have a selection of **OBJECTIVE QUESTIONS** (including Multiple Choice Questions). Make good use of the **HELPING HANDS** provided to help you answer the questions.

- There is a mark allocation for each question. Each mark carries with it a time allocation of 1.2 minutes. A 2 mark question should therefore be completed in 2.4 minutes.

- 70% of the exam consists of **objective questions**, including Multiple Choice Questions. You should attempt each bank of objective test questions to ensure you are familiar with their styles and to practise your technique. Ensure you read **Tackling Multiple Choice Questions** on page xi to get advice on how best to approach them.

- Once you have completed all of the questions in the body of this Practice & Revision Kit, you should attempt the **MOCK EXAMS** under examination conditions. Check your answers against our answers to find out how well you did.

Passing the FFA/FA exam

FA Financial Accounting aims to develop your knowledge and understanding of the underlying principles, concepts and regulations relating to financial accounting. You will need to demonstrate technical proficiency in the use of double entry techniques, including the preparation of basic financial statements for incorporated and unincorporated entities, as well as simple consolidated financial statements for group entities. You also need to be able to conduct a basic interpretation of financial statements. If you plan to progress through the ACCA qualification, the skills you learn at FA will be built upon in the exams *FR Financial Reporting* and *SBR Strategic Business Reporting*.

To access Foundations in Accountancy syllabi, visit the ACCA website www2.accaglobal.com/students/fia

The exam

All questions in the exam are compulsory. This means you cannot avoid any topic, but also means that you do not need to dedicate time in the exam deciding which questions to attempt. There are thirty-five objective test questions in the exam, including a mixture of MCQs and other types of objective questions (for example, number entry, multiple response and multiple response matching) in the CBE. This means that the examining team is able to test most of the syllabus at each sitting, so you need to have revised right across the syllabus for this exam.

Revision

This Practice and Revision kit has been reviewed by the FA examining team and contains the ACCA Specimen Exam, so if you just work through it to the end you would be very well prepared for the exam. It is important to tackle questions under exam conditions. Allow yourself just the number of minutes shown next to the questions in the index and don't look at the answers until you have finished. Then correct your answer and go back to the Interactive Text for any topic you are having trouble with. Try the same questions again a week later – you will be surprised how much better you are getting. Doing the questions like this will really show you what you know, and will make the exam experience less worrying.

Doing the exam

If you have diligently done your revision you can pass this exam. There are a couple of points to bear in mind:

- Read the question properly.

- Don't spend more than the allotted time on each question. If you are having trouble with a question leave it and carry on. You can come back to it at the end.

Approach to examining the syllabus

FFA/FA is a two-hour exam.

The exam is structured as follows:

	No of marks
Section A – 35 compulsory objective questions of 2 marks each	70
Section B – 2 compulsory multi-task questions of 15 marks each	30
	100

Tackling Multiple Choice Questions

MCQs are part of all Foundations in Accountancy exams and the first three ACCA exams (AB, MA and FA). MCQs may feature in the CBE, along with other types of question.

The MCQs in your exam contain four possible answers. You have to **choose the option that best answers the question**. The three incorrect options are called distractors. There is a skill in answering MCQs quickly and correctly. By practising MCQs you can develop this skill, giving you a better chance of passing the exam.

You may wish to follow the approach outlined below, or you may prefer to adapt it.

Step 1	Skim read all the MCQs and identify what appear to be the easier questions.
Step 2	Attempt each question – **starting with the easier questions** identified in Step 1. Read the question **thoroughly**. You may prefer to work out the answer before looking at the options, or you may prefer to look at the options at the beginning. Adopt the method that works best for you.
Step 3	Read the four options and see if one matches your own answer. Be careful with numerical questions as the distractors are designed to match answers that incorporate common errors. Check that your calculation is correct. Have you followed the requirement exactly? Have you included every stage of the calculation?
Step 4	You may find that none of the options matches your answer. • Re-read the question to ensure that you understand it and are answering the requirement • Eliminate any obviously wrong answers • Consider which of the remaining answers is the most likely to be correct and select the option
Step 5	If you are still unsure make a note and continue to the next question
Step 6	Revisit unanswered questions. When you come back to a question after a break you often find you are able to answer it correctly straight away. If you are still unsure have a guess. You are not penalised for incorrect answers, so **never leave a question unanswered!**

After extensive practice and revision of MCQs, you may think that you recognise a question when you sit the exam. Be aware that the detail and/or requirement may be different. If the question seems familiar read the requirement and options carefully – do not assume that it is identical. Although it may be similar to one you have done previously, it may not be exactly the same.

Using your BPP products

This Practice & Revision Kit gives you the question practice and guidance you need in the exam. Our other products can also help you pass:

- **Interactive Text** introduces and explains the knowledge required for your exam
- **Passcards** provide you with clear topic summaries and exam tips

You can purchase these products by visiting www.bpp.com/learning-media.

Questions

Do you know? – The context and purpose of financial reporting

Check that you can fill in the blanks in the statements below before you attempt any questions. If in doubt, you should go back to your BPP Interactive Text and revise first.

- F............... r .... is a way of recording, analysing and summarising financial data.

- F.......... entities of whatever size or nature exist to make a p......

- N............. entities exist for the achievement of specific objectives rather than to make a profit.

- P.............. is the excess of .... over expenditure. When e............... exceeds .... the business is running at a l.......

- A s......... t............... is a business owned and run by one individual, perhaps employing one or two assistants and controlling their work.

- L .... l............ status means that the business's debts and the personal debts of the business's owners (shareholders) are legally separate.

- .... are arrangements between individuals to carry on business in common with a view to profit. Partnerships are governed by a ....

- Financial accounting is mainly a method of reporting the .... and .... of a business. Financial accounts provide .... information.

- There are various groups of people who need .... about the activities of a business.

- Those charged with g.................. of a company are responsible for the preparation of the financial statements.

- The statement of financial position is simply a list of all the a............ owned and all the l............... owed by a business as at a particular date.

- An .... is a resource controlled by an entity as a result of past events and from which future economic benefits are expected to flow to the entity.

- A .... is a present obligation of the entity arising from past events, the settlement of which is expected to result in an outflow from the entity of resources embodying economic benefits.

- E............. is the residual interest in the assets of the entity after deducting all its liabilities.

- A statement of profit or loss is a record of .... generated and .... incurred over a given period.

- Accounting standards were developed to try to address s..............y

- The IASB develops ....

- The main objectives of the IFRS Foundation are to:

    - .... a single set of high quality, understandable, enforceable and globally accepted l..... through its standard-setting body, the l......

    - Promote the .... and rigorous application of those standards

    - Take account of the financial reporting needs of emerging economies and .... and .... entities

    - Bring about c.................. of national accounting standards and IFRSs to high quality solutions.

Did you know? – The context and purpose of financial reporting

Could you fill in the blanks? The answers are in bold. Use this page for revision purposes as you approach the exam.

- **Financial reporting** is a way of recording, analysing and summarising financial data.

- **For-profit** entities of whatever size or nature exist to make a **profit**.

- **Not-for-profit** entities exist for the achievement of specific objectives rather than to make a profit.

- **Profit** is the excess of **income** over expenditure. When **expenditure** exceeds **revenue**, the business is running at a **loss**.

- A **sole tradership** is a business owned and run by one individual, perhaps employing one or two assistants and controlling their work.

- **Limited liability** status means that the business's debts and the personal debts of the business's owners (shareholders) are legally separate.

- **Partnerships** are arrangements between individuals to carry on business in common with a view to profit. Partnerships are governed by a **partnership agreement**.

- Financial accounting is mainly a method of reporting the **financial performance** and **financial position** of a business. Financial accounts provide **historical** information.

- There are various groups of people who need **information** about the activities of a business.

- Those charged with **governance** of a company are responsible for the preparation of the financial statements.

- The statement of financial position is simply a list of all the **assets** owned and all the **liabilities** owed by a business as at a particular date.

- An **asset** is a resource controlled by an entity as a result of past events and from which future economic benefits are expected to flow to the entity.

- A **liability** is a present obligation of the entity arising from past events, the settlement of which is expected to result in an outflow from the entity of resources embodying economic benefits.

- **Equity** is the residual interest in the assets of the entity after deducting all its liabilities.

- A statement of profit or loss is a record of **income** generated and **expenditure** incurred over a given period.

- Accounting standards were developed to try to address **subjectivity**.

- The IASB develops **International Financial Reporting Standards (IFRSs)**.

- The main objectives of the IFRS Foundation are to:

  - **Develop** a single set of high quality, understandable, enforceable and globally accepted **international financial reporting standards (IFRSs)** through its standard-setting body, the **IASB**

  - Promote the **use** and rigorous application of those standards

  - Take account of the financial reporting needs of emerging economies and **small** and **medium-sized** entities **(SMEs)**

  - Bring about **convergence** of national accounting standards and IFRSs to high quality solutions.

1 The context and purpose of financial reporting — 34 mins

1.1 Who issues International Financial Reporting Standards?

    A   The IFRS Advisory Committee
    B   The stock exchange
    C   The International Accounting Standards Board
    D   The government   **(2 marks)**

1.2 Which groups of people are most likely to be interested in the financial statements of a sole trader?

    1   Shareholders of the company
    2   The business's bank manager
    3   The tax authorities
    4   Financial analysts

    A   1 and 2 only
    B   2 and 3 only
    C   2, 3 and 4 only
    D   1, 2 and 3 only   **(2 marks)**

1.3 Identify, by indicating the relevant box in the table below, whether each of the following statements is true or false.

	True	False
A supplier of goods on credit is interested only in the statement of financial position, ie an indication of the current state of affairs.		
The objective of financial statements is to provide information about the financial position, performance and changes in financial position of an entity that is useful to a wide range of users in making economic decisions.		

    (2 marks)

1.4 Which of the following are advantages of trading as a limited liability company?

    1   Operating as a limited liability company makes raising finance easier because additional shares can be issued to raise additional cash.

    2   Operating as a limited liability company is more risky than operating as a sole trader because the shareholders of a business are liable for all the debts of the business whereas the sole trader is only liable for the debts up to the amount he has invested.

    A   1 only
    B   2 only
    C   Both 1 and 2
    D   Neither 1 or 2   **(2 marks)**

1.5   Which of the following best describes corporate governance?

A   Corporate governance is the system of rules and regulations surrounding financial reporting.

B   Corporate governance is the system by which companies and other entities are directed and controlled.

C   Corporate governance is carried out by the finance department in preparing the financial statements.

D   Corporate governance is the system by which an entity monitors its impact on the natural environment.
(2 marks)

1.6   Identify which of the following statements are true or false.

1   The directors of a company are ultimately responsible for the preparation of financial statements, even if the majority of the work on them is performed by the finance department.

2   If financial statements are audited, then the responsibility for those financial statements instead falls on the auditors instead of the directors.

3   There are generally no laws surrounding the duties of directors in managing the affairs of a company.

A   1 only
B   2 only
C   2 and 3 only
D   1 and 3 only
(2 marks)

1.7   Which **ONE** of the following statements correctly describes the contents of the Statement of Financial Position?

A   A list of ledger balances shown in debit and credit columns
B   A list of all the assets owned and all the liabilities owed by a business
C   A record of income generated and expenditure incurred over a given period
D   A record of the amount of cash generated and used by a company in a given period
(2 marks)

1.8   Which **ONE** of the following statements correctly describes the contents of the Statement of Profit or Loss?

A   A list of ledger balances shown in debit and credit columns
B   A list of all the assets owned and all the liabilities owed by a business
C   A record of income generated and expenditure incurred over a given period
D   A record of the amount of cash generated and used by a company in a given period
(2 marks)

1.9   Which of the following are TRUE of partnerships?

1   The partners' individual exposure to debt is limited.
2   Financial statements for the partnership by law must be produced and made public.
3   A partnership is not a separate legal entity from the partners themselves.

A   1 and 2 only
B   2 only
C   3 only
D   1 and 3 only
(2 marks)

1.10 Which of the following statements is/are true?

    1   Directors of companies have a duty of care to show reasonable competence in their management of the affairs of a company.

    2   Directors of companies must act honestly in what they consider to be the best interest of the company.

    3   A Director's main aim should be to create wealth for the shareholders of the company.

    A   1 and 2 only
    B   2 only
    C   1, 2 and 3
    D   1 and 3 only   **(2 marks)**

1.11 Which of the following statements is/are true?

    1   The IFRS Interpretations Committee is a forum for the IASB to consult with the outside world.

    2   The IFRS Foundation produces IFRSs. The IFRS Foundation is overseen by the IASB.

    3   One of the objectives of the IFRS Foundation is to bring about convergence of national accounting standards and IFRSs.

    A   1 and 3 only
    B   2 only
    C   2 and 3 only
    D   3 only   **(2 marks)**

1.12 What is the role of the IASB?

    A   Oversee the standard setting and regulatory process
    B   Formulate international financial reporting standards
    C   Review defective accounts
    D   Control the accountancy profession   **(2 marks)**

1.13 Which **ONE** of the following is **NOT** an objective of the IFRS Foundation?

    A   Through the IASB, develop a single set of globally accepted International Financial Reporting Standards (IFRSs)

    B   Promote the use and rigorous application of International Financial Reporting Standards (IFRSs)

    C   Ensure International Financial Reporting Standards (IFRSs) focus primarily on the needs of global, multi-national organisations

    D   Bring about the convergence of national accounting standards and IFRSs   **(2 marks)**

1.14 Which **ONE** of the following statements correctly describes how International Financial Reporting Standards (IFRSs) should be used?

    A   To provide examples of best financial reporting practice for national bodies who develop their own requirements

    B   To ensure high ethical standards are maintained by financial reporting professionals internationally

    C   To facilitate the enforcement of a single set of global financial reporting standards

    D   To prevent national bodies from developing their own financial reporting standards   **(2 marks)**

(Total = 28 marks)

Do you know? – The qualitative characteristics of financial information

Check that you can fill in the blanks in the statements below before you attempt any questions. If in doubt, you should go back to your BPP Interactive Text and revise first.

- In preparing financial statements, accountants follow certain fundamental **a**.................

- The IASB's **C**..........*l* **f**...............**k** provides the basis for its IFRSs.

- The main underlying assumption is ....

- The *Conceptual framework* states that .... characteristics are the attributes that make the information provided in financial statements useful to users.

- The four enhancing qualitative characteristics are ...., ..., ...
and ....

- Other important qualitative characteristics and concepts include fair ...., **c**..................
and the business .... concept.

- A .... between qualitative characteristics is often necessary, the aim being to achieve an appropriate balance to meet the objective of financial statements.

Did you know? – The qualitative characteristics of financial information

Could you fill in the blanks? The answers are in bold. Use this page for revision purposes as you approach the exam.

- In preparing financial statements, accountants follow certain fundamental **assumptions**.

- The IASB's *Conceptual framework* provides the basis for its IFRSs.

- The main underlying assumption is **going concern**.

- The *Conceptual framework* states that **qualitative** characteristics are the attributes that make the information provided in financial statements useful to users.

- The four enhancing qualitative characteristics are **understandability, verifiability**, **timeliness** and **comparability**.

- Other important qualitative characteristics and concepts include fair **presentation**, **consistency** and the business **entity** concept.

- A **trade off** between qualitative characteristics is often necessary, the aim being to achieve an appropriate balance to meet the objective of financial statements.

2 The qualitative characteristics of financial information   31 mins

2.1 Which accounting concept should be considered if the owner of a business takes goods from inventory for their own personal use?

    A   The fair presentation concept
    B   The accruals concept
    C   The going concern concept
    D   The business entity concept   **(2 marks)**

2.2 Sales revenue should be recognised when goods and services have been supplied; costs are incurred when goods and services have been received.

Which accounting concept governs the above?

    A   The business entity concept
    B   The materiality concept
    C   The accruals concept
    D   The duality concept   **(2 marks)**

2.3 Which accounting concept states that omitting or misstating this information could influence users of the financial statements?

    A   The consistency concept
    B   The accruals concept
    C   The materiality concept
    D   The going concern concept   **(2 marks)**

2.4 According to the IASB's *Conceptual Framework for Financial Reporting*, which **TWO** of the following are part of faithful representation?

    1   It is neutral
    2   It is relevant
    3   It is presented fairly
    4   It is free from material error

    A   1 and 2
    B   2 and 3
    C   1 and 4
    D   3 and 4   **(2 marks)**

2.5 Which of the following accounting concepts means that similar items should receive a similar accounting treatment?

    A   Conformity
    B   Accruals
    C   Matching
    D   Consistency   **(2 marks)**

2.6 Listed below are some characteristics of financial information.

    1   Relevance
    2   Consistency
    3   Faithful representation
    4   Accuracy

Which **TWO** of these are qualitative characteristics of financial information according to the IASB's *Conceptual Framework for Financial Reporting*?

    A   1 and 2
    B   2 and 4
    C   3 and 4
    D   1 and 3   **(2 marks)**

2.7 Which **ONE** of the following statements describes faithful representation, a qualitative characteristic of faithful representation?

A   Revenue earned must be matched against the expenditure incurred in earning it.

B   Having information available to decision-makers in time to be capable of influencing their decisions.

C   The presentation and classification of items in the financial statements should stay the same from one period to the next.

D   Financial information should be complete, neutral and free from error.   **(2 marks)**

2.8 Listed below are some comments on accounting concepts.

1   Financial statements always treat the business as a separate entity.

2   Materiality means that only items having a physical existence may be recognised as assets.

3   Provisions are estimates and therefore can be altered to make the financial results of a business more attractive to investors.

Which, if any, of these comments is correct, according to the IASB's *Conceptual Framework for Financial Reporting*?

A   1 only
B   2 only
C   3 only
D   None of them   **(2 marks)**

2.9 Which of the following statements about accounting concepts and the characteristics of financial information are correct?

1   The concept of accruals requires transactions to be reflected in the financial statements once the cash or its equivalent is received or paid.

2   Information is material if its omission or misstatement could influence the economic decisions of users taken on the basis of the financial statements.

3   Based on faithful representation, it may sometimes be necessary to exclude material information from financial statements due to difficulties establishing an accurate figure.

A   1 only
B   1 and 2 only
C   2 only
D   2 and 3 only   **(2 marks)**

2.10 The IASB's *Conceptual Framework for Financial Reporting* gives six qualitative characteristics of financial information. What are these six characteristics?

A   Relevance, Faithful representation, Comparability, Verifiability, Timeliness and Understandability
B   Accuracy, Faithful representation, Comparability, Verifiability, Timeliness and Understandability
C   Relevance, Faithful representation, Consistency, Verifiability, Timeliness and Understandability
D   Relevance, Comparability, Consistency, Verifiability, Timeliness and Understandability

(2 marks)

2.11 Which one of the following is **NOT** a qualitative characteristic of financial information according to the *Conceptual framework for Financial Reporting*?

A   Faithful representation
B   Relevance
C   Timeliness
D   Accruals   **(2 marks)**

2.12 According to the IASB *Conceptual framework* which of the following is **NOT** an objective of financial statements?

    A   Providing information regarding the financial position of a business

    B   Providing information regarding the performance of a business

    C   Enabling users to assess the performance of management to aid decision making

    D   Providing reliable investment advice   **(2 marks)**

2.13 Identify, by indicating the relevant box in the table below, whether each of the following statements is correct or incorrect.

	Correct	**Incorrect**
Companies should never change the presentation or classification of items in their financial statements, even if there is a significant change in the nature of operations.		
Companies should create provisions in times of company growth to be utilised in more difficult times, to smooth profits.		

               (2 marks)

               (Total = 26 marks)

Do you know? – The use of double entry and accounting systems

Check that you can fill in the blanks in the statements below before you attempt any questions. If in doubt, you should go back to your BPP Interactive Text and revise first.

- Business transactions are recorded on **s**.......... **d**................ Examples include sales and purchase orders, ... and ....

- Books of .... are books in which we first record transactions.

- The main books of prime entry are:

  (a) .... day book
  (b) .... day book
  (c) .... day book
  (d) .... day book
  (e) **J**.........**l**
  (f) .... book
  (g) .... book

- Entries in the .... are totalled and analysed before posting to the **n**......... ledger.

- The .... and .... ledgers contain the personal accounts of individual customers and suppliers. They do not normally form part of the double-entry system.

- The **b**........... **e**......... concept means that a business is always treated separately from its owner(s).

- The accounting equation is: .... = ... + LIABILITIES – .... + PROFIT

- Trade accounts payable are **l**................ Trade accounts receivable are **a**.........

- In double entry bookkeeping every transaction is recorded .... so that every .... is balanced by a ....

- A debit entry will:

  – .... an asset
  – .... a liability
  – .... an expense

- A credit entry will:

  – .... an asset
  – .... a liability
  – .... income

- A trial balance can be used to test the .... of the double entry accounting records.

- A .... and .... ledger account is opened up to gather all items relating to income and expenses. When rearranged, the items make up the ....

Did you know? – The use of double entry and accounting systems

Could you fill in the blanks? The answers are in bold. Use this page for revision purposes as you approach the exam.

- Business transactions are recorded on **source documents**. Examples include sales and purchase orders, **invoices** and **credit notes**.

- Books of **prime entry** are books in which we first record transactions.

- The main books of prime entry are:

  (a) **Sales** day book
  (b) **Purchase** day book
  (c) **Sales returns** day book
  (d) **Purchase returns** day book
  (e) **Journal**
  (f) **Cash** book
  (g) **Petty cash** book

- Entries in the **day books** are totalled and analysed before posting to the **nominal** ledger.

- The **receivables** and **payables** ledgers contain the personal accounts of individual customers and suppliers. They do not normally form part of the double-entry system.

- The **business entity** concept means that a business is always treated separately from its owner(s).

- The accounting equation is: **ASSETS** = **CAPITAL** + LIABILITIES – **DRAWINGS** + PROFIT

- Trade accounts payable are **liabilities**. Trade accounts receivable are **assets**.

- In double entry bookkeeping every transaction is recorded **twice** so that every **debit** is balanced by a **credit**.

- A debit entry will:

  - **Increase** an asset
  - **Decrease** a liability
  - **Increase** an expense

- A credit entry will:

  - **Decrease** an asset
  - **Increase** a liability
  - **Increase** income

- A trial balance can be used to test the **accuracy** of the double entry accounting records.

- A **profit** and **loss** ledger account is opened up to gather all items relating to income and expenses. When rearranged, the items make up the **statement of profit or loss**.

3 Double entry bookkeeping I
46 mins

3.1 Which one of the following can the accounting equation can be rewritten as?

A   Assets + profit – drawings – liabilities = closing capital
B   Assets – liabilities – drawings = opening capital + profit
C   Assets – liabilities – opening capital + drawings = profit
D   Assets – profit – drawings = closing capital – liabilities   **(2 marks)**

3.2 A trader's net profit for the year may be computed by using which of the following formulae?

A   Opening capital + drawings – capital introduced – closing capital
B   Closing capital + drawings – capital introduced – opening capital
C   Opening capital – drawings + capital introduced – closing capital
D   Opening capital – drawings – capital introduced – closing capital   **(2 marks)**

3.3 The profit earned by a business in 20X7 was $72,500. The proprietor injected new capital of $8,000 during the year and withdrew goods for his private use which had cost $2,200.

If net assets at the beginning of 20X7 were $101,700, what were the closing net assets?

A $35,000
B $39,400
C $168,400
D $180,000   **(2 marks)**

3.4 The profit made by a business in 20X7 was $35,400. The proprietor injected new capital of $10,200 during the year and withdrew a monthly salary of $500.

If net assets at the end of 20X7 were $95,100, what was the proprietor's capital at the beginning of the year?

$_____   **(2 marks)**

3.5 A sole trader took some goods costing $800 from inventory for his own use. The normal selling price of the goods is $1,600.

Which of the following journal entries would correctly record this?

		Dr $	Cr $
A	Inventory account	800	
	Purchases account		800
B	Drawings account	800	
	Purchases account		800
C	Sales account	1,600	
	Drawings account		1,600
D	Drawings account	800	
	Sales account		800

(2 marks)

3.6 A business can make a profit and yet have a reduction in its bank balance. Which **ONE** of the following might cause this to happen?

A   The sale of non-current assets at a loss
B   The charging of depreciation in the statement of profit or loss
C   The lengthening of the period of credit given to customers
D   The lengthening of the period of credit taken from suppliers   **(2 marks)**

3.7 The net assets of Altese, a trader, at 1 January 20X2 amounted to $128,000. During the year to 31 December 20X2 Altese introduced a further $50,000 of capital and made drawings of $48,000. At 31 December 20X2 Altese's net assets totalled $184,000.

What is Altese's total profit or loss for the year ended 31 December 20X2?

A $54,000 profit
B $54,000 loss
C $42,000 loss
D $58,000 profit   (2 marks)

3.8 Jones Co has the following transactions:

1   Payment of $400 to J Bloggs for a cash purchase
2   Payment of $250 to J Doe in respect of an invoice for goods purchased last month

What are the correct ledger entries to record these transactions?

A   Dr Cash $650
         Cr Purchases $650
B   Dr Purchases $650
         Cr Cash $650
C   Dr Purchases $400
     Dr Trade Payables $250
         Cr Cash $650
D   Dr Cash $650
         Cr Trade Payables $250
         Cr Purchases $400   (2 marks)

3.9 T Tallon had the following transactions:

1   Sale of goods on credit for $150 to F Rogit
2   Return of goods from B Blendigg originally sold for $300 in cash to B Blendigg

What are the correct ledger entries to record these transactions?

A   Dr Receivables $150
     Dr Sales Returns $300
         Cr Sales $150
         Cr Cash $300
B   Dr Sales $150
     Dr Cash $300
         Cr Receivables $150
         Cr Sales Returns $300
C   Dr Receivables $450
         Cr Sales $150
         Cr Sales Returns $300
D   Dr Sales Returns $300
     Dr Sales $150
         Cr Cash $450   (2 marks)

3.10 Which of the following documents should accompany a return of goods to a supplier?

A   Debit note
B   Remittance advice
C   Purchase invoice
D   Credit note   (2 marks)

3.11 Which of the following are books of prime entry?

    1   Sales day book
    2   Cash book
    3   Journal
    4   Purchase ledger

    A   1, 2 and 3 only
    B   1, 2 and 4 only
    C   3 and 4 only
    D   All of them   **(2 marks)**

3.12 In which book of prime entry will a business record debit notes in respect of goods which have been sent back to suppliers?

    A   The sales returns day book
    B   The cash book
    C   The purchase returns day book
    D   The purchase day book   **(2 marks)**

3.13 A company's motor vehicles at cost account at 30 June 20X6 is as follows:

MOTOR VEHICLES – COST

	$		$
Balance b/d	150,500	Disposal	85,000
Additions	120,950	Balance c/d	186,450
	271,450		271,450

What opening balance should be included in the following period's trial balance for motor vehicles – cost at 1 July 20X6?

    A $271,450 DR
    B $271,450 DR
    C $186,450 CR
    D $186,450 DR   **(2 marks)**

3.14 A company's trade payables account at 30 September 20X1 is as follows:

TRADE PAYABLES ACCOUNT

	$		$
Cash at bank	21,600	Balance b/d	14,000
Balance c/d	11,900	Purchases	19,500
	33,500		33,500

What was the balance for trade payables in the trial balance at 1 October 20X0?

    A $14,000 DR
    B $14,000 CR
    C $11,900 DR
    D $11,900 CR   **(2 marks)**

3.15 Which of the following would be recorded in the sales day book?

    A   Cash received
    B   Sales invoices
    C   Credit notes received
    D   Trade discounts   **(2 marks)**

3.16 Identify, by indicating the relevant box in the table below, whether each of the following statements is true or false.

A debit records an increase in liabilities.	True	False
A debit records a decrease in assets.	True	False
A credit records an increase in liabilities.	True	False
A credit records an decrease in capital.	True	False

(2 marks)

3.17 How is the total of the purchases day book posted to the nominal ledger?

A   Debit purchases, Credit cash
B   Debit payables control, Credit purchases
C   Debit cash, Credit purchases
D   Debit purchases, Credit payables control   (2 marks)

3.18 Which one of the following statements about an imprest system of petty cash is correct?

A   An imprest system for petty cash controls small cash expenditures because a fixed amount is paid into petty cash at the beginning of each period.

B   The imprest system provides a control over petty cash spending because the amount of cash held in petty cash at any time must be equal to the value of the petty cash vouchers for the period.

C   An imprest system for petty cash can operate without the need for petty cash vouchers or receipts for spending.

D   An imprest system for petty cash helps with management of small cash expenditures and reduces the risk of fraud.   (2 marks)

3.19 Which one of the following provides evidence that an item of expenditure on petty cash has been approved or authorised?

A   Petty cash voucher
B   Record of the transaction in the petty cash book
C   Receipt for the expense
D   Transfer of cash from the bank account into petty cash   (2 marks)

(Total = 38 marks)

4 Double entry bookkeeping II
43 mins

The following information is relevant for Questions 4.1 and 4.2.

On 1 May 20X9 Marshall's cash book showed a cash balance of $224 and an overdraft of $336. During the week ended 6 May the following transactions took place.

May 1   Sold $160 of goods to P Dixon on credit.
May 1   Withdrew $50 of cash from the bank for business use.
May 2   Purchased goods priced at $380 from A Clarke, on credit, less 15% trade discount.
May 2   Repaid a debt of $120 owing to R Hill, taking advantage of a 10% settlement discount. The payment was by cheque.
May 3   Sold $45 of goods for cash.
May 4   Sold $80 of goods to M Maguire on credit, offering a $12^{1}/_{2}$% discount if payment made within 7 days. Marshall expects Maguire to take up this discount.
May 4   Paid a telephone bill of $210 by cheque.

May 4   Purchased $400 of goods on credit from D Daley.
May 5   Received a cheque from H Larkin for $180.
May 5   Sold $304 of goods to M Donald on credit.
May 5   Purchased $135 of goods from Honour Co by cheque.
May 6   Received a cheque from D Randle for $482.
May 6   Purchased $100 of goods on credit from G Perkins.

4.1   What is the total of the sales day book?

$_____   **(2 marks)**

4.2   What is the total of the purchases day book?

$_____   **(2 marks)**

4.3   Smith Co has the following transactions:

1   Purchase of goods on credit from T Rader: $450
2   Return of goods purchased on credit last month to T Rouble: $700

What are the correct ledger entries to record these transactions?

A	Dr Purchases	$450	
	Dr Purchase Returns	$700	
	Cr Cash		$450
	Cr Trade Payables		$700
B	Dr Purchases	$450	
	Dr Trade Payables	$700	
	Cr Purchase Returns		$1,150
C	Dr Purchases	$450	
	Dr Trade Payables	$250	
	Cr Purchase Returns		$700
D	Dr Purchase Returns	$700	
	Dr Purchases	$450	
	Cr Trade Payables		$1,150

(2 marks)

4.4   Mew Ling has the following transactions:

1   Receipt of cash from R Singh in respect of an invoice for goods sold three weeks ago
2   Receipt of cash from S Kalu for cash sales

What are the ledger entries required to record the above transactions?

A   Dr Cash
        Cr Sales
B   Dr Cash
        Cr Sales
        Cr Trade Receivables
C   Dr Sales
        Cr Cash
D   Dr Trade Receivables
        Dr Sales
        Cr Cash   **(2 marks)**

4.5 How is the total of the sales day book recorded in the nominal ledger?

	Debit	Credit
A	Receivables Ledger	Receivables Control Account
B	Receivables Control Account	Receivables Ledger
C	Sales	Receivables Control Account
D	Receivables Control Account	Sales

(2 marks)

4.6 Identify, by indicating the relevant box in the table below, whether each of the statements is true or false.

A debit entry in the cash book will increase an overdraft in the accounts.	True	False
A debit entry in the cash book will increase a bank balance in the accounts.	True	False

(2 marks)

4.7 An accountant has inserted all the relevant figures into the trade payables account, but has not yet balanced off the account.

TRADE PAYABLES ACCOUNT

	$		$
Cash at bank	100,750	Balance b/d	250,225
		Purchases	325,010

Assuming there are no other entries to be made, other than to balance off the account, what is the closing balance on the trade payables account?

A $474,485 DR
B $575,235 DR
C $474,485 CR
D $575,235 CR

(2 marks)

4.8 You are given the following information:

Receivables at 1 January 20X3	$10,000
Receivables at 31 December 20X3	$9,000
Total receipts during 20X3 (including cash sales of $5,000)	$85,000

What are sales on credit during 20X3?

A $81,000
B $86,000
C $79,000
D $84,000

(2 marks)

4.9 A business sells $100 worth of goods to a customer, the customer pays $50 in cash immediately and will pay the remaining $50 in 30 days' time.

What is the double entry to record the purchase in the customer's accounting records?

A Debit cash $50, credit payables $50, credit purchases $50
B Debit payables $50, debit cash $50, credit purchases $100
C Debit purchases $100, credit payables $50, credit cash $50
D Debit purchases $100, credit cash $100

(2 marks)

4.10   Tin Co purchases $250 worth of metal from Steel Co. Tin Co agrees to pay Steel Co in 60 days' time.

From the list of tokens below, identify the tokens needed to record the correct entries in Steel Co's books.

TOKEN	DEBIT ENTRY	CREDIT ENTRY
Sales $250	Debit entry	
Receivables $250		Credit entry
Purchases $250		
Payables $250		
Cash $250		

(2 marks)

4.11   The following totals appear in the day books for March 20X8.

	$
Sales day book	40,000
Purchases day book	20,000
Returns inwards day book	2,000
Returns outward day book	4,000

Opening and closing inventories are both $3,000. What is the gross profit for March 20X8?

A $22,000
B $24,000
C $20,000
D $18,000   **(2 marks)**

4.12   William's trial balance at 30 September 20X5 includes the following balances:

Trade receivables $75,943
Receivables allowance $4,751

How should these balances be reported in William's statement of financial position as at 30 September 20X5?

A   An asset of $71,192
B   An asset of $75,943 and a liability of $4,751
C   A liability of $71,192
D   A liability of $75,943 and an asset of $4,751   **(2 marks)**

4.13   A trial balance is made up of a list of debit balances and credit balances.

Which of the following statements is correct?

A   Every debit balance represents an expense.
B   Assets are represented by debit balances.
C   Liabilities are represented by debit balances.
D   Income is included in the list of debit balances.   **(2 marks)**

4.14   At 30 November 20X5 Jenny had a bank loan of $8,500 and a balance of $678 in hand in her bank account.

How should these amounts be recorded on Jenny's opening trial balance at 1 December 20X5?

A   Debit $7,822
B   Credit $7,822
C   Credit $8,500 and Debit $678
D   Debit $8,500 and Credit $678   **(2 marks)**

4.15 Bert has extracted the following list of balances from his general ledger at 31 October 20X5:

	$
Sales	258,542
Opening inventory	9,649
Purchases	142,958
Expenses	34,835
Non-current assets (carrying amount)	63,960
Receivables	31,746
Payables	13,864
Cash at bank	1,783
Capital	12,525

What is the total of the debit balances in Bert's trial balance at 31 October 20X5?

A $267,049
B $275,282
C $283,148
D $284,931   **(2 marks)**

4.16 At 31 October 20X6 Roger's trial balance included the following balances:

	$
Machinery at cost	12,890
Accumulated depreciation	8,950
Inventory	5,754
Trade receivables	11,745
Trade payables	7,830
Bank overdraft	1,675
Cash at bank	150

What is the value of Roger's current assets at 31 October 20X6?

A $17,649
B $17,499
C $15,974
D $13,734   **(2 marks)**

4.17 Which **ONE** of the following statements does **NOT** describe a way in which an effective accounting system facilitates the provision of useful accounting information?

A   By requiring authorisation in line with organisational policies
B   By processing and recording transactions in accordance with accounting rules
C   By preventing transactions from being processed inaccurately
D   By enabling transactions to be recorded as necessary to permit preparation of financial
    statements   **(2 marks)**

4.18 Which of the following statements is/are TRUE or FALSE?

1   Cash purchases are recorded in the purchases day book.
2   The sales day books is used to keep a list of invoices received from suppliers.

A   Both statements are TRUE
B   Both statements are FALSE
C   Statement 1 is TRUE and statement 2 is FALSE
D   Statement 1 is FALSE and statement 2 is TRUE   **(2 marks)**

(Total = 36 marks)

Do you know? – Recording transactions and events

Check that you can fill in the blanks in the statements below before you attempt any questions. If in doubt, you should go back to your BPP Interactive Text and revise first.

- S......... t...... is an indirect tax levied on the sale of goods and services.

- R................. businesses charge .... sales tax on sales and suffer .... sales tax on purchases.

- The c...... of g...... s.......is calculated as: Opening inventory + purchases – closing inventory.

- Carriage .... is included in the cost of purchases. Carriage .... is a selling expense.

- The value of inventories is calculated at the l......... of c......... and n...... r............ v........

- The cost of inventories can be arrived at by using .... or ....

- C.......... expenditure is expenditure which forms part of the cost of non-current assets. R................. expenditure is expenditure incurred for the purpose of the trade or to maintain non current assets.

- The ...... of a non-current asset, less its estimated residual value, is allocated fairly between accounting periods by means of d...................

- D................. costs must be capitalised as an i................. asset if the criteria in IAS 38 are satisfied.

- A................. are expenses which relate to an accounting period but have not yet been paid for. They are shown in the statement of financial position as a l.................

- P.................are expenses which have already been paid but relate to a future accounting period. They are shown in the statement of financial position as an ....

- I................. debts are specific debts owed to a business which it decides are never going to be paid. They are written off as an .... in the statement of profit or loss.

- An .... in the allowance for receivables is shown as an expense in the statement of profit or loss.

- According to IAS 37, a provision should be recognised when:
    - An entity has a p......... o............
    - It is p.......... that a transfer of economic benefits will be required to settle it
    - A r......... e......... can be made of its amount

- According to IAS 37, a c................. liability must not be recognised as a liability in the financial statements. Instead it should be d............. in the notes to the financial statements.

Did you know? – Recording transactions and events

Could you fill in the blanks? The answers are in bold. Use this page for revision purposes as you approach the exam.

- **Sales tax** is an indirect tax levied on the sale of goods and services.

- **Registered** businesses charge **output** sales tax on sales and suffer **input** sales tax on purchases.

- The **cost of goods sold** is calculated as: Opening inventory + purchases – closing inventory.

- Carriage **inwards** is included in the cost of purchases. Carriage **outwards** is a selling expense.

- The value of inventories is calculated at the **lower** of **cost** and **net realisable value**.

- The cost of inventories can be arrived at by using **FIFO (first in-first out)** or **AVCO (weighted average costing, both periodic weighted average and continuous weighted average)**.

- **Capital** expenditure is expenditure which forms part of the cost of non-current assets. **Revenue** expenditure is expenditure incurred for the purpose of the trade or to maintain non current assets.

- The **cost** of a non-current asset, less its estimated residual value, is allocated fairly between accounting periods by means of **depreciation**.

- **Development** costs must be capitalised as an **intangible** asset if the criteria in IAS 38 are satisfied.

- **Accruals** are expenses which relate to an accounting period but have not yet been paid for. They are shown in the statement of financial position as a **liability**.

- **Prepayments** are expenses which have already been paid but relate to a future accounting period. They are shown in the statement of financial position as an **asset**.

- **Irrecoverable** debts are specific debts owed to a business which it decides are never going to be paid. They are written off as an **expense** in the statement of profit or loss.

- An **increase** in the allowance for receivables is shown as an expense in the statement of profit or loss.

- According to IAS 37, a **provision** should be recognised when:
    - An entity has a **present obligation**
    - It is **probable** that a transfer of economic benefits will be required to settle it
    - A **reliable estimate** can be made of its amount

- According to IAS 37, a **contingent** liability must not be recognised as a liability in the financial statements. Instead it should be **disclosed** in the notes to the financial statements.

5 Sales tax   19 mins

5.1   W is registered for sales tax. The managing director has asked four staff in the accounts department why
       the output tax for the last quarter does not equal 20% of sales (20% is the rate of tax). Which one of
       the following four replies she received was **NOT** correct?

       A   The company had some exports that were not liable to sales tax.
       B   The company made some sales of zero-rated products.
       C   The company made some sales of exempt products.
       D   The company sold some products to businesses not registered for sales tax.   **(2 marks)**

5.2   The following information relates to Eva Co's sales tax for the month of March 20X3:

                                                                $
       Sales (including sales tax)   109,250
       Purchases (net of sales tax)   64,000

       Sales tax is charged at a flat rate of 15%. Eva Co's sales tax account showed an opening credit balance
       of $4,540 at the beginning of the month and a closing debit balance of $2,720 at the end of the
       month.

       What was the total sales tax paid to regulatory authorities during the month of March 20X3?

       $_____   **(2 marks)**

5.3   Alana is not registered for sales tax purposes. She has recently received an invoice for goods for resale
       which cost $500 before sales tax, which is levied at 15%. The total value was therefore $575.

       What is the correct entry to be made in Alana's general ledger in respect of the invoice?

       A   Dr Purchases $500, Dr Sales tax $75, Cr Payables $575
       B   Dr Purchases $575, Cr Sales tax $75, Cr Payables $500
       C   Dr Purchases $500, Cr Payables $500
       D   Dr Purchases $575, Cr Payables $575   **(2 marks)**

5.4   Information relating to Lauren Co's transactions for the month of May 20X4 is shown below:

                                                                $
       Sales (including sales tax)   140,000*
       Purchases (net of sales tax)   65,000

       Sales tax is charged at a flat rate of 20%. Lauren Co's sales tax account had a zero balance at the
       beginning of the month and at the end of the month.

       * Lauren Co's sales for the month of $140,000 included $20,000 of sales exempt from sales tax.

       What was the total sales tax paid to regulatory authorities at the end of May 20X4 (to the nearest $)?

       A $7,000
       B $20,000
       C $23,333
       D $13,000   **(2 marks)**

5.5   A business commenced with capital in cash of $1,000. Inventory costing $800 plus sales tax is
       purchased on credit, and half is sold for $1,000 plus sales tax, the customer paying in cash at once.
       The sales tax rate is 20%.

       What would the accounting equation after these transactions show?

       A   Assets $1,800 less Liabilities $200 equals Capital $1,600
       B   Assets $2,200 less Liabilities $1,000 equals Capital $1,200
       C   Assets $2,600 less Liabilities $800 equals Capital $1,800
       D   Assets $2,600 less Liabilities $1,000 equals Capital $1,600   **(2 marks)**

5.6 Trade receivables and payables in the financial statements of a sales tax registered trader will appear as described by which of the following?

A   Inclusive of sales tax in the statement of financial position

B   Exclusive of sales tax in the statement of financial position

C   The sales tax is deducted and added to the sales tax account in the statement of financial position

D   Sales tax does not appear in the statement of financial position because the business simply acts as a collector on behalf of the tax authorities   **(2 marks)**

5.7 Which of the following correctly describe the entry in the sales account for a sale for a sales tax registered trader?

A   Credited with the total of sales made, including sales tax
B   Credited with the total of sales made, excluding sales tax
C   Debited with the total of sales made, including sales tax
D   Debited with the total of sales made, excluding sales tax   **(2 marks)**

5.8 Sales (including sales tax) amounted to $27,612.50, and purchases (excluding sales tax) amounted to $18,000. What is the balance on the sales tax account, assuming all items are subject to sales tax at 17.5%?

A $962.50 debit
B $962.50 credit
C $1,682.10 debit
D $1,682.10 credit   **(2 marks)**

(Total = 16 marks)

6 Inventory   46 mins

6.1 The inventory value for the financial statements of Global Co for the year ended 30 June 20X3 was based on a inventory count on 7 July 20X3, which gave a total inventory value of $950,000.

Between 30 June and 7 July 20X3, the following transactions took place.

	$
Purchase of goods	11,750
Sale of goods (mark up on cost at 15%)	14,950
Goods returned by Global Co to supplier	1,500

What figure should be included in the financial statements for inventories at 30 June 20X3?

$_____   **(2 marks)**

6.2 Which of the following costs may be included when arriving at the cost of finished goods inventory for inclusion in the financial statements of a manufacturing company?

1 Carriage inwards
2 Carriage outwards
3 Depreciation of factory plant
4 Finished goods storage costs
5 Factory supervisors' wages

A 1 and 5 only
B 2, 4 and 5 only
C 1, 3 and 5 only
D 1, 2, 3 and 4 only   (2 marks)

6.3 The closing inventory at cost of a company at 31 January 20X3 amounted to $284,700.

The following items were included at cost in the total:

1 400 coats, which had cost $80 each and normally sold for $150 each. Owing to a defect in manufacture, they were all sold after the reporting date at 50% of their normal price. Selling expenses amounted to 5% of the proceeds.

2 800 skirts, which had cost $20 each. These too were found to be defective. Remedial work in February 20X3 cost $5 per skirt, and selling expenses for the batch totalled $800. They were sold for $28 each.

What should the inventory value be according to IAS 2 *Inventories* after considering the above items?

A $276,400
B $281,200
C $282,800
D $329,200   (2 marks)

6.4 A company values its inventory using the first in, first out (FIFO) method. At 1 May 20X2 the company had 700 engines in inventory, valued at $190 each.

During the year ended 30 April 20X3 the following transactions took place:

20X2
1 July   Purchased 500 engines at $220 each
1 November   Sold 400 engines for $160,000

20X3
1 February   Purchased 300 engines at $230 each
15 April   Sold 250 engines for $125,000

What is the value of the company's closing inventory of engines at 30 April 20X3?

A $188,500
B $195,500
C $166,000
D None of these figures   (2 marks)

6.5 Identify, by indicating the relevant box in the table below, whether each of the following statements about the valuation of inventory are correct or incorrect, according to IAS 2 *Inventories*.

Inventory items are normally to be valued at the higher of cost and net realisable value.	Correct	Incorrect
The cost of goods manufactured by an entity will include materials and labour only. Overhead costs cannot be included.	Correct	Incorrect
LIFO (last in, first out) cannot be used to value inventory.	Correct	Incorrect
Selling price less estimated profit margin may be used to arrive at cost if this gives a reasonable approximation to actual cost.	Correct	Incorrect

(2 marks)

6.6 A company with an accounting date of 31 October carried out a physical check of inventory on 4 November 20X3, leading to an inventory value at cost at this date of $483,700.

Between 1 November 20X3 and 4 November 20X3 the following transactions took place:

1 Goods costing $38,400 were received from suppliers.

2 Goods that had cost $14,800 were sold for $20,000.

3 A customer returned, in good condition, some goods which had been sold to him in October for $600 and which had cost $400.

4 The company returned goods that had cost $1,800 in October to the supplier, and received a credit note for them.

What figure should appear in the company's financial statements at 31 October 20X3 for closing inventory, based on this information?

A $458,700
B $505,900
C $508,700
D $461,500 **(2 marks)**

6.7 In preparing its financial statements for the current year, a company's closing inventory was understated by $300,000.

What will be the effect of this error if it remains uncorrected?

A The current year's profit will be overstated and next year's profit will be understated.
B The current year's profit will be understated but there will be no effect on next year's profit.
C The current year's profit will be understated and next year's profit will be overstated.
D The current year's profit will be overstated but there will be no effect on next year's profit.

(2 marks)

6.8 The financial year of Mitex Co ended on 31 December 20X1. An inventory count on January 4 20X2 gave a total inventory value of $527,300.

The following transactions occurred between January 1 and January 4.

	$
Purchases of goods	7,900
Sales of goods (gross profit margin 40% on sales)	15,000
Goods returned to a supplier	800

What inventory value should be included in Mitex Co's financial statements at 31 December 20X1?

A $525,400
B $527,600
C $529,200
D $535,200 **(2 marks)**

6.9 Which of the following statements about IAS 2 *Inventories* is correct?

A Production overheads should be included in cost on the basis of a company's normal level of activity in the period.

B In determining the cost of inventories, trade discounts received must be deducted and selling costs must be added.

C In arriving at the cost of inventories, FIFO, LIFO and weighted average cost formulas are acceptable.

D It is permitted to value finished goods inventories at materials plus labour cost only, without adding production overheads. **(2 marks)**

6.10 You are preparing the financial statements for a business. The cost of the items in closing inventory is $41,875. This includes some items which cost $1,960 and which were damaged in transit. You have estimated that it will cost $360 to repair the items, and they can then be sold for $1,200.

What is the correct inventory valuation for inclusion in the financial statements?

A $39,915
B $40,755
C $41,515
D $42,995 **(2 marks)**

6.11 S sells three products – Basic, Super and Luxury. The following information was available at the year end.

	Basic $ per unit	Super $ per unit	Luxury $ per unit
Original cost	6	9	18
Estimated selling price	9	12	15
Selling and distribution costs	1	4	5
	units	units	units
Units of inventory	200	250	150

What is the value of inventory at the year end?

A $4,200
B $4,700
C $5,700
D $6,150 **(2 marks)**

6.12   An inventory record card shows the following details.

February   1   50 units in stock at a cost of $40 per unit
            7   100 units purchased at a cost of $45 per unit
            14   80 units sold
            21   50 units purchased at a cost of $50 per unit
            28   60 units sold

What is the value of inventory at 28 February using the FIFO method?

A $2,450
B $2,700
C $2,950
D $3,000   (2 marks)

6.13   IAS 2 *Inventories* defines the items that may be included in computing the cost of an inventory of finished goods manufactured by a business.

Which one of the following lists consists only of items which may be included in the cost of inventories, according to IAS 2?

A   Supervisor's wages, carriage inwards, carriage outwards, raw materials
B   Raw materials, carriage inwards, costs of storage of finished goods, plant depreciation
C   Plant depreciation, carriage inwards, raw materials, Supervisor's wages
D   Carriage outwards, raw materials, Supervisor's wages, plant depreciation   (2 marks)

6.14   The closing inventory of X amounted to $116,400 **excluding** the following two inventory lines:

1   400 items which had cost $4 each. All were sold after the reporting period for $3 each, with selling expenses of $200 for the batch.

2   200 different items which had cost $30 each. These items were found to be defective at the end of the reporting period. Rectification work after the statement of financial position amounted to $1,200, after which they were sold for $35 each, with selling expenses totalling $300.

Which of the following total figures should appear in the statement of financial position of X for inventory?

A $122,300
B $121,900
C $122,900
D $123,300   (2 marks)

6.15   The inventory value for the financial statements of Q for the year ended 31 December 20X4 was based on an inventory count on 4 January 20X5, which gave a total inventory value of $836,200.

Between 31 December and 4 January 20X5, the following transactions took place:

	$
Purchases of goods	8,600
Sales of goods (profit margin 30% on sales)	14,000
Goods returned by Q to supplier	700

What adjusted figure should be included in the financial statements for inventories at 31 December 20X4?

A $838,100
B $853,900
C $818,500
D $834,300   (2 marks)

6.16 A company has decided to switch from using the FIFO method of inventory valuation to using the average cost method (AVCO).

In the first accounting period where the change is made, opening inventory valued by the FIFO method was $53,200. Closing inventory valued by the AVCO method was $59,800.

Total purchases and during the period were $136,500. Using the continuous AVCO method, opening inventory would have been valued at $56,200.

What is the cost of materials that should be included in the statement of profit or loss for the period?

A $129,900
B $132,900
C $135,900
D $140,100   **(2 marks)**

6.17 Which one of the following statements about the use of a continuous inventory system is **INCORRECT**?

A   In a retail organisation, a continuous inventory system can be used to keep track of the quantity of each stock item available in its distribution centres.

B   Under continuous inventory, the cost of each receipt of inventory and the cost of each issue from inventory is recorded individually.

C   A continuous inventory system removes the need for periodic physical inventory counts.

D   Both the FIFO and average cost (AVCO) methods of pricing inventory may be used within a continuous inventory system.   **(2 marks)**

6.18 The information below relates to inventory item Z.

March   1   50 units held in opening inventory at a cost of $40 per unit
           17   50 units purchased at a cost of $50 per unit
           31   60 units sold at a selling price of $100 per unit

Under AVCO, what is the value of inventory held for item Z at the end of March 31?

A $4,000
B $1,800
C $2,000
D $2,500   **(2 marks)**

6.19 A firm has the following transactions with its product R.

1 January 20X1   Opening inventory: nil
1 February 20X1   Buys 10 units at $300 per unit
11 February 20X1   Buys 12 units at $250 per unit
1 April 20X1   Sells 8 units at $400 per unit
1 August 20X1   Buys 6 units at $200 per unit
1 December 20X1   Sells 12 units at $400 per unit

The firm uses periodic weighted average cost (AVCO) to value its inventory.

What is the inventory value at the end of the year? (Give your answer to 2 decimal places)

$_____   **(2 marks)**

(Total = 38 marks)

7 Tangible non-current assets I

46 mins

7.1 What is the purpose of charging depreciation in financial statements?

A To allocate the cost of a non-current asset over the accounting periods expected to benefit from its use

B To ensure that funds are available for the eventual replacement of the asset

C To reduce the cost of the asset in the statement of financial position to its estimated market value

D To account for the 'wearing-out' of the asset over its life **(2 marks)**

7.2 Which of the statements below correctly states the purpose of the asset register?

A An internal control to ensure details of all assets are readily available in the event of loss or theft

B To ensure the organisation is aware of the age of plant and machinery

C An internal control to ensure information relating to non-current assets in the nominal ledger and the financial statements is correct

D To enable the organisation to comply with IAS 16 Property, plant and equipment **(2 marks)**

7.3 An asset register showed a carrying amount of $67,460. A non-current asset costing $15,000 had been sold for $4,000, making a loss on disposal of $1,250. No entries had been made in the asset register for this disposal.

What is the correct balance on the asset register, once the disposal has been accounted for?

$_____. **(2 marks)**

7.4 An organisation's asset register shows a carrying amount of $145,600. The non-current asset account in the nominal ledger shows a carrying amount of $135,600. The difference could be due to a disposed asset not having been deducted from the asset register.

Which one of the following could represent that asset?

A Asset with disposal proceeds of $15,000 and a profit on disposal of $5,000
B Asset with disposal proceeds of $15,000 and a carrying amount of $5,000
C Asset with disposal proceeds of $15,000 and a loss on disposal of $5,000
D Asset with disposal proceeds of $5,000 and a carrying amount of $5,000 **(2 marks)**

7.5 Which one of the following would occur if the purchase of computer stationary was debited to the computer equipment at cost account?

A An overstatement of profit and an overstatement of non-current assets
B An understatement of profit and an overstatement of non-current assets
C An overstatement of profit and an understatement of non-current assets
D An understatement of profit and an understatement of non-current assets **(2 marks)**

7.6 Which one of the following statements correctly defines non-current assets?

A Assets that are held for use in the production of goods or services and are expected to be used during more than one accounting period

B Assets which are intended to be used by the business on a continuing basis, including both tangible and intangible assets that do not meet the IASB definition of a current asset

C Non-monetary assets without physical substance that are controlled by the entity and from which future benefits are expected to flow

D Assets in the form of materials or supplies to be consumed in the production process **(2 marks)**

7.7 A company bought a property four years ago on 1 January for $ 170,000. Since then property prices have risen substantially and the property has been revalued at $210,000.

The property was estimated as having a useful life of 20 years when it was purchased. What is the balance on the revaluation surplus reported in the statement of financial position?

A $210,000
B $136,000
C $74,000
D $34,000 **(2 marks)**

7.8 A business purchased a motor car on 1 July 20X3 for $20,000. It is to be depreciated at 20 per cent per year on the straight line basis, assuming a residual value at the end of five years of $4,000, with a proportionate depreciation charge in the years of purchase and disposal.

The $20,000 cost was correctly entered in the cash book but posted to the debit of the motor vehicles repairs account.

How will the business profit for the year ended 31 December 20X3 be affected by the error?

A Understated by $18,400
B Understated by $16,800
C Overstated by $18,400
D Overstated by $16,800 **(2 marks)**

7.9 A company's policy is to charge depreciation on plant and machinery at 20% per year on cost, with proportional depreciation for items purchased or sold during a year.

The company's plant and machinery at cost account for the year ended 30 September 20X3 is shown below.

PLANT AND MACHINERY – COST

		$			$
20X2			20X3		
1 Oct	Balance	200,000	30 Jun	Transfer disposal account	40,000
			30 Sep	Balance	210,000
20X3					
1 Apr	Cash-purchase of plant	50,000			
		250,000			250,000

What should be the depreciation charge for plant and machinery (excluding any profit or loss on the disposal) for the year ended 30 September 20X3?

A $43,000
B $51,000
C $42,000
D $45,000 **(2 marks)**

7.10 The plant and machinery at cost account of a business for the year ended 30 June 20X4 was as follows:

PLANT AND MACHINERY – COST

20X3		$	20X3		$
1 Jul	Balance	240,000	30 Sep Transfer disposal account		60,000
20X4			20X4		
1 Jan	Cash – purchase of plant	160,000	30 Jun Balance		340,000
		400,000			400,000

The company's policy is to charge depreciation at 20% per year on the straight line basis, with proportionate depreciation in the years of purchase and disposal.

What should be the depreciation charge for the year ended 30 June 20X4?

A $68,000
B $64,000
C $61,000
D $55,000   (2 marks)

7.11 A manufacturing company receives an invoice on 29 February 20X2 for work done on one of its machines. $25,500 of the cost is actually for a machine upgrade, which will improve efficiency. The accounts department do not notice and charge the whole amount to maintenance costs. Machinery is depreciated at 25% per annum on a straight-line basis, with a proportional charge in the years of acquisition and disposal.

By what amount will the profit for the year to 30 June 20X2 be understated?

A $19,125
B $25,500
C $23,375
D $21,250   (2 marks)

7.12 W bought a new printing machine. The machine was purchased for $80,000. The installation costs were $5,000 and the employees received training on how to use the machine, at a cost of $2,000. Before using the machine to print customers' orders, a test was undertaken and the paper and ink cost $1,000.

What should be the cost of the machine in the company's statement of financial position?

$_____   (2 marks)

7.13 What are the correct ledger entries to record an acquisition of a non-current asset on credit?

	Debit	Credit
A	Non-current assets – cost	Receivables
B	Payables	Non-current assets – cost
C	Non-current assets – cost	Payables
D	Non-current assets – cost	Revaluation surplus

(2 marks)

7.14 Alpha sells machine B for $50,000 cash on 30 April 20X4. Machine B cost $100,000 when it was purchased and has a carrying amount of $65,000 at the date of disposal. What are the journal entries to record the disposal of machine B?

A	Dr Accumulated depreciation	$35,000	
	Dr Loss on disposal (SPL)	$15,000	
	Dr Cash	$50,000	
	Cr Non-current assets – cost		$100,000
B	Dr Accumulated depreciation	$65,000	
	Dr Loss on disposal (SPL)	$35,000	
	Cr Non-current assets – cost		$100,000
C	Dr Accumulated depreciation	$35,000	
	Dr Cash	$50,000	
	Cr Non-current assets		$65,000
	Cr Profit on disposal (SPL)		$20,000
D	Dr Non-current assets	$65,000	
	Dr Accumulated depreciation	$35,000	
	Cr Cash	$50,000	
	Cr Profit on disposal (SPL)	$50,000	**(2 marks)**

7.15 Identify, by indicating the relevant box in the table below, whether each of the following statements is true or false.

	True	False
IAS 16 *Property, plant and equipment* requires entities to disclose the purchase date of each asset.	**True**	**False**
The carrying amount of a non-current asset is the cost or valuation of that asset less accumulated depreciation.	**True**	**False**
IAS 16 *Property, plant and equipment* permits entities to make a transfer from the revaluation surplus to retained earnings for excess depreciation on revalued assets.	**True**	**True**
Once decided, the useful life of a non-current asset should not be changed.	**True**	**False**

(2 marks)

The following information is relevant for Questions 7.16 and 7.17.

Gusna Co purchased a building on 31 December 20X1 for $750,000. At the date of acquisition, the useful life of the building was estimated to be 25 years and depreciation is calculated using the straight-line method. At 31 December 20X6, an independent valuer valued the building at $1,000,000 and the revaluation was recognised in the financial statements. Gusna's accounting policies state that excess depreciation arising on revaluation of non-current assets can be transferred from the revaluation surplus to retained earnings.

7.16 What is the depreciation charge on the building for the year ended 31 December 20X7?

    A $40,000
    B $50,000
    C $30,000
    D $42,500   **(2 marks)**

7.17 From the list of tokens below, identify the correct debit / credit entries to record the transfer of excess depreciation.

TOKEN		DEBIT ENTRY	CREDIT ENTRY
Retained earnings $20,000		Debit entry	
Revaluation surplus $20,000			Credit entry
Revaluation surplus $12,500			
Retained earnings $12,500			

(2 marks)

7.18 Which of the following should be disclosed for tangible non-current assets according to IAS 16 *Property, plant and equipment*?

1 Depreciation methods used and the total depreciation allocated for the period

2 A reconciliation of the carrying amount of non-current assets at the beginning and end of the period

3 For revalued assets, whether an independent valuer was involved in the valuation

4 For revalued assets, the effective date of the revaluation

A 2 and 4 only
B 1 and 2 only
C 1, 2, 3 and 4
D 3 and 4 only

(2 marks)

7.19 On 1 October 2011, X Co purchased a property for $400,000. The property had a useful life of 40 years and was depreciated on a straight-line basis. On 1 October 2015, the property was revalued to $432,000. The remaining useful life at that date was 36 years. The company wishes to make the allowed transfer of excess depreciation between the revaluation surplus and retained earnings.

Which of the following correctly records the transfer at 30 September 2016?

	Debit	Credit
A	Retained earnings $2,000	Revaluation surplus $2,000
B	Revaluation surplus $2,000	Retained earnings $2,000
C	Retained earnings $12,000	Revaluation surplus $12,000
D	Revaluation surplus $12,000	Retained earnings $12,000

(2 marks)

(Total = 38 marks)

8 Tangible non-current assets II

48 mins

8.1 A car was purchased by a newsagent business in May 20X0 for:

	$
Cost	10,000
Road tax	150
Total	10,150

The business adopts a date of 31 December as its year end.

The car was traded in for a replacement vehicle in August 20X3 at an agreed value of $5,000.

It has been depreciated at 25% per annum on the reducing balance method, charging a full year's depreciation in the year of purchase and none in the year of sale.

What was the profit or loss on disposal of the vehicle during the year ended December 20X3?

$_____ profit. **(2 marks)**

8.2 The carrying amount of a company's non-current assets was $200,000 at 1 August 20X0. During the year ended 31 July 20X1, the company sold non-current assets for $25,000 on which it made a loss of $5,000. The depreciation charge for the year was $20,000. What was the carrying amount of non-current assets at 31 July 20X1?

A $150,000
B $155,000
C $160,000
D $180,000 **(2 marks)**

8.3 Y purchased some plant on 1 January 20X0 for $38,000. The payment for the plant was correctly entered in the cash book but was entered on the debit side of the plant repairs account.

Y charges depreciation on the straight line basis at 20% per year, with a proportionate charge in the years of acquisition and disposal, and assuming no scrap value at the end of the life of the asset.

How will Y's profit for the year ended 31 March 20X0 be affected by the error?

A Understated by $30,400
B Understated by $36,100
C Understated by $38,000
D Overstated by $1,900 **(2 marks)**

8.4 B acquired a lorry on 1 May 20X0 at a cost of $30,000. The lorry has an estimated useful life of four years, and an estimated resale value at the end of that time of $6,000. B charges depreciation on the straight line basis, with a proportionate charge in the period of acquisition.

What will the depreciation charge for the lorry be in B's accounting period to 30 September 20X0?

A $3,000
B $2,500
C $2,000
D $5,000 **(2 marks)**

8.5 At 31 December 20X3 Q, a limited liability company, owned a building that had cost $800,000 on 1 January 20W4.

It was being depreciated at 2% per year.

On 31 December 20X3 a revaluation to $1,000,000 was recognised. At this date the building had a remaining useful life of 40 years.

What is the balance on the revaluation surplus at 31 December 20X3 and the depreciation charge in the statement of profit or loss for the year ended 31 December 20X4?

	Depreciation charge for year ended 31 December 20X4 (statement of profit or loss) $	Revaluation surplus as at 31 December 20X3 (statement of financial position) $
A	25,000	200,000
B	25,000	360,000
C	20,000	200,000
D	20,000	360,000

(2 marks)

8.6 Which of the following best explains what is meant by 'capital expenditure'?

A Expenditure on non-current assets, including repairs and maintenance
B Expenditure on expensive assets
C Expenditure relating to the issue of share capital
D Expenditure relating to the acquisition or improvement of non-current assets

(2 marks)

8.7 Which of the following costs would be classified as capital expenditure for a restaurant business?

A A replacement for a broken window
B Repainting the restaurant
C An illuminated sign advertising the business name
D Cleaning of the kitchen floors

(2 marks)

8.8 Which one of the following costs would be classified as revenue expenditure on the invoice for a new company car?

A Road tax
B Number plates
C Fitted stereo
D Delivery costs

(2 marks)

8.9 Lance is entering an invoice for a new item of equipment in the accounts. The invoice shows the following costs:

Water treatment equipment	$39,800
Delivery	$1,100
Maintenance charge	$3,980
Sales tax	$7,854
Invoice total	$52,734

Lance is registered for sales tax. What is the total value of capital expenditure on the invoice?

A $39,800
B $40,900
C $44,880
D $52,734

(2 marks)

8.10 Which one of the following assets may be classified as a non-current asset in the financial statements of a business?

    A   A tax refund due next year
    B   A motor vehicle held for resale
    C   A computer used in the office
    D   Cleaning products used to clean the office floors   **(2 marks)**

8.11 Which of the following items should be included in current assets?

    (i)   Assets which are not intended to be converted into cash
    (ii)   Assets which will be converted into cash in the long term
    (iii)   Assets which will be converted into cash in the near future

    A   (i) only
    B   (ii) only
    C   (iii) only
    D   (ii) and (iii)   **(2 marks)**

8.12 Which of the following statements describes current assets?

    A   Assets which are currently located on the business premises
    B   Assets which are used to conduct the organisation's current business
    C   Assets which are expected to be converted into cash in the short-term
    D   Assets which are not expected to be converted into cash in the short-term   **(2 marks)**

8.13 Gamma purchases a motor vehicle on 30 September 20X1 for $15,000 on credit. Gamma has a policy of depreciating motor vehicles using the reducing balance method at 15% per annum, pro rata in the years of purchase and sale.

What are the correct ledger entries to record the purchase of the vehicle at 30 September 20X1 and what is the depreciation charge for the year ended 30 November 20X1?

	Purchase of motor vehicle on 30.9.X1			Depreciation charge for year ended 30.11.X1
A	Dr Non-current assets – cost	$15,000		$2,250
	Cr Payables		$15,000	
B	Dr Payables	$15,000		$2,250
	Cr Non-current assets – cost		$15,000	
C	Dr Non-current assets – cost	$15,000		$375
	Cr Payables		$15,000	
D	Dr Payables	$15,000		$375
	Cr Non-current assets – cost		$15,000	**(2 marks)**

8.14 Banjo Co purchased a building on 30 June 20X8 for $1,250,000. At acquisition, the useful life of the building was 50 years. Depreciation is calculated on the straight-line basis. 10 years later, on 30 June 20Y8 when the carrying amount of the building was $1,000,000, the building was revalued to $1,600,000. Banjo Co has a policy of transferring the excess depreciation on revaluation from the revaluation surplus to retained earnings.

Assuming no further revaluations take place, what is the balance on the revaluation surplus at 30 June 20Y9?

    A $335,000
    B $310,000
    C $560,000
    D $585,000   **(2 marks)**

8.15 A non-current asset (cost $15,000, depreciation $10,000) is given in part exchange for a new asset costing $20,500. The agreed trade-in value was $5,500. Which of the following will be included in the statement of profit or loss?

A   A profit on disposal $5,500
B   A loss on disposal $4,500
C   A loss on purchase of a new asset $5,500
D   A profit on disposal $500   **(2 marks)**

8.16 Baxter Co purchased an asset for $100,000 on 1.1.X1. It had an estimated useful life of 5 years and it was depreciated using the straight line method. On 1.1.X3 Baxter Co revised the remaining estimated useful life to 8 years.

What is the carrying amount of the asset at 31.12.X3?

A $40,000
B $52,500
C $40,000
D $62,500   **(2 marks)**

8.17 Senakuta Co purchased a machine with an estimated useful life of 5 years for $34,000 on 30 September 20X5. Senakuta Co planned to scrap the machine at the end of its useful life and estimated that the scrap value at the purchase date was $4,000. On 1 October 20X8, Senakuta revised the scrap value to $2,000 due to the decreased value of scrap metal.

What is the depreciation charge for the year ended 30 September 20X9?

A $7,000
B $6,800
C $2,800
D $6,400   **(2 marks)**

8.18 Evans Co purchased a machine with an estimated useful life of 10 years for $76,000 on 30 September 20X5. The machine had a residual value of $16,000.

What are the ledger entries to record the depreciation charge for the machine in the year ended 30 September 20X8?

A   Dr Depreciation charge $6,000
               Cr Accumulated depreciation $6,000

B   Dr Depreciation charge $6,000
               Dr Non-current assets $12,000
               Cr Accumulated depreciation $18,000

C   Dr Accumulated depreciation $6,000
               Cr Depreciation charge $6,000

D   Dr Accumulated depreciation $18,000
               Cr Non-current assets $18,000   **(2 marks)**

8.19 Banter Co purchased an office building on 1 January 20X1. The building cost was $1,600,000 and this was depreciated by the straight line method at 2% per year, assuming a 50-year life and nil residual value. The building was re-valued to $2,250,000 on 1 January 20X6. The useful life was not revised. The excess depreciation charge will be transferred from the revaluation surplus to retained earnings each year. The company's financial year ends on 31 December.

What is the balance on the revaluation surplus at 31 December 20X6?

$_____   **(2 marks)**

8.20 A company purchased an asset on 1 January 20X3 at a cost of $1,000,000. It is depreciated over 50 years by the straight line method (nil residual value), with a proportionate charge for depreciation in the year of acquisition and the year of disposal. At 31 December 20X4 the asset was re-valued to $1,200,000. There was no change in the expected useful life of the asset.

The asset was sold on 30 June 20X5 for $1,195,000.

What profit or loss on disposal of the asset will be reported in the statement of profit or loss of the company for the year ended 31 December 20X5?

A   Profit of $7,500
B   Profit of $235,000
C   Profit of $247,500
D   Loss of $5,000   **(2 marks)**

(Total = 40 marks)

9   Intangible non-current assets   34 mins

9.1   Identify, by clicking on the relevant box in the table below, whether each of the following statements about research and development expenditure are true or false, according to IAS 38 *Intangible assets*.

	True	False
Research expenditure, other than capital expenditure on research facilities, should be recognised as an expense as incurred.		
In deciding whether development expenditure qualifies to be recognised as an asset, it is necessary to consider whether there will be adequate finance available to complete the project.		
Development expenditure recognised as an asset must be amortised over a period not exceeding five years.		

(2 marks)

9.2   According to IAS 38 *Intangible assets,* which of the following statements about research and development expenditure are correct?

1   If certain conditions are met, an entity may decide to capitalise development expenditure.

2   Research expenditure, other than capital expenditure on research facilities, must be written off as incurred.

3   Capitalised development expenditure must be amortised over a period not exceeding 5 years.

4   Capitalised development expenditure must be disclosed in the statement of financial position under intangible non-current assets.

A   1, 2 and 4 only
B   1 and 3 only
C   2 and 4 only
D   3 and 4 only   **(2 marks)**

9.3 According to IAS 38 *Intangible assets,* which of the following statements concerning the accounting treatment of research and development expenditure are TRUE?

1 Development costs recognised as an asset must be amortised over a period not exceeding five years.

2 Research expenditure, other than capital expenditure on research facilities, should be recognised as an expense as incurred.

3 In deciding whether development expenditure qualifies to be recognised as an asset, it is necessary to consider whether there will be adequate finance available to complete the project.

4 Development projects must be reviewed at each reporting date, and expenditure on any project no longer qualifying for capitalisation must be amortised through the statement of profit or loss and other comprehensive income over a period not exceeding five years.

A   1 and 4
B   2 and 4
C   2 and 3
D   1 and 3   (2 marks)

9.4 According to IAS 38 *Intangible assets,* which of the following statements is/are correct?

1 Capitalised development expenditure must be amortised over a period not exceeding five years.

2 If all the conditions specified in IAS 38 are met, development expenditure may be capitalised if the directors decide to do so.

3 Capitalised development costs are shown in the statement of financial position under the heading of non-current assets.

4 Amortisation of capitalised development expenditure will appear as an item in a company's statement of changes in equity.

A   3 only
B   2 and 3
C   1 and 4
D   1 and 3   (2 marks)

9.5 According to IAS 38 *Intangible assets*, which of the following are intangible non-current assets in the financial statements of Iota Co?

1 A patent for a new glue purchased for $20,000 by Iota Co
2 Development costs capitalised in accordance with IAS 38
3 A licence to broadcast a television series, purchased by Iota Co for $150,000
4 A state of the art factory purchased by Iota Co for $1.5million

A   1 and 3 only
B   1, 2 and 3 only
C   2 and 4 only
D   2, 3 and 4 only   (2 marks)

9.6 According to IAS 38 *Intangible assets,* which of the following statements about intangible assets are correct?

1 If certain criteria are met, research expenditure must be recognised as an intangible asset.
2 If certain criteria are met, development expenditure must be capitalised
3 Intangible assets must be amortised if they have a definite useful life

A   2 and 3 only
B   1 and 3 only
C   1 and 2 only
D   1, 2, and 3   (2 marks)

9.7 According to IAS 38 *Intangible assets,* which of the following statements concerning the accounting treatment of research and development expenditure are true?

    1   Research expenditure, other than capital expenditure on research facilities, should be recognised as an expense as incurred.

    2   In deciding whether development expenditure qualifies to be recognised as an asset, it is necessary to consider whether there will be adequate finance available to complete the project.

    3   Development expenditure recognised as an asset must be amortised over a period not exceeding five years.

    4   The financial statements should disclose the total amount of research and development expenditure recognised as an expense during the period.

    A   1, 2 and 3
    B   1, 2 and 4
    C   1, 3 and 4
    D   2, 3 and 4   **(2 marks)**

9.8 According to IAS 38 *Intangible assets,* which of the following statements are correct?

    1   Research expenditure should not be capitalised.
    2   Intangible assets are never amortised.
    3   Development expenditure must be capitalised if certain conditions are met.

    A   1 and 3 only
    B   1 and 2 only
    C   2 and 3 only
    D   All three statements are correct   **(2 marks)**

9.9 Theta Co purchased a patent on 31 December 20X3 for $250,000. Theta Co expects to use the patent for ten years, after which it will be valueless.

According to IAS 38 *Intangible assets,* what amount will be amortised in Theta Co's statement of profit or loss and other comprehensive income for the year ended 31 December 20X4?

    $_____   **(2 marks)**

9.10 PF purchased a quota for carbon dioxide emissions for $15,000 on 30 April 20X6 and capitalised it as an intangible asset in its statement of financial position. PF estimates that the quota will have a useful life of three years. What is the journal entry required to record the amortisation of the quota in the accounts for the year ended 30 April 20X9?

    A   Dr Expenses $15,000
            Cr Accumulated amortisation $15,000

    B   Dr Expenses $5,000
            Cr Accumulated amortisation $5,000

    C   Dr Intangible assets $5,000
            Cr Accumulated amortisation $5,000

    D   Dr Accumulated amortisation $15,000
            Cr Intangible assets $15,000   **(2 marks)**

9.11 What is the purpose of amortisation?

    A   To allocate the cost of an intangible non-current asset over its useful life

    B   To ensure that funds are available for the eventual purchase of a replacement non-current asset

    C   To reduce the cost of an intangible non-current asset in the statement of financial position to its estimated market value

    D   To account for the risk associated with intangible assets   **(2 marks)**

9.12 Which of the following items (that all generate future economic benefits, and whose costs can be measured reliably), is an intangible non-current asset?

1 Computer hardware owned by a business
2 Operating software that operates the computer hardware in (1)
3 A patent bought by a business
4 An extension to an office building owned by a business

A All four items
B 1, 2 and 4 only
C 1 and 2 only
D 3 only

(2 marks)

(Total = 24 marks)

10 Accruals and prepayments   36 mins

10.1 A company receives rent for subletting part of its office block.

Rent, receivable quarterly in advance, is received as follows:

Date of receipt	Period covered		$
1 October 20X1	3 months to	31 December 20X1	7,500
30 December 20X1	3 months to	31 March 20X2	7,500
4 April 20X2	3 months to	30 June 20X2	9,000
1 July 20X2	3 months to	30 September 20X2	9,000
1 October 20X2	3 months to	31 December 20X2	9,000

What figures, based on these receipts, should appear in the company's financial statements for the year ended 30 November 20X2?

	Statement of profit or loss	Statement of financial position
A	$34,000 Debit	Rent in arrears (Dr) $3,000
B	$34,500 Credit	Rent received in advance (Cr) $6,000
C	$34,000 Credit	Rent received in advance (Cr) $3,000
D	$34,000 Credit	Rent in arrears (Dr) $3,000

(2 marks)

10.2 A company pays rent quarterly in arrears on 1 January, 1 April, 1 July and 1 October each year. The rent was increased from $90,000 per year to $120,000 per year as from 1 October 20X2.

What rent expense and accrual should be included in the company's financial statements for the year ended 31 January 20X3?

	Rent expense	Accrual
	$	$
A	100,000	20,000
B	100,000	10,000
C	97,500	10,000
D	97,500	20,000

(2 marks)

10.3 At 31 March 20X2 a company had oil in hand to be used for heating costing $8,200 and an unpaid heating oil bill for $3,600.

At 31 March 20X3 the heating oil in hand was $9,300 and there was an outstanding heating oil bill of $3,200.

Payments made for heating oil during the year ended 31 March 20X3 totalled $34,600.

Based on these figures, what expense should appear in the company's statement of profit or loss and other comprehensive income for heating oil for the year?

$_____.   **(2 marks)**

10.4 A company has sublet part of its offices and in the year ended 30 November 20X3 the rent receivable was:

Until 30 June 20X3 $8,400 per year
From 1 July 20X3 $12,000 per year

Rent was paid quarterly in advance on 1 January, April, July, and October each year.

What amounts should appear in the company's financial statements for the year ended 30 November 20X3?

	Rent receivable	Statement of financial position
A	$9,900	$2,000 in sundry payables
B	$9,900	$1,000 in sundry payables
C	$10,200	$1,000 in sundry payables
D	$9,900	$2,000 in sundry receivables

(2 marks)

10.5 A business compiling its financial statements for the year to 31 July each year pays rent quarterly in advance on 1 January, 1 April, 1 July and 1 October each year. The annual rent was increased from $60,000 per year to $72,000 per year as from 1 October 20X3.

What figure should appear for rent expense in the business's statement of profit or loss and other comprehensive income for the year ended 31 July 20X4?

A $69,000
B $62,000
C $70,000
D $63,000   **(2 marks)**

10.6 One of the products a garage sells to motorists is diesel fuel. Diesel fuel in inventory at 1 November 20X7 was $12,500, and there were invoices awaited for $1,700. During the year to 31 October 20X8, diesel fuel invoices of $85,400 were paid, and a delivery worth $1,300 had yet to be invoiced. (This was the only outstanding balance on the diesel fuel payable account at the year end.) At 31 October 20X8, the inventory of diesel fuel was valued at $9,800. What is the value of diesel fuel to be charged to the garage's statement of profit or loss and other comprehensive income for the year to 31 October 20X8?

A $87,700
B $89,400
C $88,500
D $91,100   **(2 marks)**

10.7 The electricity account for the year ended 30 June 20X1 was as follows.

	$
Opening balance for electricity accrued at 1 July 20X0	300
Payments made during the year	
1 August 20X0 for three months to 31 July 20X0	600
1 November 20X0 for three months to 31 October 20X0	720
1 February 20X1 for three months to 31 January 20X1	900
30 June 20X1 for three months to 30 April 20X1	840
1 August 20X1 for three months to 31 July 20X1	840

Which of the following is the appropriate entry for electricity?

	Accrued *at 30 June 20X1*	*Charge to SPL* *year ended 30 June 20X1*
A	$Nil	$3,060
B	$460	$3,320
C	$560	$3,320
D	$560	$3,420

(2 marks)

10.8 The year end of M Co is 30 November 20X0. The company pays for its gas by a standing order of $600 per month. On 1 December 20W9, the statement from the gas supplier showed that M Co had overpaid by $200. M Co received gas bills for the four quarters commencing on 1 December 20W9 and ending on 30 November 20X0 for $1,300, $1,400, $2,100 and $2,000 respectively.

Which of the following is the correct charge for gas in M Inc's statement of profit or loss for the year ended 30 November 20X0?

A $6,800
B $7,000
C $7,200
D $7,400

(2 marks)

10.9 A business compiling its financial statements for the year to 31 January each year pays rent quarterly in advance on 1 January, 1 April, 1 July and 1 October each year. After remaining unchanged for some years, the rent was increased from $24,000 per year to $30,000 per year as from 1 July 20X0.

Which of the following figures is the rent expense which should appear in the statement of profit or loss for year ended 31 January 20X1?

A $27,500
B $29,500
C $28,000
D $29,000

(2 marks)

10.10 Blint, a limited liability company, receives rent for subletting part of its office premises to a number of tenants.

In the year ended 31 December 20X4 Blint received cash of $318,600 from its tenants.

Details of rent in advance and in arrears at the beginning and end of 20X4 are as follows:

	31 December	
	20X4	*20X3*
	$	*$*
Rent received in advance	28,400	24,600
Rent owing by tenants	18,300	16,900

All rent owing was subsequently received

What is the figure for rental income that Blint should include in its statement of profit or loss for 20X4?

$_____

(2 marks)

10.11 During 20X4, Hild Co paid a total of $60,000 for rent, covering the period from 1 October 20X3 to 31 March 20X5.

What figures should appear in Hild Co's financial statements for the year ended 31 December 20X4?

	Statement of profit or loss and other comprehensive income	Statement of financial position
	$	$
A	40,000	10,000 Prepayment
B	40,000	15,000 Prepayment
C	50,000	10,000 Accrual
D	50,000	15,000 Accrual

(2 marks)

10.12 The trainee accountant at Judd Co has forgotten to make an accrual for rent for December in the financial statements for the year ended 31 December 20X2. Rent is charged in arrears at the end of February, May, August and November each year. The bill payable in February is expected to be $30,000. Judd Co's draft statement of profit or loss shows a profit of $25,000 and draft statement of financial position shows net assets of $275,000.

What is the profit or loss for the year and what is the net asset position after the accrual has been included in the financial statements?

	Profit for the year	Net asset position
A	$15,000	$265,000
B	$15,000	$285,000
C	$35,000	$265,000
D	$35,000	$285,000

(2 marks)

10.13 Buster's draft financial statements for the year to 31 October 20X5 report a loss of $1,486. When he prepared the financial statements, Buster did not include an accrual of $1,625 and a prepayment of $834.

What is Buster's profit or loss for the year to 31 October 20X5 following the inclusion of the accrual and prepayment?

A   A loss of $695
B   A loss of $2,277
C   A loss of $3,945
D   A profit of $1,807

(2 marks)

10.14 Bookz Co pays royalties to writers annually, in February, the payment covering the previous calendar year.

As at the end of December 20X2, Bookz Co had accrued $100,000 in royalties due to writers. However, a check of the royalty calculation performed in January 20X3 established that the actual figure due to be paid by Bookz Co to writers was $150,000.

Before this under-accrual was discovered, Bookz Co's draft statement of profit or loss for the accounting year ended 31 December 20X2 showed a profit of $125,000 and their draft statement of financial position showed net assets of $375,000.

What will Bookz Co's profit and net asset position be after an entry to correct the under-accrual has been processed?

	Profit for the year	Net asset position
A	$175,000	$425,000
B	$125,000	$375,000
C	$75,000	$325,000
D	$25,000	$225,000

(2 marks)

10.15 Danya owns a small shop and the following information concerns the heat and light account for the year to 31 March 2017:

	Gas	Electricity
At 31 March 2016	1,000 prepayment	500 accrual
At 31 March 2017	2,000 accrual	1,200 prepayment

During the year, Danya made payments of $5,000 for gas and $7,800 for electricity.

What is the total heat and light expense for the year ended 31 March 2017?

A $14,100
B $13,100
C $12,500
D $11,500

(2 marks)

(Total = 30 marks)

11 Receivables and payables   48 mins

11.1 Identify, by indicating the relevant box in the table below, whether each of the following statements is true or false.

Payables represent money the business owes.	True	False
Payables are an asset.	True	False
Receivables represent money owed to the business.	True	False

(2 marks)

11.2 At 31 December 20X2 a company's receivables totalled $400,000 and an allowance for receivables of $50,000 had been brought forward from the year ended 31 December 20X1.

It was decided to write off debts totalling $38,000. The allowance for receivables was to be adjusted to the equivalent of 10% of the receivables.

What charge for receivables expense should appear in the company's statement of profit or loss for the year ended 31 December 20X2?

A $74,200
B $51,800
C $28,000
D $24,200

(2 marks)

11.3 At 1 July 20X2 the receivables allowance of Q was $18,000.

During the year ended 30 June 20X3 debts totalling $14,600 were written off. The receivables allowance required was to be $16,000 as at 30 June 20X3.

What amount should appear in Q's statement of profit or loss for receivables expense for the year ended 30 June 20X3?

A $12,600
B $16,600
C $48,600
D $30,600

(2 marks)

11.4 At 30 September 20X2 a company's allowance for receivables amounted to $38,000, which was equivalent to five per cent of the receivables at that date.

At 30 September 20X3 receivables totalled $868,500. It was decided to write off $28,500 of debts as irrecoverable. The allowance for receivables required was to be the equivalent of five per cent of receivables.

What should be the charge in the statement of profit or loss for the year ended 30 September 20X3 for receivables expense?

$_____   (2 marks)

11.5 At 1 July 20X3 a limited liability company had an allowance for receivables of $83,000.

During the year ended 30 June 20X4 debts totalling $146,000 were written off. At 30 June 20X4 a receivables allowance of $218,000 was required.

What figure should appear in the company's statement of profit or loss for the year ended 30 June 20X4 for receivables expense?

A $155,000
B $364,000
C $281,000
D $11,000   (2 marks)

11.6 A company has received cash for a debt that was previously written off. Which of the following is the correct double entry to record the cash received?

	Debit	Credit
A	Irrecoverable debts expense	Accounts receivable
B	Cash	Irrecoverable debts expense
C	Allowance for receivables	Accounts receivable
D	Cash	Allowance for receivables

(2 marks)

11.7 At 31 December 20X4 a company's trade receivables totalled $864,000 and the allowance for receivables was $48,000.

It was decided that debts totalling $13,000 were to be written off. The allowance for receivables was to be adjusted to the equivalent of five per cent of the receivables.

What figures should appear in the statement of financial position for trade receivables (after deducting the allowance) and in the statement of profit or loss for receivables expense?

	Statement of profit or loss $	Statement of financial position $
A	8,200	807,800
B	7,550	808,450
C	18,450	808,450
D	55,550	808,450

(2 marks)

11.8 Which of the following would a decrease in the allowance for receivables result in?

A   An increase in liabilities
B   A decrease in working capital
C   A decrease in net profit
D   An increase in net profit   (2 marks)

11.9 A company has been notified that a customer has been declared bankrupt. The company had previously made an allowance for this debt. Which of the following is the correct double entry to account for this new information?

	Debit	Credit	
A	Irrecoverable debts	Receivables	
B	Receivables	Irrecoverable debts	
C	Allowance for receivables	Receivables	
D	Receivables	Allowance for receivables	**(2 marks)**

11.10 An increase in an allowance for receivables of $8,000 has been treated as a reduction in the allowance in the financial statements. Which of the following explains the resulting effects?

A   Net profit is overstated by $16,000, receivables overstated by $8,000
B   Net profit understated by $16,000, receivables understated by $16,000
C   Net profit overstated by $16,000, receivables overstated by $16,000
D   Gross profit overstated by $16,000, receivables overstated by $16,000   **(2 marks)**

11.11 At 1 January 20X1, there was an allowance for receivables of $3,000. During the year, $1,000 of debts were written off as irrecoverable, and $800 of debts previously written off were recovered. At 31 December 20X1, it was decided to adjust the allowance for receivables to 5% of receivables which are $20,000.

What figure should be included in the statement of profit or loss as the receivables expense for the year?

$_____ debit / credit   **(2 marks)**

11.12 Top Co has total receivables outstanding of $280,000. The accountant believes that approximately 1% of these balances will not be collected, so wishes to make an allowance of $28,000. No previous allowance has been made for receivables.

Which of the following is the correct double entry to create this allowance?

	Debit	Credit	
A	Irrecoverable debts	Allowance for receivables	
B	Allowance for receivables	Receivables	
C	Irrecoverable debts	Receivables	
D	Receivables	Allowance for receivables	**(2 marks)**

11.13 At the beginning of the year, the allowance for receivables was $850. At the year-end, the allowance required was $1,000. During the year $500 of debts were written off, which includes $100 previously included in the allowance for receivables.

What is the charge to statement of profit or loss for receivables expense for the year?

A $1,500
B $1,000
C $650
D $550   **(2 marks)**

11.14 Which **TWO** of the following statements are correct?

A   An aged receivables analysis shows how long invoices for each customer have been outstanding.

B   A credit limit is a tool applied by the credit control department to make suppliers provide goods on time.

C   Receivables are included in the statement of financial position net of the receivables allowance.

D   Credit limits are applied to customers who purchase goods using cash only.   **(2 marks)**

11.15 At 31 May 20X7 Roberta's trial balance included the following items.

	$
Inventory at 1 June 20X6	23,856
Trade receivables	55,742
Trade payables	32,165
Bank overdraft	5,855
Loan due for repayment in 20X9	15,000

What is the value of Roberta's current liabilities at 31 May 20X7?

A $38,020
B $53,020
C $61,597
D $76,597   **(2 marks)**

11.16 Which one of the following statements is **NOT** a benefit of offering credit facilities to customers?

A   Improved convenience for the customer
B   The separation of product and service delivery from payment
C   Provides time for appropriate payment approval procedures
D   Fewer irrecoverable debts   **(2 marks)**

11.17 What is the correct double entry for discounts received?

	Debit	*Credit*
A	Payables control account	Expenses
B	Expenses	Payables control account
C	Discounts received (income)	Payables control account
D	Payables control account	Discounts received (income)

(2 marks)

11.18 Which of the following is/are examples of payables of a business?

1   Interest owed from the bank
2   Loans and advances to employees
3   Money owed from customers
4   Tax owed to the tax authority

A   1 and 3 only
B   2 and 3 only
C   2 and 4 only
D   4 only   **(2 marks)**

11.19 Which of the following is/are examples of payables of a business?

1   An estimation of tax owed to the tax authority for the year just ended
2     $500 owed to a supplier for invoiced goods
3   An estimation of probable repair costs under warranty claims

A   1 and 2 only
B   1 and 3 only
C   2 only
D   1, 2 and 3   **(2 marks)**

11.20 A business commenced trading on 01 January 20X1. The following transactions with Supplier A have been recorded in the purchase ledger.

	01 January 20X1	Opening balance	$nil
(1)	01 January 20X1	Purchase of goods	$50
(2)	01 February 20X1	Purchase of goods	$435
(3)	30 March 20X1	Payment	$385
	31 March 20X1	Closing balance	$100

On 31 March 20X1, the business receives the following statement from the supplier.

	Opening balance		$nil
(4)	1 January 20X1	Invoice #365	$50
(5)	1 February 20X1	Invoice #490	$435
(6)	31 March 20X1	Invoice #533	$35
	Closing balance		$520

Which transactions should be noted as reconciling items on the supplier statement reconciliation at 31 March 20X1?

A   3 only
B   6 only
C   3 and 6 only
D   1 to 6   **(2 marks)**

(Total = 40 marks)

12   Provisions and contingencies   31 mins

12.1   Identify, by indicating the relevant box in the table below, whether each of the following statements about provisions and contingencies is true or false.

	True	False
A company should disclose details of the change in carrying amount of a provision from the beginning to the end of the year.	True	False
Contingent assets must be recognised in the financial statements in accordance with the prudence concept.	True	False
Contingent liabilities must be treated as actual liabilities and provided for if it is probable that they will arise.	True	False

(2 marks)

12.2 Which of the following statements about contingent assets and contingent liabilities are correct?

1   A contingent asset should be disclosed by note if an inflow of economic benefits is probable.

2   A contingent liability should be disclosed by note if it is probable that a transfer of economic benefits to settle it will be required, with no provision being made.

3   No disclosure is required for a contingent liability if it is not probable that a transfer of economic benefits to settle it will be required.

4   No disclosure is required for either a contingent liability or a contingent asset if the likelihood of a payment or receipt is remote.

A   1 and 4 only
B   2 and 3 only
C   2, 3 and 4
D   1, 2 and 4   **(2 marks)**

12.3 A former director of Biss Co has commenced an action against the company claiming substantial damages for wrongful dismissal. The company's solicitors have advised that the former director is unlikely to succeed with his claim, although the chance of Biss Co paying any monies to the ex-director is not remote. The solicitors' estimates of Biss Co's potential liabilities are:

	$
Legal costs (to be incurred whether the claim is successful or not)	50,000
Settlement of claim if successful	500,000
	550,000

According to IAS 37 *Provisions, contingent liabilities and continent assets*, how should this claim be treated in Bliss Co's financial statements?

A   Provision of $550,000
B   Disclose a contingent liability of $550,000
C   Disclose a provision of $50,000 and a contingent liability of $500,000
D   Provision for $500,000 and a contingent liability of $50,000   **(2 marks)**

12.4 The following items have to be considered in finalising the financial statements of Q, a limited liability company:

1   The company gives warranties on its products. The company's statistics show that about 5% of sales give rise to a warranty claim.

2   The company has guaranteed the overdraft of another company. The likelihood of a liability arising under the guarantee is assessed as possible.

According to IAS 37 *Provisions, contingent liabilities and continent assets*, what is the correct action to be taken in the financial statements for these items?

	Create a provision	*Disclose by note only*	*No action*
A	1	2	
B		1	2
C	1, 2		
D	2	1	

(2 marks)

12.5 Which of the following statements about the requirements of IAS 37 *Provisions, contingent liabilities and contingent assets* are correct?

1   A contingent asset should be disclosed by note if an inflow of economic benefits is probable.

2   No disclosure of a contingent liability is required if the possibility of a transfer of economic benefits arising is remote.

3   Contingent assets must not be recognised in financial statements unless an inflow of economic benefits is virtually certain to arise.

A   All three statements are correct
B   1 and 2 only
C   1 and 3 only
D   2 and 3 only   **(2 marks)**

12.6 Wanda Co allows customers to return faulty goods within 14 days of purchase. At 30 November 20X5 a provision of $6,548 was made for sales returns. At 30 November 20X6, the provision was re-calculated and should now be $7,634.

What should be reported in Wanda Co's statement of profit or loss for the year to 31 October 20X6 in respect of the provision?

A   A charge of $7,634
B   A credit of $7,634
C   A charge of $1,086
D   A credit of $1,086   **(2 marks)**

12.7 Doggard Co is a business that sells second hand cars. If a car develops a fault within 30 days of the sale, Doggard Co will repair it free of charge.

At 30 April 20X4 Doggard Co had made a provision for repairs of $2,500. At 30 April 20X5 Doggard Co calculated that the provision should be $2,000.

What entry should be made for the provision in Doggard Co's statement of profit or loss for the year to 30 April 20X5?

A   A charge of $500
B   A credit of $500
C   A charge of $2,000
D   A credit of $2,000   **(2 marks)**

12.8 Which of the following best describes a provision according to IAS 37 *Provisions, contingent liabilities and contingent assets*?

A   A provision is a liability of uncertain timing or amount.

B   A provision is a possible obligation of uncertain timing or amount.

C   A provision is a credit balance set up to offset a contingent asset so that the effect on the statement of financial position is nil.

D   A provision is a possible asset that arises from past events.   **(2 marks)**

12.9 Which of the following items does the statement below describe?

According to IAS 37 *Provisions, contingent liabilities and contingent assets*, 'A possible obligation that arises from past events and whose existence will be confirmed only by the occurrence or non-occurrence of one or more uncertain future events not wholly within the entity's control'

A   A provision
B   A current liability
C   A contingent liability
D   A contingent asset   **(2 marks)**

12.10 Montague's paint shop has suffered some bad publicity as a result of a customer claiming to be suffering from skin rashes as a result of using a new brand of paint sold by Montague's shop. The customer launched a court action against Montague in November 20X3, claiming damages of $5,000. Montague's lawyer has advised him that the most probable outcome is that he will have to pay the customer $3,000.

What amount should Montague include as a provision in his financial statements for the year ended 31 December 20X3?

$_____

(2 marks)

12.11 Mobiles Co sells goods with a one year warranty under which customers are covered for any defect that becomes apparent within a year of purchase. In calendar year 20X4, Mobiles Co sold 100,000 units.

The company expects warranty claims for 5% of units sold. Half of these claims will be for a major defect, with an average claim value of $50. The other half of these claims will be for a minor defect, with an average claim value of $10.

What amount should Mobiles Co include as a provision in the statement of financial position for the year ended 31 December 20X4?

A $125,000
B $ 25,000
C $300,000
D $150,000

(2 marks)

12.12 When a provision is needed that involves a number of outcomes, the provision is calculated using the expected value of expenditure. The expected value of expenditure is the total expenditure of:

A   Each possible outcome
B   Each possible outcome weighted according to the probability of each outcome happening
C   Each possible outcome divided by the number of outcomes
D   Each possible outcome multiplied by the number of outcomes

(2 marks)

12.13 X Co sells goods with a one year warranty and had a provision for warranty claims of $64,000 at 31 December 20X0. During the year ended 31 December 20X1, $25,000 in claims were paid to customers. On 31 December 20X1, X Co estimated that the following claims will be paid in the following year:

Scenario	Probability	Anticipated cost
Worst case	5%	$150,000
Best case	20%	$25,000
Most likely	75%	$60,000

What amount should X Co record in the statement of profit or loss for the year ended 31 December 20X1 in respect of the provision?

A $57,500
B $6,500
C $18,500
D $39,000

(2 marks)

(Total = 26 marks)

13 Capital structure and finance costs 34 mins

13.1 The issued share capital of Alpha, a limited liability company, is as follows:

	$
Ordinary shares of 10c each	1,000,000
8% Redeemable preference shares of 50c each	500,000

In the year ended 31 October 20X2, the company has paid the preference dividend for the year and an interim dividend of 2c per share on the ordinary shares. A final ordinary dividend of 3c per share was proposed, after the reporting date.

What amount will be recognised for dividends in the equity section of the statement of financial position at 31 October 20X2?

$_____ **(2 marks)**

13.2 When a company makes a rights issue of equity shares which of the following effects will the issue have?

1 Assets are increased
2 Retained earnings are reduced
3 Share premium account is reduced
4 Investments are increased

A 1 only
B 1 and 2
C 3 only
D 1 and 4 **(2 marks)**

13.3 A company made an issue for cash of 1,000,000 50c shares at a premium of 30c per share.

Which one of the following journal entries correctly records the issue?

		Debit $	Credit $
A	Share capital	500,000	
	Share premium	300,000	
	Bank		800,000
B	Bank	800,000	
	Share capital		500,000
	Share premium		300,000
C	Bank	1,300,000	
	Share capital		1,000,000
	Share premium		300,000
D	Share capital	1,000,000	
	Share premium		300,000
	Bank		1,300,000

(2 marks)

13.4 At 31 December 20X1 the capital structure of a company was as follows:

	$
Ordinary share capital	
100,000 shares of 50c each	50,000
Share premium account	180,000

During 20X2 the company made a bonus issue of one share for every two held, using the share premium account for the purpose, and later issued for cash another 60,000 shares at 80c per share.

What is the company's capital structure at 31 December 20X2?

	Ordinary share capital	Share premium account
	$	$
A	130,000	173,000
B	105,000	173,000
C	130,000	137,000
D	105,000	137,000

(2 marks)

13.5 An organisation's year end is 30 September. On 1 January 20X6 the organisation took out a loan of $100,000 with annual interest of 12%. The interest is payable in equal instalments on the first day of April, July, October and January in arrears.

How much should be charged to the statement of profit or loss (SPL) for the year ended 30 September 20X6, and how much should be accrued on the statement of financial position (SOFP)?

	SPL	SOFP
A	$12,000	$3,000
B	$9,000	$3,000
C	$9,000	NIL
D	$6,000	$3,000

(2 marks)

13.6 Identify, by indicating the relevant box in the table below, whether each of the following statements about company financial statements is true or false, according to International Financial Reporting Standards.

	True	False
Dividends paid on ordinary shares should be included in the statement of profit or loss and other comprehensive income.		
Dividends paid on redeemable preference shares are treated in the same way as dividends paid on ordinary shares.		
The statement of profit or loss and other comprehensive income shows the gain on revaluation of non-current assets for the period.		

(2 marks)

13.7 At 30 June 20X2 a company's capital structure was as follows:

	$
Ordinary share capital	
500,000 shares of 25c each	125,000
Share premium account	100,000

In the year ended 30 June 20X3 the company made a rights issue of one share for every two held at $1 per share and this was taken up in full. Later in the year the company made a bonus issue of one share for every five held, using the share premium account for the purpose.

What was the company's capital structure at 30 June 20X3?

	Ordinary share capital	Share premium account
	$	$
A	450,000	25,000
B	225,000	325,000
C	225,000	250,000
D	212,500	262,500

(2 marks)

13.8 At 30 June 20X2 a company had $1m 8% loan notes in issue, interest being paid half-yearly on 30 June and 31 December.

On 30 September 20X2 the company redeemed $250,000 of these loan notes at par, paying interest due to that date.

On 1 April 20X3 the company issued $500,000 7% loan notes, interest payable half-yearly on 31 March and 30 September.

What figure should appear in the company's statement of profit or loss for interest payable in the year ended 30 June 20X3?

$_____

(2 marks)

13.9 A limited liability company issued 50,000 ordinary shares of 25c each at a premium of 50c per share. The cash received was correctly recorded but the full amount was credited to the ordinary share capital account.

Which one of the following journal entries is needed to correct this error?

		Debit	Credit
		$	$
A	Share premium account	25,000	
	Share capital account		25,000
B	Share capital account	25,000	
	Share premium account		25,000
C	Share capital account	37,500	
	Share premium account		37,500
D	Share capital account	25,000	
	Cash		25,000

(2 marks)

13.10 Which one of the following journal entries could correctly record a bonus issue of shares?

		Debit	Credit
		$	$
A	Cash	100,000	
	Ordinary share capital		100,000
B	Ordinary share capital	100,000	
	Share premium		100,000
C	Share premium	100,000	
	Ordinary share capital		100,000
D	Investments	100,000	
	Cash		100,000

(2 marks)

13.11 Which of these statements about limited liability companies is/are correct?

1   A company might make a bonus issue of shares to raise funds for expansion.

2   No cash is received when a company makes a rights issue of shares, instead other reserves (usually share premium) are capitalised and reclassified as share capital.

3   A rights issue of shares dilutes the shareholding of existing shareholders if they do not take up their rights.

A   1 and 3
B   2 and 3
C   1 and 2
D   3 only   **(2 marks)**

13.12 At 1 January 20X0 the capital structure of Q, a limited liability company, was as follows:

	$
Issued share capital 1,000,000 ordinary shares of 50c each	500,000
Share premium account	300,000

On 1 April 20X0 the company made an issue of 200,000 50c shares at $1.30 each, and on 1 July the company made a bonus (capitalisation) issue of one share for every four in issue at the time, using the share premium account for the purpose.

Which of the following correctly states the company's share capital and share premium account at 31 December 20X0?

	Share capital	Share premium account
A	$750,000	$230,000
B	$875,000	$285,000
C	$750,000	$310,000
D	$750,000	$610,000

(2 marks)

13.13 According to the illustrative financial structure in IAS 1 Presentation of financial statements, where should dividends paid during the year should be disclosed?

A   Statement of profit or loss and other comprehensive income
B   Statement of changes in equity
C   Statement of financial position
D   None of these   **(2 marks)**

13.14 On 31 March 2016, Yellow, a limited liability company, issued share capital of $50,000 (25c ordinary shares). The company also has an investment of 50,000 50c shares in Blue, a limited liability company.

The following is an extract from Yellow's ledger accounts:

Dividend	
	30 September 2016 Bank $5,000

Which of the following statements is correct?

A   Yellow has paid an interim dividend of 5c per share
B   Yellow has received a 20% interim dividend
C   Yellow has received a 10% interim dividend
D   Yellow has paid a 10% interim dividend   **(2 marks)**

(Total = 28 marks)

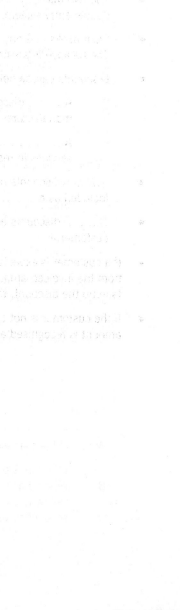

Do you know? – Preparing a trial balance

Check that you can fill in the blanks in the statements below before you attempt any questions. If in doubt, you should go back to your BPP Interactive Text and revise first.

- A ...... reconciliation is a comparison of a **b**...... **s**............. (sent monthly, weekly or even daily by the bank) with the cash book. Differences between the balance on the bank statement and the balance in the cash book will be errors or .... differences, and they should be identified and satisfactorily explained.

- Differences between the cash book and the bank statement arise for three reasons:
    - .... – usually in the cash book
    - Omissions – such as **b**...... **c**...........not posted in the cash book
    - **T**........... differences – such as unpresented cheques

- There are five main types of error: errors of **t**..............., **o**..........., **pr**..........., **c**..........., and **comp**........... errors.

- A suspense account is an account showing a balance equal to the difference in a **t** ...... **b**...........

- Suspense accounts are only .... None should exist when it comes to drawing up the financial statements at the end of the accounting period.

- The two most important control accounts are those for .... and .... They are part of the double entry system.

- Cash books and day books are totalled periodically and the totals posted to the **c**........... accounts. The balance totals on the **p**........... accounts should agree to the balance on the **c**.............. account.

- Discounts can be defined as follows:
    - A......... discount is a reduction in the list price of an article, given by a wholesaler or manufacturer to a retailer.
    - A.................... discount is a reduction in the amount payable for the purchase of goods or services in return for payment in cash, or within an agreed period.

- .... discounts received are **d**........... from the cost of purchases. **C**...... discounts received are included as **o**........ **i**......... of the period in the statement of profit or loss.

- .... discounts allowed are **d**........... from the gross sales price, and this amount is invoiced to the customer.

- If a customer is expected to take up a .... or .... discount allowed, the discount is deducted from the invoiced amount when recording the revenue for the sale. If the customer subsequently does not take up the discount, the discount is then recorded as revenue.

- If the customer is not expected to take up a .... or .... discount allowed, the full invoiced amount is recognised as revenue when recording the sale.

Did you know? – Preparing a trial balance

Could you fill in the blanks? The answers are in bold. Use this page for revision purposes as you approach the exam.

- A **bank** reconciliation is a comparison of a **bank statement** (sent monthly, weekly or even daily by the bank) with the cash book. Differences between the balance on the bank statement and the balance in the cash book will be errors or **timing** differences, and they should be identified and satisfactorily explained.

- Differences between the cash book and the bank statement arise for three reasons:

    - **Errors** – usually in the cash book
    - Omissions – such as **bank charges** not posted in the cash book
    - **Timing** differences – such as unpresented cheques

- There are five main types of error: errors of **transposition**, **omission**, **principle**, **commission** and **compensating** errors.

- A suspense account is an account showing a balance equal to the difference in a **trial balance**.

- Suspense accounts are only **temporary**. None should exist when it comes to drawing up the financial statements at the end of the accounting period.

- The two most important control accounts are those for **receivables** and **payables**. They are part of the double entry system.

- Cash books and day books are totalled periodically and the totals posted to the **control** accounts. The balance totals on the **personal** accounts should agree to the balance on the **control** account.

- Discounts can be defined as follows:

    - A **trade** discount is a reduction in the list price of an article, given by a wholesaler or manufacturer to a retailer.

    - A **cash (settlement)** discount is a reduction in the amount payable for the purchase of goods or services in return for payment in cash, or within an agreed period.

- **Trade** discounts received are **deducted** from the cost of purchases. **Cash (or settlement)** discounts received are included as **other income** of the period in the statement of profit or loss.

- **Trade** discounts allowed are **deducted** from the gross sales price, and this amount is invoiced to the customer.

- If a customer is expected to take up a **cash** or **settlement** discount allowed, the discount is deducted from the invoiced amount when recording the revenue for the sale. If the customer subsequently does not take up the discount, the discount is then recorded as revenue.

- If the customer is not expected to take up a **cash** or **settlement** discount allowed, the full invoiced amount is recognised as revenue when recording the sale.

14   15 mark question: trial balance   18 mins

14.1   Mr Yousef

The following balances have been extracted from the ledger of Mr Yousef, a sole trader at 31 May 20X6.

Task 1

Indicate whether each of these balances are debit or credit balances (Mr Yousef is not overdrawn at the bank).

	$	DR	CR
Sales	138,078	O	O
Purchases	82,350	O	O
Carriage	5,144	O	O
Drawings	7,800	O	O
Rent and insurance	6,622	O	O
Postage and stationery	3,001	O	O
Advertising	1,330	O	O
Salaries and wages	26,420	O	O
Irrecoverable debts	877	O	O
Allowance for receivables	130	O	O
Receivables	12,120	O	O
Payables	6,471	O	O
Cash on hand	177	O	O
Cash at bank	1,002	O	O
Inventory as at 1 June 20X5	11,927	O	O
Equipment at cost	58,000	O	O
Accumulated depreciation	19,000	O	O
Capital at 1 June 20X5	53,091	O	O

The following additional information as at 31 May 20X6 is available.

1   Rent is accrued by $210.
2   Insurance has been prepaid by $880.
3    $2,211 of carriage represents carriage inwards on purchases.
4   Equipment is to be depreciated at 15% per annum using the straight-line method.
5   The allowance for receivables is to be increased by $40.
6   Inventory at the close of business has been valued at $13,551.   **(6 marks)**

Task 2

Calculate cost of sales at 31 May 20X6

$ [   ]   **(3 marks)**

Task 3

Complete this sentence

Profit for the year will be (increased/decreased) by the rent accrual and (increased/decreased) by the insurance prepayment.   **(2 marks)**

Task 4

If profit for the year ended 31 May 20X6 is $5,888, what will be the capital balance at 31 May 20X6?

$ [   ]   **(2 marks)**

Task 5

What will be the carrying amount of equipment at 31 May 20X6?

$ [   ]   **(2 marks)**

(Total = 15 marks)

15 Control accounts   53 mins

15.1 You are given the following information:

Receivables at 1 January 20X3	$10,000
Receivables at 31 December 20X3	$9,000
Total receipts during 20X3 (including cash sales of $5,000)	$85,000

What is the figure for sales on credit during 20X3?

$_____   **(2 marks)**

15.2 A supplier sends you a statement showing a balance outstanding of $14,350. Your own records show a balance outstanding of $14,500.

Which one of the following could be the reason for this difference?

A   The supplier sent an invoice for $150 which you have not yet received.
B   The supplier has allowed you $150 cash discount which you had omitted to enter in your ledgers.
C   You have paid the supplier $150 which he has not yet accounted for.
D   You have returned goods worth $150 which the supplier has not yet accounted for.   **(2 marks)**

15.3 Your payables control account has a balance at 1 October 20X8 of $34,500 credit. During October, credit purchases were $78,400, cash purchases were $2,400 and payments made to suppliers, excluding cash purchases, and after deducting settlement discounts of $1,200, were $68,900. Purchase returns were $4,700.

What was the closing balance?

A $38,100
B $40,500
C $47,500
D $49,900   **(2 marks)**

15.4 A receivables ledger control account had a closing balance of $8,500. It contained a contra to the payables ledger of $400, but this had been entered on the wrong side of the control account.

What should be the correct balance on the control account?

A $7,700 debit
B $8,100 debit
C $8,400 debit
D $8,900 debit   **(2 marks)**

15.5 Which of the following items could appear on the credit side of a receivables ledger control account?

1   Cash received from customers
2   Irrecoverable debts written off
3   Increase in allowance for receivables
4   Sales
5   Credits for goods returned by customers
6   Cash refunds to customers

A   1, 2, and 5
B   1, 2, 3 and 6
C   3, 4 and 5
D   4 and 6   **(2 marks)**

15.6 An inexperienced bookkeeper has drawn up the following receivables ledger control account:

RECEIVABLES LEDGER CONTROL ACCOUNT

	$		$
Opening balance	180,000	Credit sales	190,000
Cash from credit customers	232,200	Irrecoverable debts written off	1,500
Sales returns	8,000	Contras against payables	2,400
Cash refunds to credit customers	3,300	Closing balance (balancing figure)	229,600
	423,500		423,500

What should the closing balance be after correcting the errors made in preparing the account?

A $130,600
B $129,200
C $142,400
D $214,600   (2 marks)

15.7 The payables ledger control account below contains a number of errors:

PAYABLES LEDGER CONTROL ACCOUNT

	$		$
Opening balance (amounts owed to suppliers)	318,600	Purchases	1,268,600
Cash paid to suppliers	1,364,300	Contras against debit balances in receivables ledger	48,000
Purchases returns	41,200	Discounts received	8,200
Refunds received from suppliers	2,700	Closing balance	402,000
	$1,726,800		$1,726,800

All items relate to credit purchases.

What should the closing balance be when all the errors are corrected?

A $128,200
B $509,000
C $224,200
D $144,600   (2 marks)

15.8 The following control account has been prepared by a trainee accountant:

RECEIVABLES LEDGER CONTROL ACCOUNT

	$		$
Opening balance	308,600	Cash received from credit customers	148,600
Credit sales	154,200		
Cash sales	88,100	Interest charged on overdue accounts	2,400
Contras against credit balances in payables ledger	4,600	Irrecoverable debts written off	4,900
		Allowance for receivables	2,800
		Closing balance	396,800
	555,500		555,500

Once all the errors made in preparing the receivables ledger control account have been corrected, what should the closing balance be?

$_____   (2 marks)

15.9 The following receivables ledger control account prepared by a trainee accountant contains a number of errors:

RECEIVABLES LEDGER CONTROL ACCOUNT

	$		$
20X4		*20X4*	
1 Jan Balance	614,000	31 Dec Credit sales	301,000
31 Jan Cash from credit customers	311,000		
Contras against amounts		Irrecoverable debts	
due to suppliers in		written off	35,400
payables ledger	8,650	Interest charged on overdue	
		accounts	1,600
		Balance	595,650
	933,650		933,650

What should the closing balance on the control account be after the errors in it have been corrected?

A $561,550
B $578,850
C $581,550
D $568,350

(2 marks)

15.10 Your organisation sold goods to PQ Co for $800 less trade discount of 20% and settlement discount of 5% for payment within 14 days. At the time of the sale, you expect PQ to take up the settlement discount. The invoice was settled by cheque five days later. Which one of the following gives the entries required to record **BOTH** of these transactions?

		DEBIT	CREDIT
		$	$
A	PQ Co	608	
	Sales		608
	Bank	608	
	PQ Co		608
B	PQ Co	640	
	Sales		640
	Bank	640	
	PQ Co		640
C	PQ Co	608	
	Sales		608
	Bank	640	
	PQ Co		608
	Sales		32
D	PQ Co	640	
	Sales		640
	Bank	608	
	Sales	32	
	PQ Co		640

(2 marks)

15.11 Which one of the following is **NOT** a purpose of a receivables ledger control account?

A   A receivables ledger control account provides a check on the overall accuracy of the personal ledger accounts.

B   A receivables ledger control account ensures the trial balance balances.

C   A receivables ledger control account aims to ensure there are no errors in the personal ledger.

D   Control accounts help deter fraud.

(2 marks)

15.12 Which of the following lists is composed only of items which would appear on the credit side of the receivables control account?

A   Cash received from customers, sales returns, irrecoverable debts written off, contras against amounts due to suppliers in the accounts payable ledger

B   Sales, cash refunds to customers, irrecoverable debts written off

C   Cash received from customers, interest charged on overdue accounts, irrecoverable debts written off

D   Sales, cash refunds to customers, interest charged on overdue accounts, contras against amounts due to suppliers in the accounts payable ledger   **(2 marks)**

15.13 The following receivables ledger control account has been prepared by a trainee accountant:

RECEIVABLES LEDGER CONTROL ACCOUNT

20X5		$	20X5		$
1 Jan	Balance	318,650	31 Jan	Cash from credit customers	181,140
	Credit sales	163,010		Interest charged on overdue accounts	280
	Cash sales	84,260		Irrecoverable debts written off	1,390
				Sales returns from credit customers	3,990
				Balance	379,120
		565,920			565,920

What should the closing balance at 31 January 20X5 be after correcting the errors in the account?

A $294,860
B $298,200
C $295,420
D $379,680   **(2 marks)**

15.14 At 1 April 20X9, the payables ledger control account showed a balance of $142,320.

At the end of April the following totals are extracted from the subsidiary books for April:

	$
Purchases day book	183,800
Returns outwards day book	27,490
Returns inwards day book	13,240
Payments to payables, after deducting $1,430 cash discount	196,360

It is also discovered that:

(a)   The purchase day book figure is net of sales tax at 17.5%; the other figures all include sales tax.

(b)   A customer's balance of $2,420 has been offset against his balance of $3,650 in the payables ledger.

(c)   A supplier's account in the payables ledger, with a debit balance of $800, has been included on the list of payables as a credit balance.

What is the corrected balance on the payables ledger control account?

A $130,585
B $144,835
C $98,429
D $128,985   **(2 marks)**

15.15 The balance on Jude Co's payables ledger control account is $31,554. The accountant at Jude Co has discovered that she has not recorded:

A settlement discount of $53 received from a supplier; and
A supplier's invoice for $622.

What amount should be reported for payables on Jude Co's statement of financial position?

   A $30,879
   B $30,985
   C $32,123
   D $32,229

(2 marks)

15.16 The accountant at Borris Co has prepared the following reconciliation between the balance on the trade payables ledger control account in the general ledger and the list of balances from the suppliers ledger:

	$
Balance on general ledger control account	68,566
Credit balance omitted from list of balances from payables ledger	(127)
	68,439
Undercasting of purchases day book	99
Total of list of balances	68,538

What balance should be reported on Borris Co's statement of financial position for trade payables?

   A $68,439
   B $68,538
   C $68,566
   D $68,665

(2 marks)

15.17 How should the balance on the payables ledger control account be reported in the final financial statements?

   A   As an expense account
   B   As a non-current liability
   C   As a current asset
   D   As a current liability

(2 marks)

15.18 Y Ltd keeps a receivables ledger control account as part of its accounting system.

The following transactions take place in March:

(a)   Invoices totalling $5,000 are raised to Customer X in March. These invoices offer the customer a 5% discount if they pay within 14 days. Of these invoices, Y Ltd expects invoices amounting to $2,000 to be paid with the discount taken.

(b)   Customer Z pays cash of $2,850 for invoices with face values of $3,000. They took advantage of discounts totalling $150 for early payment, however Y Ltd had not expected Customer Z to take up the discounts.

Which of the following entries correctly record these transactions?

   A   Debit receivables ledger control $5,000, credit sales $5,000, debit cash $2,850, credit receivables ledger control $2,850

   B   Debit receivables ledger control $4,900, credit sales $4,900, debit cash $2,850, debit sales $150, credit receivables ledger control $3,000

   C   Debit receivables ledger control $5,000, credit sales $5,000, debit cash $2,850, debit sales $150, credit receivables ledger control $3,000

   D   Debit receivables ledger control $4,900, credit sales $4,900, debit cash $2,850, credit receivables ledger control $2,850

(2 marks)

15.19 You are an accounts assistant at Cuppa Supplies, a company that sells cups and mugs. The following is an extract from a sales invoice raised by the bookkeeper in your company to a customer, Oasis Café.

Invoice No: 3242

Date: 31 October 20X6

Description	Qty	Unit Price $		Net amt $
Coffee cups	200	5.00		1,000.00
			Sales Value	1,000.00
			Sales Tax	0.00
			Amt payable	1,000.00

A discount of 5% of the full price applies if payment is made within 7 days.

If you pay within 7 days, the discounted price is: 950.00

Senior management at your company do not expect Oasis Café to take advantage of the discount. However, you receive a payment from Oasis Café on 3 November 20X6.

Which one of the following gives the entries required to record **BOTH** of these transactions?

		DEBIT $	CREDIT $
A	Trade receivables	950	
	Sales		950
	Bank	950	
	Trade receivables		950
B	Trade receivables	1,000	
	Sales		1,000
	Bank	950	
	Trade receivables		950
C	Trade receivables	1,000	
	Sales		1,000
	Bank	950	
	Sales	50	
	Trade receivables		1,000
D	Trade receivables	950	
	Sales		950
	Bank	950	
	Sales	50	
	Trade receivables		1,000

(2 marks)

(Total = 38 marks)

16 Bank reconciliations

36 mins

16.1 Your cash book at 31 December 20X3 shows a bank balance of $565 overdrawn. On comparing this with your bank statement at the same date, you discover the following.

1   A cheque for $57 drawn by you on 29 December 20X3 has not yet been presented for payment.

2   A cheque for $92 from a customer, which was paid into the bank on 24 December 20X3, has been dishonoured on 31 December 20X3.

What is the correct bank balance to be shown in the statement of financial position at 31 December 20X3?

A $714 overdrawn
B $657 overdrawn
C $473 overdrawn
D $53 overdrawn

(2 marks)

16.2 The cash book shows a bank balance of $5,675 overdrawn at 31 August 20X5. It is subsequently discovered that a standing order for $125 has been entered twice, and that a dishonoured cheque for $450 has been debited in the cash book instead of credited.

What is the correct bank balance?

$_____ overdrawn.

(2 marks)

16.3 A business had a balance at the bank of $2,500 at the start of the month. During the following month, it paid for materials invoiced at $1,000 less trade discount of 20% and settlement discount of 10%. It received a cheque from a customer in respect of an invoice for $200, subject to settlement discount of 5%.

What was the balance at the bank at the end of the month?

A $1,970
B $1,980
C $1,990
D $2,000

(2 marks)

16.4 The bank statement on 31 October 20X7 showed an overdraft of $800. On reconciling the bank statement, it was discovered that a cheque drawn by your company for $80 had not been presented for payment, and that a cheque for $130 from a customer had been dishonoured on 30 October 20X7, but that this had not yet been notified to you by the bank.

What is the correct bank balance to be shown in the statement of financial position at 31 October 20X7?

A $1,010 overdrawn
B $880 overdrawn
C $750 overdrawn
D $720 overdrawn

(2 marks)

16.5 The following information relates to a bank reconciliation.

(i) The bank balance in the cashbook before taking the items below into account was $8,970 overdrawn.

(ii) Bank charges of $550 on the bank statement have not been entered in the cashbook.

(iii) The bank has credited the account in error with $425 which belongs to another customer.

(iv) Cheque payments totalling $3,275 have been entered in the cashbook but have not been presented for payment.

(v) Cheques totalling $5,380 have been correctly entered on the debit side of the cashbook but have not been paid in at the bank.

What was the balance as shown by the bank statement **before** taking the above items into account?

A $9,520 overdrawn
B $11,200 overdrawn
C $9,520 in credit
D $11,200 in credit   **(2 marks)**

16.6 The following bank reconciliation statement has been prepared by a trainee accountant:

BANK RECONCILIATION 30 SEPTEMBER 20X2

	$
Balance per bank statement (overdrawn)	36,840
Add: lodgements credited after date	51,240
	88,080
Less: unpresented cheques	43,620
Balance per cash book (credit)	44,460

Assuming the amounts stated for items other than the cash book balance are correct, what should the cash book balance be?

A $44,460 credit as stated
B $60,020 credit
C $29,220 debit
D $29,220 credit   **(2 marks)**

16.7 Listed below are some possible causes of difference between the cash book balance and the bank statement balance when preparing a bank reconciliation.

Which **TWO** of these items require an entry in the cash book?

A   Cheque paid in, subsequently dishonoured
B   Error by bank
C   Bank charges
D   Lodgements credited after date
E   Cheques not yet presented   **(2 marks)**

16.8 In preparing a company's bank reconciliation statement at March 20X3, the following items are causing the difference between the cash book balance and the bank statement balance:

1 Bank charges $380
2 Error by bank $1,000 (cheque incorrectly debited to the account)
3 Lodgements not credited $4,580
4 Unpresented cheques $1,475
5 Direct debit $350
6 Cheque paid in by the company and dishonoured $400

Which of these items will require an entry in the cash book?

A 2, 4 and 6
B 1, 5 and 6
C 3 and 4
D 3 and 5 **(2 marks)**

16.9 The following bank reconciliation statement has been prepared by a trainee accountant:

	$
Overdraft per bank statement	3,860
Less: unpresented cheques	9,160
	5,300
Add: deposits credited after date	16,690
Cash at bank as calculated above	21,990

What should be the correct balance per the cash book?

A $21,990 balance at bank as stated
B $3,670 balance at bank
C $11,390 balance at bank
D $3,670 overdrawn **(2 marks)**

16.10 Which of the following statements about bank reconciliations are correct?

1 A difference between the cash book and the bank statement must be corrected by means of a journal entry.

2 In preparing a bank reconciliation, lodgements recorded before date in the cash book but credited by the bank after date should reduce an overdrawn balance in the bank statement.

3 Bank charges not yet entered in the cash book should be dealt with by an adjustment in the bank reconciliation statement.

4 If a cheque received from a customer is dishonoured after date, a credit entry in the cash book is required.

A 2 and 4
B 1 and 4
C 2 and 3
D 1 and 3 **(2 marks)**

16.11 The following information relates to a bank reconciliation.

(i) The bank balance in the cashbook before taking the items below into account was $8,970 overdrawn.

(ii) Bank charges of $550 on the bank statement have not been entered in the cashbook.

(iii) The bank has credited the account in error with $425 which belongs to another customer.

(iv) Cheque payments totalling $3,275 have been entered in the cashbook but have not been presented for payment.

(v) Cheques totalling $5,380 have been correctly entered on the debit side of the cashbook but have not been paid in at the bank.

What was the balance as shown by the bank statement **before** taking the items above into account?

$_____ overdrawn **(2 marks)**

16.12 The following attempt at a bank reconciliation statement has been prepared by Q Co:

	$
Overdraft per bank statement	38,600
Add: deposits not credited	41,200
	79,800
Less: unpresented cheques	3,300
Overdraft per cash book	76,500

Assuming the bank statement balance of $38,600 to be correct, what **should** the cash book balance be?

A $76,500 overdrawn, as stated
B $5,900 overdrawn
C $700 overdrawn
D $5,900 cash at bank   **(2 marks)**

16.13 After checking a business cash book against the bank statement, which of the following items could require an entry in the cash book?

1   Bank charges
2   A cheque from a customer which was dishonoured
3   Cheque not presented
4   Deposits not credited
5   Credit transfer entered in bank statement
6   Standing order entered in bank statement.

A   1, 2, 5 and 6
B   3 and 4
C   1, 3, 4 and 6
D   3, 4, 5 and 6   **(2 marks)**

16.14 The following bank reconciliation statement has been prepared for a company:

	$
Overdraft per bank statement	39,800
Add: Deposits credited after date	64,100
	103,900
Less: Unpresented cheques presented after date	44,200
Overdraft per cash book	59,700

Assuming the amount of the overdraft per the bank statement of $39,800 is correct, what should be the balance in the cash book?

A $158,100 overdrawn
B $19,900 overdrawn
C $68,500 overdrawn
D $59,700 overdrawn   **(2 marks)**

16.15 Listed below are five potential causes of difference between a company's cash book balance and its bank statement balance as at 30 November 20X3:

1   Cheques recorded and sent to suppliers before 30 November 20X3 but not yet presented for payment

2   An error by the bank in crediting to another customer's account a lodgement made by the company

3   Bank charges

4   Cheques paid in before 30 November 20X3 but not credited by the bank until 3 December 20X3

5   A cheque recorded and paid in before 30 November 20X3 but dishonoured by the bank

Which one of the following alternatives correctly analyses these items into those requiring an entry in the cash book and those that would feature in the bank reconciliation?

	Cash book entry	Bank reconciliation
A	1, 2, 4	3, 5
B	3, 5	1, 2, 4
C	3, 4	1, 2, 5
D	2, 3, 5	1, 4

(2 marks)

(Total = 30 marks)

17 Correction of errors
44 mins

17.1 The debit side of a trial balance totals $800 more than the credit side.

Which one of the following errors would fully account for the difference?

A $400 paid for plant maintenance has been correctly entered in the cash book and credited to the plant asset account.

B   Credit note issued to a customer of $400 has been debited to trade receivables.

C   A receipt of $800 for commission receivable has been omitted from the records.

D   The petty cash balance of $800 has been omitted from the trial balance.

(2 marks)

17.2 The bookkeeper of Peri made the following mistakes:

Sales returns of $384 were credited to the purchases returns account.
Purchases returns of $296 were debited to the sales returns account.

Which one of the following journal entries will correct the errors?

		Dr $	Cr $
A	Sales returns	768	
	Purchases returns		592
	Suspense account		176
B	Sales returns	88	
	Purchases returns	88	
	Suspense account		176
C	Sales returns	680	
	Purchases returns		680
D	Suspense account	176	
	Sales returns		88
	Purchases returns		88

(2 marks)

17.3 A company's trial balance failed to agree, the totals being:

Debit	$815,602
Credit	$808,420

Which one of the following errors could fully account for the difference?

A   The omission from the trial balance of the balance on the insurance expense account $7,182 debit

B   Settlement discounts received from suppliers of $3,591 were credited in error to the purchases account

C   No entries made in the records for cash sales totalling $7,182

D   The returns outwards total of $3,591 was included in the trial balance as a debit balance

(2 marks)

17.4 The debit side of a trial balance totals $50 more than the credit side. Which one of the following could this be due to?

A   A purchase of goods for $50 being omitted from the payables control account
B   A sale of goods for $50 being omitted from the receivables control account
C   An invoice of $25 for electricity being credited to the electricity account
D   A receipt for $50 from a customer being omitted from the cash book   **(2 marks)**

17.5 Which one of the following is an error of principle?

A   Plant and machinery purchased was credited to a non-current assets account.
B   Plant and machinery purchased was debited to the purchases account.
C   Plant and machinery purchased was debited to the equipment account.
D   Plant and machinery purchased was credited to the equipment account.   **(2 marks)**

17.6 What is an error of commission?

A   An error where a transaction has not been recorded

B   An error where one side of a transaction has been recorded in the wrong account, and that account is of a different class to the correct account

C   An error where one side of a transaction has been recorded in the wrong account, and that account is of the same class as the correct account

D   An error where the numbers in the posting have been transposed   **(2 marks)**

17.7 Where a transaction is entered into the correct ledger accounts, but the wrong amount is used, what is the error known as?

A   An error of omission
B   An error of original entry
C   An error of commission
D   An error of principle   **(2 marks)**

17.8 A company's statement of profit or loss and other comprehensive income for the year ended 31 December 20X4 showed a net profit of $83,600. It was later found that $18,000 paid for the purchase of a motor van had been debited to motor expenses account. It is the company's policy to depreciate motor vans at 25 per cent per year, with a full year's charge in the year of acquisition.

What is the company's net profit after adjusting for this error?

$_____   **(2 marks)**

17.9 An organisation restores its petty cash balance to $250 at the end of each month. During October, the total expenditure column in the petty cash book was calculated as being $210, and the imprest was restored by this amount. The analysis columns posted to the nominal ledger totalled only $200.

Which one of the following would this error cause?

A   The trial balance being $10 higher on the debit side
B   The trial balance being $10 higher on the credit side
C   No imbalance in the trial balance
D   The petty cash balance being $10 lower than it should be   **(2 marks)**

17.10 Net profit was calculated as being $10,200. It was later discovered that capital expenditure of $3,000 had been treated as revenue expenditure, and revenue receipts of $1,400 had been treated as capital receipts.

What is the net profit after correcting this error?

A $5,800
B $8,600
C $11,800
D $14,600   **(2 marks)**

17.11 The accountant at Investotech discovered the following errors after calculating the company's profit for 20X3:

(a)   A non-current asset costing $50,000 has been included in the purchases account

(b)   Stationery costing $10,000 has been included as closing inventory of raw materials, instead of stationery expenses

What is the effect of these errors on gross profit and net profit?

A   Understatement of gross profit by $40,000 and understatement of net profit by $30,000
B   Understatement of both gross profit and net profit by $40,000
C   Understatement of gross profit by $60,000 and understatement of net profit by $50,000
D   Overstatement of both gross profit and net profit by $60,000   **(2 marks)**

17.12 A purchase return of $48 has been wrongly posted to the debit of the sales returns account, but has been correctly entered in the supplier's account.

Which of the following statements about the trial balance would be correct?

A   The credit side to be $48 more than the debit side
B   The debit side to be $48 more than the credit side
C   The credit side to be $96 more than the debit side
D   The debit side to be $96 more than the credit side   **(2 marks)**

17.13 Two types of common errors in bookkeeping are errors of **principle** and errors of **transposition**.

Which of the following correctly states whether or not these errors will be revealed by extracting a trial balance?

	Errors of principle	*Errors of transposition*
A	Will be revealed	Will not be revealed
B	Will be revealed	Will be revealed
C	Will not be revealed	Will not be revealed
D	Will not be revealed	Will be revealed

(2 marks)

17.14 The following are balances on the accounts of Luigi, a sole trader, as at the end of the current financial year and after all entries have been processed and the profit for the year has been calculated.

	$
Non-current assets	85,000
Receivables	7,000
Trade payables	3,000
Bank loan	15,000
Allowance for depreciation, non-current assets	15,000
Inventory	4,000
Accruals	1,000
Prepayments	2,000
Bank overdraft	2,000

What is the balance on Luigi's capital account?

A $59,000
B $66,000
C $62,000
D $64,000   (2 marks)

17.15 The following balances have been extracted from the nominal ledger accounts of Tanya, but the figure for bank loan is unknown. There are no other accounts in the main ledger.

	$
Payables	27,000
Capital	66,000
Purchases	160,000
Sales	300,000
Other expenses	110,000
Receivables	33,000
Purchase returns	2,000
Non-current assets	120,000
Cash in bank	18,000
Bank loan	[Unknown]

What is the credit balance on the bank loan account?

$_____   (2 marks)

17.16 Beta Co has total assets of $650,000 and profit for the year of $150,000 recorded in the financial statements for the year ended 31 December 20X3. Inventory costing $50,000, with a resale value of $75,000, was received into the warehouse on 2 January 20X4 and included in the inventory value that was recorded in the financial statements at 31 December 20X3.

What would the total assets figure in the Statement of Financial Position, and the adjusted profit for the year figure, be after adjusting for this error?

	Total assets (SOFP)	Profit for year
A	$700,000	$200,000
B	$600,000	$100,000
C	$725,000	$225,000
D	$600,000	$75,000

(2 marks)

17.17 The electricity account for Jingles Co for the year ended 30 June 20X1 was as follows.

	$
Opening balance for electricity accrued at 1 July 20X0	300
Payments made during the year	
1 August 20X0 for three months to 31 July 20X0	600
1 November 20X0 for three months to 31 October 20X0	720
1 February 20X1 for three months to 31 January 20X1	900
30 June 20X1 for three months to 30 April 20X1	840

Jingles Co expects the next bill due in September to be for the same amount as the bill received in June.

What are the appropriate amounts for electricity to be included in the financial statements of Jingles Co for the year ended 30 June 20X1?

	Statement of financial position	*Statement of profit or loss*
A	$560	$3,320
B	$560	$3,060
C	$860	$3,320
D	$860	$3,060

(2 marks)

17.18 Paula Co is reconciling its receivables control account and has discovered the following items:

(1) An invoice for $110 had been recorded in the receivables ledger as $1,100
(2) A cash sale of $100 to a customer had been posted to the receivables ledger

Where should each of the corrections be recorded?

	Item 1	Item 2
A	Control account	Receivables ledger
B	Receivables ledger	Control account
C	Control account	Control account
D	Receivables ledger	Receivables ledger

(2 marks)

(Total = 36 marks)

18 Suspense accounts

27 mins

The following information is relevant for Questions 18.1 and 18.2.

When Q's trial balance failed to agree, a suspense account was opened for the difference. The trial balance totals were:

Debit	$864,390
Credit	$860,930

The company does not have control accounts for its receivables and payables ledgers.

The following errors were found:

1 In recording an issue of shares at par, cash received of $333,000 was credited to the ordinary share capital account as $330,000.

2 Cash $2,800 paid for plant repairs was correctly accounted for in the cash book but was credited to the plant asset account.

3 The petty cash book balance $500 had been omitted from the trial balance.

4 A cheque for $78,400 paid for the purchase of a motor car was debited to the motor vehicles account as $87,400.

5 A contra between the receivables ledger and the payables ledger for $1,200 which should have been credited in the receivables ledger and debited in the payables ledger was actually debited in the receivables ledger and credited in the payables ledger.

18.1 Which of these errors will require an entry to the suspense account to correct them?

    A   All five items
    B   3 and 5 only
    C   2, 4 and 5 only
    D   1, 2, 3 and 4 only   **(2 marks)**

18.2 What will the balance on the suspense account be after making the necessary entries to correct the errors affecting the suspense account?

    A $2,440 Debit
    B $15,560 Credit
    C $13,640 Debit
    D $3,440 Debit   **(2 marks)**

18.3 A company's trial balance totals were:

Debit $387,642
Credit $379,511

A suspense account was opened for the difference.

Which one of the following errors would have the effect of reducing the difference when corrected?

    A   The petty cash balance of $500 has been omitted from the trial balance.

    B $4,000 received for rent of part of the office has been correctly recorded in the cash book and debited to rent account.

    C $3,000 paid for repairs to plant has been debited to the plant asset account.

    D   An invoice for Mr A Smith for $400 has been posted to the account of Mrs B Smith in error.   **(2 marks)**

18.4 A trial balance extracted from a sole trader's records failed to agree, and a suspense account was opened for the difference.

Which of the following errors would require an entry in the suspense account in correcting them?

    1   Sales returns were mistakenly debited to the purchases returns account.

    2   Cash received from the sale of a non-current asset was correctly entered in the cash book but was debited to the disposal account.

    3   The balance on the rent account was omitted from the trial balance.

    4   Goods taken from inventory by the proprietor had been recorded by crediting drawings account and debiting purchases account.

    A   All four items
    B   2 and 3 only
    C   2 and 4 only
    D   1 and 3 only   **(2 marks)**

18.5 A suspense account was opened when a trial balance failed to agree. The following errors were later discovered.

    •   A gas bill of $420 had been recorded in the gas account as $240.
    •   A sales invoice to a customer for $50 had been credited to accounts receivable.
    •   Interest received of $70 had been entered in the bank account only.

What was the original balance on the suspense account?

    A   Debit $210
    B   Credit $210
    C   Debit $160
    D   Credit $160   **(2 marks)**

18.6 A company's trial balance failed to agree, the out of balance difference of $25,000 being posted to a suspense account.

Subsequent investigation revealed the difference was due to one side of an entry to record the purchase of machinery for $25,000, by cheque, failing to post to the plant and machinery account.

Which of the following journal entries would correct the error?

		Debit $	Credit $
A	Plant and machinery	25,000	
	Bank current account		25,000
B	Suspense account	25,000	
	Plant and machinery		25,000
C	Plant and machinery	25,000	
	Suspense account		25,000
D	Bank current account	25,000	
	Suspense account		25,000

(2 marks)

18.7 The trial balance of Z failed to agree, the totals being: DEBIT $836,200
CREDIT $819,700

A suspense account was opened for the amount of the difference and the following errors were found and corrected:

1 The total of the cash discount received column in the cash book had not been posted to the discount received account. The figure for discounts received was $5,100.

2 A cheque for $19,000 received from a customer was correctly entered in the cash book but was posted to the control account as $9,100.

What will the remaining balance be on the suspense after the correction of these errors?

$_____ credit (2 marks)

18.8 The trial balance of C, a limited liability company, did not agree, and a suspense account was opened for the difference. Checking in the bookkeeping system revealed a number of errors.

Which TWO of the following errors would require an entry to the suspense account as part of the process of correcting them?

A $4,600 paid for motor van repairs was correctly treated in the cash book but was credited to motor vehicles asset account.

B $360 received from B, a customer, was credited in error to the account of BB.

C $9,500 paid for rent was debited to the rent account as $5,900.

D Sales returns had been debited in error to the purchases returns account.

E No entries have been made to record a cash sale of $100. (2 marks)

18.9 The suspense account shows a debit balance of $100. What could this balance be due to?

A Entering $50 received from A Turner on the debit side of A Turner's account
B Entering $50 received from A Turner on the credit side of A Turner's account
C Undercasting the sales day book by $100
D Undercasting the purchases account by $100 (2 marks)

18.10 A suspense account shows a credit balance of $130. Which of the following could be due to?

    A   Omitting a sale of $130 from the sales ledger

    B   Recording a purchase of $130 twice in the purchases account

    C   Failing to write off a bad debt of $130

    D   Recording an electricity bill paid of $65 by debiting the bank account and crediting the electricity account   **(2 marks)**

18.11 A company has a suspense account balance in its trial balance of $560 credit.

It was discovered that discounts allowed of $700 have been debited to, instead of credited to, the receivables control account.

What is the remaining balance on the suspense account after this error has been adjusted for?

    A $140 debit
    B $840 debit
    C $1,260 credit
    D $1,960 credit   **(2 marks)**

(Total = 22 marks)

Do you know? – Preparing basic financial statements

Check that you can fill in the blanks in the statements below before you attempt any questions. If in doubt, you should go back to your BPP Interactive Text and revise first.

- There are some important differences between the accounts of a l............ l............ c........... and those of sole traders or partnerships.

- .... liability means that the maximum amount that an owner stands to lose, in the event that the company becomes insolvent and cannot pay off its debts, is his share of the capital in the business.

- .... capital and .... are 'owned' by the shareholders. They are known collectively as 'shareholders' equity'.

- A company can increase its share capital by means of a .... issue or a .... issue.

- .... are included in a set of financial statements to give users extra information.

- IFRS 15 is concerned with the recognition of ....

- Events after the reporting date but before the date the financial statements are approved that provide further **e**........... of conditions that existed at the reporting date should be .... for in the financial statements.

- Events which do not affect the situation at the reporting date should not be .... for, but should be .... in the financial statements.

- The approach to incomplete records questions is to build up the information given so as to complete the necessary .... entry.

- ....-......... is the profit as a percentage of cost.

- **G**......... **p**.......... .... is the profit as a percentage of sales.

- Where no trading records have been kept, profit can be derived from opening and closing net assets by use of the **b**........... **e**.............

- The business equation is Profit = increase in .... – capital introduced + ...

- Statements of **c**...... **f**........ are a useful addition to the financial statements of companies because it is recognised that accounting profit is not the only indicator of a company's performance.

- .... activities are the principal revenue-producing activities of the enterprise and other activities that are not investing or financing activities.

- .... activities are the acquisition and disposal of non-current assets and other investments not included in cash equivalents.

- .... activities are activities that result in changes in the size and composition of the equity capital and borrowings of the entity.

Did you know? – Preparing basic financial statements

Could you fill in the blanks? The answers are in bold. Use this page for revision purposes as you approach the exam.

- There are some important differences between the accounts of a **limited liability company** and those of sole traders or partnerships.

- **Limited** liability means that the maximum amount that an owner stands to lose, in the event that the company becomes insolvent and cannot pay off its debts, is his share of the capital in the business.

- **Share** capital and **reserves** are 'owned' by the shareholders. They are known collectively as 'shareholders' equity'.

- A company can increase its share capital by means of a **bonus** issue or a **rights** issue.

- **Notes** are included in a set of financial statements to give users extra information.

- IFRS 15 is concerned with the recognition of **revenue from contracts with customers**.

- Events after the reporting date but before the date the financial statements are approved that provide further **evidence** of conditions that existed at the reporting date should be **adjusted** for in the financial statements.

- Events which do not affect the situation at the reporting date should not be **adjusted** for, but should be **disclosed** in the financial statements.

- The approach to incomplete records questions is to build up the information given so as to complete the necessary **double** entry.

- **Mark-up** is the profit as a percentage of cost.

- **Gross profit margin** is the profit as a percentage of sales.

- Where no trading records have been kept, profit can be derived from opening and closing net assets by use of the **business equation**.

- The business equation is Profit = increase in **net assets** – capital introduced + **drawings**

- Statements of **cash flows** are a useful addition to the financial statements of companies because it is recognised that accounting profit is not the only indicator of a company's performance.

- **Operating** activities are the principal revenue-producing activities of the enterprise and other activities that are not investing or financing activities.

- **Investing** activities are the acquisition and disposal of non-current assets and other investments not included in cash equivalents.

- **Financing** activities are activities that result in changes in the size and composition of the equity capital and borrowings of the entity.

15 mark questions: preparing basic financial statements 126 mins

19.1 Shuswap

Exam focus point. This question provides excellent practise of the knowledge and skills required to tackle the longer questions that appear in Section B of the exam.

The draft statement of financial position shown below has been prepared for Shuswap, a limited liability company, as at 31 December 20X4:

	Cost $'000	Accumulated depreciation $'000	Carrying value $'000
Assets			
Non-current assets			
Land and buildings	9,000	1,000	8,000
Plant and equipment	21,000	9,000	12,000
	30,000	10,000	20,000
Current assets			
Inventories			3,000
Receivables			2,600
Cash at bank			1,900
Total assets			27,500
Equity and liabilities			
Equity			
Issued share capital (ordinary shares of 50c each)			6,000
Retained earnings			12,400
Non-current liabilities			
Loan notes (redeemable 20Y0)			2,000
Current liabilities			
Trade payables			2,100
			22,500
Suspense account			5,000
			27,500

Task 1

Some inventory items included in the draft statement of financial position at cost $500,000 were sold after the reporting date for $400,000, with selling expenses of $40,000.

Which of the following statements is correct?

O   Inventory should be debited with $140,000 at 31.12.20X4
O   Inventory should be credited with $140,000 at 31.12.20X4
O   Cash should be credited with $140,000 at 31.12.20X4
O   No adjustment should be made because the inventory was sold after the year end.   **(2 marks)**

Task 2

The suspense account is made up of two items:

(a)   The proceeds of issue of 4,000,000 50c shares at $1.10 per share, credited to the suspense account from the cash book.

(b)   The balance of the account is the proceeds of sale of some plant on 1 January 20X4 with a carrying amount at the date of sale of $700,000 and which had originally cost $1,400,000. No other accounting entries have yet been made for the disposal apart from the cash book entry for the receipt of the proceeds. Depreciation on plant has been charged at 25% (straight line basis) in preparing the draft statement of financial position without allowing for the sale. The depreciation for the year relating to the plant sold should be adjusted for in full.

BPP
LEARNING MEDIA

What is the profit or loss on disposal of the plant?

$ [   ] Profit / Loss

What is the amount of the depreciation adjustment that should be made for the year to 31.12.20X4?

$ [   ]

(3 marks)

Task 3

A year end journal to clear the suspense account is given below.

Prepare the double entry by selecting the correct option for each row. (Use the information given under Task 2 to help you.)

	DR	CR	Neither DR nor CR
Issued share capital	O	O	O
Share premium	O	O	O
Cash	O	O	O
Plant and equipment – cost	O	O	O
Plant and equipment – disposal account	O	O	O
Suspense account	O	O	O

After the suspense account has been cleared, what will be the balances on these accounts?

Share capital $ [   ]

Share premium $ [   ]

(7 marks)

Task 4

Irrecoverable debts of $200,000 are to be written off at 31.12.20X4

Will the following adjustments be debited or credited to retained earnings?

	DR	CR	Neither DR nor CR
Irrecoverable debts	O	O	O
Depreciation adjustment (Task 2)	O	O	O
Inventory adjustment (Task 1)	O	O	O

(3 marks)

19.2   Malright

You are presented with the following trial balance of Malright, a limited liability company, at 31 October 20X7.

Task 1

Do each of these items belong on the statement of financial position (SOFP) as at 31 October 20X7?

	Dr $'000	Cr $'000	On SOFP	Not on SOFP
Buildings at cost	740		O	O
Buildings, accumulated depreciation, 1 November 20X6		60	O	O
Plant at cost	220		O	O
Plant, accumulated depreciation, 1 November 20X6		110	O	O
Bank balance		70	O	O
Revenue		1,800	O	O
Purchases	1,140		O	O
Inventory at 1 November 20X6	160		O	O
Cash	20		O	O
Trade payables		250	O	O
Trade receivables	320		O	O
Administrative expenses	325		O	O
Allowance for receivables, at 1 November 20X6		10	O	O
Retained earnings at 1 November 20X6		130	O	O
$1 ordinary shares		415	O	O
Share premium account		80	O	O
	2,925	2,925		

(4 marks)

Task 2

The allowance for receivables is to be increased to 5% of trade receivables. The allowance for receivables is treated as an administrative expense.

The year-end journal for allowance for receivables is given below. Prepare the double entry by selecting the correct option for each row.

	DR	CR	Neither DR nor CR
Trade receivables	O	O	O
Administrative expenses	O	O	O
Allowance for receivables	O	O	O
Revenue	O	O	O

Complete the following:

The amount included in the statement of profit or loss after the allowance is increased to 5% of trade

receivables is $ [   ] **(3 marks)**

Task 3

Plant is depreciated at 20% per annum using the reducing balance method and buildings are depreciated at 5% per annum on their original cost. Depreciation is treated as a cost of sales expense.

The year-end journal for buildings and plant depreciation is given below. Using the information above, prepare the double entry by selecting the correct option for each row.

	DR	CR	Neither DR nor CR
Administrative expenses	O	O	O
Cost of sales	O	O	O
Buildings cost	O	O	O
Plant cost	O	O	O
Buildings accumulated depreciation	O	O	O
Plant accumulated depreciation	O	O	O

Calculate the depreciation charge for the below for the year ended 31 October 20X7. Use the information above to help you.

Buildings $ [   ]

Plant $ [   ] **(5 marks)**

Task 4

Closing inventory is $75,000.

Ignoring the depreciation charge calculated earlier, what is the cost of sales for the year?

$ [   ] **(1.5 marks)**

Task 5

An invoice of $15,000 for energy costs relating to the quarter ended 30 November 20X7 was received on 2 December 20X7. Energy costs are included in administrative expenses.

Complete the following statements:

The double entry to post the year end adjustments for energy costs is:

	DR	CR
Accrual	O	O
Administrative expenses	O	O

The amount to be posted within the year end adjustment double entry above is $ [   ] **(1.5 marks)**

19.3 Tonson

The information below has been extracted from the books of Tonson, a limited liability company, as at 31 October 20X6.

Task 1

Do each of these items belong in the profit or loss account (P/L) as at 31 October 20X6?

	Dr $'000	Cr $'000	P/L	Not P/L
Inventory at 1 November 20X5	350		O	O
Administrative expenses	1,106		O	O
Share premium account		200	O	O
Retained earnings at 1 November 20X5		315	O	O
Allowance for receivables at 1 November 20X5		40	O	O
Sales revenue		5,780	O	O
Bank		79	O	O
Returns inward	95		O	O
Trade payables		340	O	O
Loan note interest	33		O	O
Trade receivables	900		O	O
Purchases	3,570		O	O
7% loan notes		470	O	O
Irrecoverable debts	150		O	O
$1 ordinary shares		1,800	O	O
Accumulated depreciation at 1 November 20X5				
Buildings		360	O	O
Motor Vehicles		80	O	O
Furniture and equipment		420	O	O
Land at cost	740		O	O
Buildings at cost	1,500		O	O
Motor vehicles at cost	240		O	O
Furniture and equipment at cost	1,200		O	O
	9,884	9,884		

(5 marks)

Task 2

Buildings are depreciated at 5% of cost. At 31 October 20X6 the buildings were professionally valued at $1,800,000 and the directors wish this valuation to be incorporated into the financial statements.

Depreciation is to be charged as follows:

(i)   Motor vehicles at 20% of carrying amount
(ii)   Furniture and equipment at 20% of cost

What will be the carrying amount of the following assets in the financial statements at 31 October 20X6?

Land $ [   ]

Buildings $ [   ]

Motor vehicles $ [   ]

Furniture and equipment $ [   ]

(4 marks)

Task 3

Inventory at 31 October 20X6 was valued at $275,000 based on its original cost. However, $45,000 of this inventory has been in the warehouse for over two years and the directors have agreed to sell it in November 20X6 for a cash price of $20,000.

The administrative expenses include $5,000 which relates to November 20X6.
The allowance for receivables is to be increased to the equivalent of 5% of trade receivables.
There are wages and salaries outstanding of $40,000 for the year ended 31 October 20X6.

Will the following items be debited or credited to profit for the year?

	Debit	Credit
Inventory valuation adjustment	O	O
Administrative expenses relating to November 20X6	O	O
Increase in allowance for receivables	O	O
Outstanding wages and salaries	O	O

(3 marks)

Task 4

During October 20X6 a bonus issue of one for ten shares was made to ordinary shareholders. This has not been entered into the books. The share premium account was used for this purpose.

Complete this sentence:

The bonus issue will (increase / decrease / not affect) Tonson's cash balance.

What will be the balances on these accounts following the bonus issue?

Share capital $ [   ]

Share premium $ [   ]

(3 marks)

19.4 Emma

Set out below are the financial statements of Emma, a limited liability company.

STATEMENT OF PROFIT OR LOSS FOR THE YEAR ENDED 31 DECEMBER 20X2

	$'000
Sales revenue	2,553
Cost of sales	1,814
Gross profit	739
Distribution costs	125
Administrative expenses	264
Profit before tax	350
Income tax expense	240
Profit for the year	110

STATEMENTS OF FINANCIAL POSITION AS AT 31 DECEMBER

	20X2 $'000	20X1 $'000
Non-current assets		
Tangible assets	380	305
Intangible assets	250	200
Investments	–	25
	630	530
Current assets		
Inventories	150	102
Receivables	390	315
Cash in hand	52	1
	592	418
	1,222	948
Equity and liabilities		
Share capital ($1 ordinary shares)	200	150
Share premium account	160	150
Revaluation surplus	100	91
Retained earnings	160	100
	620	491
Non-current liabilities		
Long-term loan	100	–
Current liabilities		
Trade payables	127	119
Bank overdraft	85	98
Taxation	290	240
	502	457
	1,222	948

Additional information.

(1) The proceeds of the sale of non-current asset investments amounted to $30,000.

(2) Fixtures and fittings, with an original cost of $85,000 and a carrying amount of $45,000, were sold for $32,000 during the year.

(3) The following information relates to property, plant and equipment.

	31.12.20X2	31.12.20X1
	$'000	$'000
Cost	720	595
Accumulated depreciation	340	290
Carrying amount	380	305

(4) 50,000 $1 ordinary shares were issued during the year at a premium of 20c per share.

Complete the following sections of the statement of cash flows for the year ended 31 December 20X2 for Emma

STATEMENT OF CASH FLOWS FOR THE YEAR ENDED 31 DECEMBER 20X2 (extracts)

	$'000	Add	Subtract
Cash flows from operating activities			
Net profit before tax / Net profit after tax (delete as applicable)			
Adjustments for:			
Depreciation		O	O
Loss on sale for non-current assets		O	O
Profit on sale of non-current asset investments		O	O
Movement in inventories		O	O
Movement in receivables		O	O
Movement in payables		O	O
Income taxes paid		O	O
Cash flows from investing activities			
Purchase of intangible non-current assets		O	O
Purchase of tangible non-current assets		O	O
Receipts from sale of non-current assets		O	O
Cash flows from financing activities			
Proceeds from issue of share capital		O	O
Long-term loan		O	O

(15 marks)

19.5 Sioux

The following information is available for Sioux, a limited liability company:

STATEMENTS OF FINANCIAL POSITION

		31 December		
		20X4		20X3
	$'000	$'000	$'000	$'000
Non-current assets				
Cost or valuation		11,000		8,000
Accumulated depreciation		(5,600)		(4,800)
Carrying amount		5,400		3,200
Current assets				
Inventories	3,400		3,800	
Receivables	3,800		2,900	
Cash at bank	400	7,600	100	6,800
		13,000		10,000

| | 31 December | | | |
| | 20X4 | | 20X3 | |
	$'000	$'000	$'000	$'000
Equity and liabilities				
Capital and reserves				
Ordinary share capital	1,000		1,000	
Revaluation surplus	1,500		1,000	
Retained earnings	3,100	5,600	2,200	4,200
Non-current liabilities				
10% Loan notes		3,000		2,000
Current liabilities				
Trade payables	3,700		3,200	
Income tax	700	4,400	600	3,800
		13,000		10,000

SUMMARISED STATEMENT OF PROFIT OR LOSS FOR THE YEAR ENDED 31 DECEMBER 20X4

	$'000
Profit from operations	2,650
Finance cost (loan note interest)	(300)
	2,350
Income tax expense	(700)
Net profit for the year	1,650

Notes

1   During the year non-current assets which had cost $800,000, with a carrying amount of $350,000, were sold for $500,000.

2   The revaluation surplus arose from the revaluation of some land that was not being depreciated.

3   The 20X3 income tax liability was settled at the amount provided for at 31 December 20X3.

4   The additional loan notes were issued on 1 January 20X4. Interest was paid on 30 June 20X4 and 31 December 20X4.

5   Dividends paid during the year amounted to $750,000.

Complete the following statement of cash flows for the year ended 31 December 20X2 for Sioux

STATEMENT OF CASH FLOWS FOR THE YEAR ENDED 31 DECEMBER 20X4

	$'000	Add	Subtract
Cash flows from operating activities			
Net profit before tax / Net profit after tax (delete as applicable)			
Adjustments for:			
Depreciation		O	O
Profit on disposal of non-current assets		O	O
Movement in inventories		O	O
Movement in receivables		O	O
Movement in payables		O	O
Income taxes paid		O	O
Cash flows from investing activities			
Purchase of tangible non-current assets		O	O
Receipts from sale of non-current assets		O	O
Cash flows from financing activities			
Issue of loan notes		O	O
Dividends paid		O	O
Net increase/decrease in cash (delete as applicable)			
Cash balance at 1 January 20X4			
Cash balance at 31 December 20X4			

(15 marks)

19.6 Snowdrop

The following information has been extracted from the draft financial statements of Snowdrop, a limited liability company.

SNOWDROP
STATEMENTS OF FINANCIAL POSITION AS AT 31 MAY

	20X5		20X4	
	$'000	$'000	$'000	$'000
Non-current assets		4,600		2,700
Current assets				
Inventory	580		500	
Trade receivables	360		230	
Bank	0		170	
		940		900
Total assets		5,540		3,600
Equity and liabilities				
Equity				
Ordinary share capital		3,500		2,370
Share premium		300		150
Retained earnings		1,052		470
		4,852		2,990
Non-current liabilities				
10% Loan note				
(redeemable 31 May 20X5)		0		100
Current liabilities				
Trade payables	450		365	
Taxation	180		145	
Bank overdraft	58		0	
		688		510
		5,540		3,600

Additional information

(1)   The statement of profit or loss for the year ended 31 May 20X5 shows the following.

	$'000
Operating profit	1,042
Interest payable	(10)
Profit before taxation	1,032
Taxation	(180)
Profit for financial year	852

(2)   During the year dividends paid were $270,000.

(3)   Profit before taxation had been arrived at after charging $700,000 for depreciation on non-current assets.

(4)   During the year non-current assets with a net book value of $200,000 were sold for $180,000.

Complete the following statement of cash flows for the year ended 31 May 20X5 for Snowdrop

STATEMENT OF CASH FLOWS FOR THE YEAR ENDED 31 MAY 20X5

	$'000	Add	Subtract
Cash flows from operating activities			
Net profit before tax / Net profit after tax (delete as applicable)	☐		
Adjustments for:			
Depreciation	☐	O	O
Loss on disposal of non-current assets	☐	O	O
Movement in inventories	☐	O	O
Movement in receivables	☐	O	O
Movement in payables	☐	O	O
Income taxes paid	☐	O	O
Dividends paid	☐	O	O
Cash flows from investing activities			
Purchase of non-current assets	☐	O	O
Receipts from sale of non-current assets	☐	O	O
Cash flows from financing activities			
Issue of share capital	☐	O	O
Repayment of loan	☐	O	O
Net increase/decrease in cash (delete as applicable)	☐		
Cash balance at 31 May 20X4	☐		
Cash balance at 31 May 20X5	☐		

(15 marks)

19.7 Geofrost

> **Exam focus point.** The statement of cash flows questions in this set have required use of the indirect method. Ensure you are also familiar with the direct method, as explained in Chapter 22 of your Study Text and tested in section 24 of this Practice and Revision Kit.

Geofrost is preparing its statement of cash flows for the year ended 31 October 20X7. You have been presented with the following information.

GEOFROST
STATEMENT OF PROFIT OR LOSS FOR THE YEAR ENDED 31 OCTOBER 20X7

	$'000
Profit before tax	15,000
Taxation	(4,350)
Profit for the year	10,650

STATEMENTS OF FINANCIAL POSITION AS AT 31 OCTOBER

| | 20X7 | | 20X6 | |
	$'000	$'000	$'000	$'000
Non-current assets		44,282		26,574
Current assets				
Inventory	3,560		9,635	
Trade receivables	6,405		4,542	
Cash	2,045		1,063	
		12,010		15,240
Total assets		56,292		41,814
Equity and liabilities				
Equity				
Ordinary share capital		19,365		17,496
Retained earnings		17,115		6,465
		36,480		23,961
Non-current liabilities				
9% loan notes		8,000		10,300
Current liabilities				
Bank overdraft	1,230		429	
Trade payables	7,562		4,364	
Taxation	3,020		2,760	
		11,812		7,553
Total equity and liabilities		56,292		41,814

Additional information

(1) Depreciation expense for the year was $4,658,000.
(2) Assets with a carrying amount of $1,974,000 were disposed of at a profit of $720,000.

Complete the following statement of cash flows for the year ended 31 October 20X7 for Geofrost

STATEMENT OF CASH FLOWS FOR THE YEAR ENDED 31 OCTOBER 20X7

	$'000	Add	Subtract
Cash flows from operating activities			
Net profit before tax / Net profit after tax (delete as applicable)			
Adjustments for:			
Depreciation		O	O
Profit on disposal of non-current assets		O	O
Movement in inventories		O	O
Movement in receivables		O	O
Movement in payables		O	O
Income taxes paid		O	O
Cash flows from investing activities			
Purchase of tangible non-current assets		O	O
Receipts from sale of non-current assets		O	O
Cash flows from financing activities			
Issue of share capital		O	O
Repayment of loan		O	O
Net increase/decrease in cash (delete as applicable)			
Cash balance at 31 October 20X6			
Cash balance at 31 October 20X7			

(15 marks)

(Total = 105 marks)

20 Incomplete records   38 mins

20.1 A business has compiled the following information for the year ended 31 October 20X2:

	$
Opening inventory	386,200
Purchases	989,000
Closing inventory	422,700

The gross profit as a percentage of sales is always 40%

Based on these figures, what is the sales revenue for the year?

A $952,500
B $1,333,500
C $1,587,500
D $1,524,000   **(2 marks)**

20.2 Which of the following calculations could produce an acceptable figure for a trader's net profit for a period if no accounting records had been kept?

A   Closing net assets plus drawings minus capital introduced minus opening net assets
B   Closing net assets minus drawings plus capital introduced minus opening net assets
C   Closing net assets minus drawings minus capital introduced minus opening net assets
D   Closing net assets plus drawings plus capital introduced minus opening net assets   **(2 marks)**

20.3 A sole trader fixes his prices to achieve a gross profit percentage on sales revenue of 40%. All his sales are for cash. He suspects that one of his sales assistants is stealing cash from sales revenue.

His trading account for the month of June 20X3 is as follows:

	$
Recorded sales revenue	181,600
Cost of sales	114,000
Gross profit	67,600

Assuming that the cost of sales figure is correct, how much cash could the sales assistant have taken?

A $5,040
B $8,400
C $22,000
D   It is not possible to calculate a figure from this information   **(2 marks)**

The following information is relevant for Questions 20.4 and 20.5.

A is a sole trader who does not keep full accounting records. The following details relate to her transactions with credit customers and suppliers for the year ended 30 November 20X3.

	$
Trade receivables, 1 December 20X2	130,000
Trade payables, 1 December 20X2	60,000
Cash received from customers	687,800
Cash paid to suppliers	302,800
Discounts received	2,960
Irrecoverable debts	4,160
Amount due from a customer who is also a supplier offset against	
an amount due for goods supplied by him	2,000
Trade receivables, 30 November 20X3	181,000
Trade payables, 30 November 20X3	84,000

20.4 Based on the above information, what should be the figure for sales revenue in A's statement of profit or loss for the year ended 30 November 20X3?

$_____   **(2 marks)**

20.5 Based on the above information, what figure should appear in A's statement of profit or loss for the year ended 30 November 20X3 for purchases?

- A $283,760
- B $325,840
- C $329,760
- D $331,760

(2 marks)

20.6 A sole trader fixes her prices by adding 50 per cent to the cost of all goods purchased. On 31 October 20X3 a fire destroyed a considerable part of the inventory and all inventory records.

Her trading account for the year ended 31 October 20X3 included the following figures:

	$	$
Sales		281,250
Opening inventory at cost	183,600	
Purchases	249,200	
	432,800	
Closing inventory at cost	204,600	
		228,200
Gross profit		53,050

Using this information, what inventory loss has occurred?

- A $61,050
- B $87,575
- C $40,700
- D $110,850

(2 marks)

20.7 A fire on 30 September 20X2 destroyed some of a company's inventory and its inventory records.

The following information is available:

	$
Inventory 1 September 20X2	318,000
Sales for September 20X2	612,000
Purchases for September 20X2	412,000
Inventory in good condition at 30 September 20X2	214,000

Standard gross profit percentage on sales is 25%

Based on this information, what is the value of inventory lost?

- A $96,000
- B $271,000
- C $26,400
- D $57,000

(2 marks)

20.8 A business's bank balance increased by $750,000 during its last financial year. During the same period it issued shares of $1 million and repaid a loan note of $750,000. It purchased non-current assets for $200,000 and charged depreciation of $100,000. Working capital (other than the bank balance) increased by $575,000.

What was its profit for the year?

- A $1,175,000
- B $1,275,000
- C $1,325,000
- D $1,375,000

(2 marks)

20.9 A sole trader's business made a profit of $32,500 during the year ended 31 March 20X8. This figure was after deducting $100 per week wages for himself. In addition, he put his home telephone bill through the business books, amounting to $400 plus sales tax at 17.5%. He is registered for sales tax and therefore has charged only the net amount to his statement of profit or loss and other comprehensive income.

His capital at 1 April 20X7 was $6,500. What was his capital at 31 March 20X8?

A $33,730
B $33,800
C $38,930
D $39,000   **(2 marks)**

20.10 Senji does not keep proper accounting records, and it is necessary to calculate her total purchases for the year ended 31 January 20X3 from the following information:

	$
Trade payables: 31 January 20X2	130,400
31 January 20X3	171,250
Payment to suppliers	888,400
Cost of goods taken from inventory by Senji for her personal use	1,000
Refunds received from suppliers	2,400
Discounts received	11,200

What should be the figure for purchases, in Senji's financial statements for the year ended 31 January 20X3?

$_____   **(2 marks)**

20.11 Aluki fixes prices to make a standard gross profit percentage on sales of 20%.

The following information for the year ended 31 January 20X3 is available to compute her sales total for the year.

	$
Inventory: 1 February 20X2	243,000
31 January 20X3	261,700
Purchases	595,400
Purchases returns	41,200

What is the sales figure for the year ended 31 January 20X3?

A $669,375
B $702,600
C $772,375
D $741,480   **(2 marks)**

20.12 Alpha is a sole trader who does not keep proper accounting records.

Alpha's first year of trading was 20X4. From reviewing Alpha's bank statements and the incomplete records relating to cash maintained, the following summary has been compiled.

Bank and cash summary, Alpha, 20X4

	$
Cash received from credit customers and paid into the bank	381,600
Expenses paid out of cash received from credit customers before banking	6,800
Cash sales	112,900

Other information, Alpha, 20X4

Irrecoverable debts written off	7,200
Closing balance of Trade receivables	0

Which of the following correctly represents Alpha's sales figure for 20X4?

A $508,500
B $112,900
C $381,600
D $494,100   **(2 marks)**

20.13 A sole trader who does not keep full accounting records wishes to calculate her sales revenue for the year. The information available is:

1	Opening inventory	$17,000
2	Closing inventory	$24,000
3	Purchases	$91,000
4	Standard gross profit percentage on sales revenue	40%

Which of the following is the sales figure for the year calculated from these figures?

A $117,600
B $108,000
C $210,000
D $140,000

(2 marks)

20.14 On 31 December 20X0 the inventory of V was completely destroyed by fire. The following information is available:

1   Inventory at 1 December 20X0 at cost $28,400
2   Purchases for December 20X0 $49,600
3   Sales for December 20X0 $64,800
4   Standard gross profit percentage on sales revenue 30%

Based on this information, which of the following is the amount of inventory destroyed?

A $45,360
B $32,640
C $40,971
D $19,440

(2 marks)

20.15 The following information is available for the year ended 31 December 20X4 for a trader who does not keep proper accounting records:

	$
Inventories at 1 January 20X4	38,000
Inventories at 31 December 20X4	45,000
Purchases	637,000

Gross profit percentage on sales = 30%

Based on this information, what was the trader's sales figure for the year?

A $900,000
B $819,000
C $920,000
D $837,200

(2 marks)

20.16 Wanda keeps no accounting records. The following information is available about her position and transactions for the year ended 31 December 20X4:

	$
Net assets at 1 January 20X4	210,000
Drawings during 20X4	48,000
Capital introduced during 20X4	100,000
Net assets at 31 December 20X4	400,000

Based on this information, what was Wanda's profit for 20X4?

A $42,000
B $242,000
C $138,000
D $338,000

(2 marks)

(Total = 32 marks)

21 Company financial statements

24 mins

21.1 Which of the following items may appear as current liabilities in a company's statement of financial position?

1   Revaluation surplus
2   Loan due for repayment within one year
3   Taxation
4   Preference dividend payable on redeemable preference shares

A   1, 2 and 3
B   1, 2 and 4
C   1, 3 and 4
D   2, 3 and 4

(2 marks)

21.2 Which **TWO** of the following might appear as an item in a company's statement of changes in equity?

A   Profit on disposal of properties
B   Surplus on revaluation of properties
C   Equity dividends proposed after the reporting date
D   Issue of share capital

(2 marks)

21.3 At 31 December 20X2 the following matters require inclusion in a company's financial statements:

1   On 1 January 20X2 the company made a loan of $12,000 to an employee, repayable on 30 April 20X3, charging interest at 2 per cent per year. On the due date she repaid the loan and paid the whole of the interest due on the loan to that date.

2   The company has paid insurance $9,000 in 20X2, covering the year ending 31 August 20X3.

3   In January 20X3 the company received rent from a tenant $4,000 covering the six months to 31 December 20X2.

For these items, what total figures should be included in the company's statement of financial position at 31 December 20X2?

	Receivables and prepayments $	Payables and accruals $
A	22,000	240
B	22,240	NIL
C	10,240	NIL
D	16,240	6,000

(2 marks)

21.4 Which of the following items are required to be disclosed by a limited liability company, either on the face of their main financial statements or in the notes, according to International Financial Reporting Standards?

1   Share capital
2   Dividends proposed
3   Depreciation and amortisation

A   1 and 2 only
B   1 and 3 only
C   2 and 3 only
D   1, 2, and 3

(2 marks)

21.5 Identify, by indicating the relevant box in the table below, whether each of the following statements about the financial statements of a limited company is true or false, according to International Financial Reporting Standards.

	True	False
In preparing a statement of cash flows, either the direct or the indirect method may be used. Both lead to the same figure for net cash from operating activities.	True	False
Loan notes can be classified as current or non-current liabilities.	True	False
Financial statements must disclose a company's total expense for depreciation, if material.	True	False
A company must disclose, by note, details of all adjusting events allowed for in the financial statements.	True	False

(2 marks)

21.6 Which **TWO** of the following could appear as separate items in the statement of changes in equity required by IAS 1 *Presentation of Financial Statements* as part of a company's financial statements?

A   Dividends on equity shares paid during the period
B   Loss on sale of investments
C   Proceeds of an issue of ordinary shares
D   Dividends proposed after the year end

(2 marks)

21.7 Which one of the following items does **NOT** appear under the heading 'equity and reserves' on a company statement of financial position?

A   Share premium account
B   Retained earnings
C   Revaluation surplus
D   Loan stock

(2 marks)

21.8 The correct ledger entries needed to record the issue of 200,000 $1 shares at a premium of 30c, and paid for in full, would be

A   Dr Ordinary share capital $200,000
     Cr Share premium account $60,000
     Cr Cash $140,000

B   Dr Cash $260,000
     Cr Ordinary share capital $200,000
     Cr Share premium account $60,000

C   Dr Ordinary share capital $200,000
     Cr Share premium account $60,000
     Cr Cash $260,000

D   Dr Cash $200,000
     Dr Share premium account $60,000
     Cr Ordinary share capital $260,000

(2 marks)

21.9 Which of the following statements about limited liability companies' accounting is/are correct?

   1   A revaluation surplus arises when a non-current asset is sold at a profit.

   2   The authorised share capital of a company is the maximum nominal value of shares and loan notes the company may issue.

   3   IAS 10 *Events after the reporting period* requires all non-adjusting events to be disclosed in the notes to the financial statements.

   A   1 and 2
   B   2 only
   C   3 only
   D   None of the statements are correct   **(2 marks)**

21.10 Fruitz Co has a tax liability relating to 20X1 brought forward in 20X2 of $16,000. This liability is finally agreed at $18,500, which is paid in 20X2.

   Fruitz's accountant estimates their tax liability for profits earned in 20X2 will be $20,000.

   What will be the charge for taxation in Fruitz's statement of profit or loss for the year ended 31 December 20X2?

   $_____   **(2 marks)**

                                                                                 (Total = 20 marks)

22 Disclosure notes   22 mins

22.1 Which of the following best describes the purpose of disclosure notes in the financial statements?

   A   To provide more detail for the users of financial statements about the information in the statement of financial position and statement of profit or loss and other comprehensive income.

   B   To allow companies to present their financial results in a more favourable way by only disclosing some things in the notes and not on the main financial statements.

   C   To give all the detail of all the transactions that occurred during the period because the main financial statements only present a summary.

   D   To explain the accounting treatment adopted where management have chosen not to apply accounting standards.   **(2 marks)**

22.2 For which class or classes of assets should a company disclose in the notes to the financial statements a reconciliation of the opening carrying amount to the closing carrying amount, showing the movements in the period?

   1   Cash
   2   Intangible assets
   3   Tangible non-current assets
   4   Trade receivables

   A   3 only
   B   2 and 3 only
   C   1 and 4 only
   D   1 only   **(2 marks)**

22.3 Which of the following should be disclosed in the note to the financial statements for inventories?

1 The date the inventories were purchased or manufactured and/or how long they have been held as inventories

2 The amount of inventories carried at net realisable value

3 The accounting policies adopted in measuring inventories

4 The useful life of the inventories

A 3 only
B 2 and 3 only
C 1 and 4 only
D 1 only   (2 marks)

22.4 Which of the following should be disclosed in the note to the financial statements for intangible assets?

1 The method of amortisation used
2 A reconciliation of the carrying amount at the beginning and end of the period
3 The useful life of the assets
4 The net realisable value of any deferred development costs capitalised

A 1, 2 and 3 only
B 2 and 3 only
C 3 and 4 only
D 2 only   (2 marks)

22.5 Which of the following statements is/are correct?

1 IAS 37 requires disclosure in the notes to the financial statements of the uncertainties affecting the outcome of a provision

2 IAS 10 requires disclosure of the nature and financial effect of a non-adjusting event after the reporting period in the notes to the financial statements

A 1 only
B 2 only
C Both 1 and 2
D Neither 1 or 2   (2 marks)

22.6 A certain IFRS requires that the following disclosure is made in a note to the financial statements:

(i)   A brief description of its nature
(ii)   Where practicable an estimate of the financial effect
(iii) An indication of the uncertainties relating to the amount or timing of any outflow
(iv)   The possibility of any reimbursement

Which of the following does the above disclosure apply to?

A Provisions
B Contingent liabilities
C Contingent assets
D Events after the reporting period   (2 marks)

22.7 Which of the following should be disclosed in the note to the financial statements for tangible non-current assets?

1   The market value of all assets classified as tangible non-current assets, whether they have been revalued or not

2   A reconciliation of the carrying amount of non-current assets at the beginning and end of the period

3   For revalued assets, the methods and significant assumptions applied in estimating the fair value

4   For revalued assets, the carrying amount of each class of assets that would have been included in the financial statements had the assets been carried at cost less depreciation

A   1, 2 and 3 only
B   2 and 3 only
C   2, 3 and 4 only
D   1 and 4 only   **(2 marks)**

22.8 Which of the following are required as disclosures by IAS 2 *Inventories*?

1   The amount of write-downs of inventories in the period that have been recognised as an expense

2   The original cost of inventories that are carried at net realisable value

3   The carrying amount of inventories classified by type (for example, raw materials, work in progress)

A   1 and 2 only
B   1 and 3 only
C   2 and 3 only
D   1, 2 and 3   **(2 marks)**

22.9 Which one of the following is a disclosure about non-adjusting events required by IAS 10 *Events after the reporting period*?

A   Dividends declared before the end of the reporting period and paid after the end of the reporting period

B   The nature of both material and non-material non-adjusting events

C   The date that the non-adjusting event occurred

D   An estimate of the financial effect of the event, unless a reasonable estimate cannot be made

     (2 marks)

     (Total = 18 marks)

23   Events after the reporting period   22 mins

23.1 Which of the following material events after the reporting period and before the financial statements are approved by the directors should be adjusted for in those financial statements?

1   A valuation of property providing evidence of impairment in value at the reporting period

2   Sale of inventory held at the end of the reporting period for less than cost

3   Discovery of fraud or error affecting the financial statements

4   The insolvency of a customer with a debt owing at the end of the reporting period which is still outstanding

A   All of them
B   1, 2 and 4 only
C   3 and 4 only
D   1, 2 and 3 only   **(2 marks)**

23.2 The draft financial statements of a limited liability company are under consideration. The accounting treatment of the following material events which occurred after the end of the reporting period needs to be determined.

According to IAS 10 *Events after the reporting period*, which **TWO** of the events require an adjustment to the figures in the draft financial statements?

A The bankruptcy of a major customer, with a substantial debt outstanding at the end of the reporting period

B A fire destroying some of the company's inventory (the company's going concern status is not affected)

C An issue of shares to finance expansion

D Sale for less than cost of some inventory held at the end of the reporting period **(2 marks)**

23.3 In finalising the financial statements of a company for the year ended 30 June 20X4, which of the following material matters should be adjusted for?

1 A customer who owed $180,000 at the end of the reporting period went bankrupt in July 20X4.

2 The sale in August 20X4 for $400,000 of some inventory items valued in the statement of financial position at $500,000.

3 A factory with a value of $3,000,000 was seriously damaged by a fire in July 20X4. The factory was back in production by August 20X4 but its value was reduced to $2,000,000.

4 The company issued 1,000,000 ordinary shares in August 20X4.

A All four items
B 1 and 2 only
C 1 and 4 only
D 2 and 3 only **(2 marks)**

23.4 IAS 10 *Events after the reporting period* regulates the extent to which events after the reporting period should be reflected in financial statements.

Which one of the following lists of such events consists only of items that, according to IAS 10, should normally be classified as non-adjusting?

A Insolvency of an account receivable which was outstanding at the end of the reporting period, issue of shares or loan notes, an acquisition of another company

B Issue of shares or loan notes, changes in foreign exchange rates, major purchases of non-current assets

C An acquisition of another company, destruction of a major non-current asset by fire, discovery of fraud or error which shows that the financial statements were incorrect

D Sale of inventory which gives evidence about its value at the end of the reporting period, issue of shares or loan notes, destruction of a major non-current asset by fire **(2 marks)**

23.5 Which of the following events occurring after the reporting period are classified as adjusting, if material?

1 The sale of inventories valued at cost at the end of the reporting period for a figure in excess of cost

2 A valuation of land and buildings providing evidence of an impairment in value at the year end

3 The issue of shares and loan notes

4 The insolvency of a customer with a balance outstanding at the year end

A 1 and 3
B 2 and 4
C 2 and 3
D 1 and 4 **(2 marks)**

23.6 The financial statements of Overexposure Co for the year ended 31 December 20X1 are to be approved on 31 March 20X2. Before they are approved, the following events take place.

1   On 14 February 20X2 the directors took the strategic decision to sell their investment in Quebec Co despite the fact that this investment generated material revenues.

2   On 15 March 20X2, a fire occurred in the eastern branch factory which destroyed a material amount of inventory. It is estimated that it will cost $505,000 to repair the significant damage done to the factory.

3   On 17 March 20X2, a customer of Overexposure Co went into liquidation. Overexposure has been advised that it is unlikely to receive payment for any of the outstanding balances owed by the customer at the year end.

How should these events reflected in the financial statements at 31 December 20X1?

	Adjust	Disclose	Do nothing
A	3	2, 3	1
B	2, 3	1	–
C	3	1, 2	–
D	2	3, 1	**(2 marks)**

23.7 Which of the following events between the reporting date and the date the financial statements are authorised for issue must be adjusted in the financial statements?

1   Declaration of equity dividends
2   Decline in market value of investments
3   The announcement of changes in tax rates
4   The announcement of a major restructuring

A   1 only
B   2 and 4
C   3 only
D   None of them   **(2 marks)**

23.8 Which of the following is the correct definition of an adjusting event after the reporting period?

A   An event that occurs between the reporting date and the date on which the financial statements are authorised for issue that provides further evidence of conditions that existed at the reporting date

B   An event that occurs between the reporting date and the date on which the financial statements are authorised for issue that provides evidence of conditions that arose subsequent to the reporting date

C   An event that occurs after the date the financial statements are authorised for issue that provides further evidence of conditions that existed at the reporting date

D   An event that occurs after the date the financial statements are authorised for issue that provides evidence of conditions that arose subsequent to the reporting date   **(2 marks)**

23.9 If a material event occurs after the reporting date but before the financial statements are authorised for issue outside the organisation, and this event does **NOT** require adjustment, what information should be disclosed in the financial statements?

A   The nature of the event and an estimate of the financial effect (or a statement that such an estimate cannot be made)

B   The nature of the event only

C   An estimate of the financial effect (or a statement that such an estimate cannot be made) only

D   No disclosure required   **(2 marks)**

(Total = 18 marks)

24 Statements of cash flows

24.1 Which of the following items appear in a company's statement of cash flows?

1   Surplus on revaluation of non-current assets
2   Proceeds of issue of shares
3   Proposed dividend
4   Irrecoverable debts written off
5   Dividends received

A   1, 2 and 5 only
B   2, 3, 4, 5 only
C   2 and 5 only
D   3 and 4 only

(2 marks)

24.2 Part of the process of preparing a company's statement of cash flows is the calculation of cash inflow from operating activities.

Which of the following statements about that calculation (using the indirect method) are correct?

1   Loss on sale of operating non-current assets should be deducted from net profit before taxation.
2   Increase in inventory should be deducted from operating profits.
3   Increase in payables should be added to operating profits.
4   Depreciation charges should be added to net profit before taxation.

A   1, 2 and 3
B   1, 2 and 4
C   1, 3 and 4
D   2, 3 and 4

(2 marks)

24.3 In the course of preparing a company's statement of cash flows, the following figures are to be included in the calculation of net cash from operating activities.

	$
Depreciation charges	980,000
Profit on sale of non-current assets	40,000
Increase in inventories	130,000
Decrease in receivables	100,000
Increase in payables	80,000

What will the net effect of these items be in the statement of cash flows?

		$
A	Addition to operating profit	890,000
B	Subtraction from operating profit	890,000
C	Addition to operating profit	1,070,000
D	Addition to operating profit	990,000

(2 marks)

24.4 Part of a company's draft statement of cash flows is shown below:

	$'000
Net profit before tax	8,640
Depreciation charges	(2,160)
Proceeds of sale of non-current assets	360
Increase in inventory	(330)
Increase in accounts payable	440

The following criticisms of the above extract have been made:

1   Depreciation charges should have been added, not deducted.

2   Increase in inventory should have been added, not deducted.

3   Increase in accounts payable should have been deducted, not added.

4   Proceeds of sale of non-current assets should not appear in this part of the statement of cash flows.

Which of these criticisms are valid?

A   2 and 3 only
B   1 and 4 only
C   1 and 3 only
D   2 and 4 only   (2 marks)

24.5 In preparing a company's statement of cash flows complying with IAS 7 *Statements of Cash Flows*, which, if any, of the following items could form part of the calculation of cash flow from financing activities?

1   Proceeds of sale of premises
2   Dividends received
3   Bonus issue of shares

A   1 only
B   2 only
C   3 only
D   None of them   (2 marks)

24.6 Which of the following assertions about statements of cash flows is/are correct?

1   A statement of cash flows prepared using the direct method produces a different figure for operating cash flow from that produced if the indirect method is used.

2   Rights issues of shares do not feature in statements of cash flows.

3   A surplus on revaluation of a non-current asset will not appear as an item in a statement of cash flows.

4   A profit on the sale of a non-current asset will appear as an item under Cash Flows from Investing Activities in a statement of cash flows.

A   1 and 4
B   2 and 3
C   3 only
D   2 and 4   (2 marks)

24.7 An extract from a statement of cash flows prepared by a trainee accountant is shown below.

Cash flows from operating activities

	$m
Net profit before taxation	28
Adjustments for: Depreciation	(9)
Operating profit before working capital changes	19
Decrease in inventories	13
Increase in receivables	(4)
Increase in payables	(8)
Cash generated from operations	10

Which **TWO** of the following criticisms of this extract are correct?

A   Depreciation charges should have been added, not deducted.
B   Decrease in inventories should have been deducted, not added.
C   Increase in receivables should have been added, not deducted.
D   Increase in payables should have been added, not deducted.   **(2 marks)**

24.8 Which of the following items could appear in a company's statement of cash flows?

1   Proposed dividends
2   Rights issue of shares
3   Bonus issue of shares
4   Repayment of loan

A   1 and 3
B   2 and 4
C   1 and 4
D   2 and 3   **(2 marks)**

24.9 IAS 7 requires the statement of cash flows to open with the calculation of net cash from operating activities, arrived at by adjusting net profit before taxation.

Which one of the following lists consists only of items which could appear in such a calculation?

A   Depreciation, increase in receivables, decrease in payables, proceeds from sale of equipment, increase in inventories

B   Increase in payables, decrease in inventories, profit on sale of plant, depreciation, decrease in receivables

C   Increase in payables, proceeds from sale of equipment, depreciation, decrease in receivables, increase in inventories

D   Depreciation, interest paid, proceeds from sale of equipment, decrease in inventories   **(2 marks)**

24.10 The following extract is from the financial statements of Pompeii, a limited liability company at 31 October:

	20X9 $'000	20X8 $'000
Equity and liabilities		
Share capital	120	80
Share premium	60	40
Retained earnings	85	68
	265	188
Non-current liabilities		
Bank loan	100	150
	365	338

What is the cash flow from financing activities to be disclosed in the statement of cash flows for the year ended 31 October 20X9?

A $60,000 inflow
B $10,000 inflow
C $110,000 inflow
D $27,000 inflow   **(2 marks)**

24.11 A draft statement of cash flows contains the following calculation of cash flows from operating activities:

	$m
Profit before tax	13
Depreciation	2
Decrease in inventories	(3)
Decrease in trade and other receivables	5
Decrease in trade payables	4
Net cash inflow from operating activities	21

Which of the following corrections need to be made to the calculation?

1   Depreciation should be deducted, not added.
2   Decrease in inventories should be added, not deducted.
3   Decrease in receivables should be deducted, not added.
4   Decrease in payables should be deducted, not added.

A   1 and 3
B   2 and 3
C   1 and 4
D   2 and 4   **(2 marks)**

24.12 The following extract is taken from a draft version of company's statement of cash flows, prepared by a trainee accountant.

	$'000
Net cash flow from operating activities	
Profit before tax	484
Depreciation charges	327
Profit on sale of property, plant and equipment	35
Increase in inventories	(74)
Decrease in trade and other receivables	(41)
Increase in trade payables	29
Cash generated from operations	760

Four possible mistakes that may have been made by the trainee accountant are listed below.

1   The profit on sale of property, plant and equipment should be subtracted, not added.
2   The increase in inventories should be added, not subtracted.
3   The decrease in trade and other receivables should be added, not subtracted.
4   The increase in trade payables should be subtracted, not added.

Which of the four mistakes did the trainee accountant make when preparing the draft statement?

A   1 and 2 only
B   1 and 3 only
C   2 and 4 only
D   3 and 4 only   **(2 marks)**

24.13 Which, if any, of the following items could be included in 'cash flows from financing activities' in a statement of cash flows that complies with IAS 7 *Statement of Cash Flows*?

1   Interest received
2   Taxation paid
3   Proceeds from sale of property

A   1 only
B   2 only
C   3 only
D   None of them   **(2 marks)**

24.14 Which one of the following statements is correct, with regard to the preparation of a statement of cash flows that complies with IAS 7 *Statement of Cash Flows*?

A   A statement of cash flows prepared using the direct method produces the same figure for net cash from operating activities as a statement produced by the indirect method.

B   An increase in a bank overdraft during the accounting period is included within cash flows from financing activities.

C   A profit on the sale of equipment is included within cash flows from investing activities.

D   A surplus on the revaluation of property will appear within cash flows from investing activities.

                                                                                    (2 marks)

24.15 The following information is available about the plant, property and equipment of Lok Co, for the year to 31 December 20X3.

	$'000
Carrying amount of assets at beginning of the year	462
Carrying amount of assets at end of the year	633
Increase in revaluation surplus during the year	50
Disposals during the year, at cost	110
Accumulated depreciation on the assets disposed of	65
Depreciation charge for the year	38

Based on this information, what amount will be included for purchases of property, plant and equipment for the year, in a statement of cash flows that complies with IAS 7 *Statement of Cash Flows?*

$_____   **(2 marks)**

24.16 A company sold warehouse premises at a loss during a financial period. How would this transaction be included in a statement of cash flows for the period that complies with IAS 7 *Statement of Cash Flows* and that uses the indirect method to present cash flows from operating activities?

	Loss on disposal	*Proceeds from sale*
A	Deduct as an adjustment in the calculation of cash flows from operating activities	Include in cash flows from investing activities
B	Deduct as an adjustment in the calculation of cash flows from operating activities	Include in cash flows from operating activities
C	Add as an adjustment in the calculation of cash flows from operating activities	Include in cash flows from investing activities
D	Add as an adjustment in the calculation of cash flows from operating activities	Include in cash flows from operating activities

(2 marks)

24.17 Big Time Co had the following transactions during the year.

- Purchases from suppliers were $18,500, of which $2,550 was unpaid at the year end. Brought forward payables were $1,000.

- Wages and salaries amounted to $9,500, of which $750 was unpaid at the year end. The financial statements for the previous year showed an accrual for wages and salaries of $1,500.

- Interest of $2,100 on a long term loan was paid in the year.

- Sales revenue was $33,400, including $900 receivables at the year end. Brought forward receivables were $400.

- Interest on cash deposits at the bank amounted to $175.

Using the direct method, what is Big Time Co's cash flow from operating activities?

A $3,425
B $3,775
C $1,425
D $6,775   **(2 marks)**

24.18 Which one of the following statements is correct?

A   If a business makes a profit, it has positive cash flow.
B   If a business makes a loss, it has negative cash flow.
C   A business may make a profit but have negative cash flow.
D   A business that breaks even has cash inflows equal to cash used.   **(2 marks)**

24.19 Toots Co has made healthy profits for the past year, although at times the company has been close to running out of cash. Because Toots Co is profitable, Adam, their accountant is unconcerned by the cash shortage. Jo, the financial controller at Toots Co, is concerned. Jo tells Adam, 'profits are fine on paper, but in the real world cash is king'. Jo believes Toots Co needs to take a more proactive approach to cash flow management.

Adam and Jo have two different views. Who is correct, and why?

A   Adam is correct. A profitable business should not waste management time on cash flow issues.

B   Adam is correct. A profitable business will always survive and prosper.

C   Jo is correct. Proactive cash flow management is required under IAS 7 *Statements of Cash Flows*.

D   Jo is correct. A business that does not have cash available to fund operations is likely to fail.

(2 marks)

24.20 Which one of the following statements correctly identifies a valid disadvantage to users of financial statements of the statement of cash flows?

A   Under IAS 7 *Statement of cash flows*, an entity may use any format for their statement.

B   There is an opportunity to reclassify some cash outflows that might have been reported in the operating section as investing cash outflows.

C   Under IAS 7 *Statement of cash flows* the statement of cash flows may cover a different period of time to the other financial statements.

D   Cash flow figures are more open to manipulation than the profit figure.   **(2 marks)**

24.21 The accountant of F Co is preparing the statement of cash flows using the direct method for reporting cash flows from operating activities. The following information is available at 31 March 2017.

	$
Sales	750,000
Purchases	400,000
Receivables at 31 March 2017	184,000
Receivables at 1 April 2016	163,000
Payables at 31 March 2017	102,000
Payables at 1 April 2016	111,000

What will be disclosed as cash receipts from customers in the statement of cash flows for the year ended 31 March 2017?

A $320,000
B $771,000
C $750,000
D $729,000   **(2 marks)**

(Total = 42 marks)

Do you know? – Preparing simple consolidated financial statements

Check that you can fill in the blanks in the statements below before you attempt any questions. If in doubt, you should go back to your BPP Interactive Text and revise first.

- .... means presenting the results, assets and liabilities of a group of companies as if they were one company.

- A .... is an entity controlled by another entity.

- An .... is an entity over which another entity exerts significant influence.

- .... are accounted for in the consolidated statements of a group using the **e**......... method.

- A **t**......... **i**..................... is a simple investment in the shares of another entity that is not an associate or a subsidiary.

- .... financial statements present the results of the **g**........., they do not replace the separate financial statements of the individual group companies.

- Basic consolidation consists of two procedures:

    - .... which appear as an asset in one company and a liability in another

    - Then adding together all the .... assets and liabilities on a line by line basis

- .... arising on consolidation is recognised as an .... asset in the consolidated statement of financial position.

- The **n**....-**c**............ **i**......... shows the extent to which net assets controlled by the group are owned by other parties.

- A consolidation adjustment is required to remove .... profit on intra-group trading and transfer of non-current assets.

- When a parent company acquires a subsidiary part way through the year, the profits for the period need to be apportioned between **p**..... and **p**...... acquisition. Only **p**..... acquisition profits are included in the group's consolidated statement of financial position.

- The .... statement of profit or loss is prepared by combining the statements of profit or loss of each group company on a line-by-line basis.

- Intra-group .... and .... are eliminated from the consolidated statement of profit or loss.

- If a .... is acquired during the year, only the post-acquisition element of statement of profit or loss balances are included on consolidation.

Did you know? – Preparing simple consolidated financial statements

Could you fill in the blanks? The answers are in bold. Use this page for revision purposes as you approach the exam.

- **Consolidation** means presenting the results, assets and liabilities of a group of companies as if they were one company.

- A **subsidiary** is an entity controlled by another entity.

- An **associate** is an entity over which another entity exerts significant influence.

- **Associates** are accounted for in the consolidated statements of a group using the **equity** method.

- A **trade investment** is a simple investment in the shares of another entity that is not an associate or a subsidiary.

- **Consolidated** financial statements present the results of the **group**, they do not replace the separate financial statements of the individual group companies.

- Basic consolidation consists of two procedures:

  - **Cancelling out items** which appear as an asset in one company and a liability in another
  - Then adding together all the **uncancelled** assets and liabilities on a line by line basis

- **Goodwill** arising on consolidation is recognised as an **intangible** asset in the consolidated statement of financial position.

- The **non-controlling interest** (**NCI**) shows the extent to which net assets controlled by the group are owned by other parties.

- A consolidation adjustment is required to remove **unrealised** profit on intra-group trading and transfer of non-current assets.

- When a parent company acquires a subsidiary part way through the year, the profits for the period need to be apportioned between **pre** and **post** acquisition. Only **post** acquisition profits are included in the group's consolidated statement of financial position.

- The **consolidated** statement of profit or loss is prepared by combining the statements of profit or loss of each group company on a line-by-line basis.

- Intra-group **sales** and **purchases** are eliminated from the consolidated statement of profit or loss.

- If a **subsidiary** is acquired during the year, only the post-acquisition element of statement of profit or loss balances are included on consolidation.

15 mark questions: preparing simple consolidated financial statements 72 mins

> **Exam focus point.** This question provides excellent practice of the knowledge and skills required to tackle long questions that may appear in Section B of the exam.

25.1 Swing and Cat

Swing purchased 80% of Cat's equity on 1 January 20X7 for $120,000 when Cat's retained earnings were $50,000. The fair value of the non-controlling interest on that date was $40,000. During the year, Swing sold goods which cost $80,000 to Cat, at an invoiced cost of $100,000. Cat had 50% of the goods still in inventories at the year end. The two companies' draft financial statements as at 31 December 20X8 are shown below.

STATEMENTS OF PROFIT OR LOSS FOR THE YEAR ENDED 31 DECEMBER 20X8

	Swing	Cat
	$'000	$'000
Revenue	5,000	1,000
Cost of sales	2,900	600
Gross profit	2,100	400
Other expenses	1,700	320
Net profit	400	80
Income tax	130	25
Profit for the year	270	55

STATEMENTS OF FINANCIAL POSITION AT 31 DECEMBER 20X8

	Swing	Cat
	$'000	$'000
Non-current assets		
Investment in Cat	120	–
Tangible non-current assets	1,880	200
	2,000	200
Current assets		
Inventory	500	120
Trade receivables	650	40
Bank and cash	390	35
	1,540	195
	3,540	395
Equity and liabilities		
Equity		
Share capital	2,000	100
Retained earnings	400	200
	2,400	300
Current liabilities		
Trade payables	910	30
Tax	230	65
	1,140	95
	3,540	395

Task 1

Complete the following to determine goodwill at acquisition

Consideration transferred on acquisition	
Fair value of non-controlling interest	Add / Subtract
Total cost of investment	
Fair value of net assets at acquisition:	
Equity share capital	
Retained earnings	
Total net assets	
Goodwill	

(4 marks)

Task 2

What is the amount of the adjustment for unrealised profit on inventory?

$ _____

(1.5 marks)

Task 3

What will be consolidated cost of sales at 31 December 20X8?

$ _____

(2.5 marks)

Task 4

Which **TWO** of the following statements concerning the non-controlling interest are correct?

☐ Non-controlling interest describes shares in the consolidated entity not held by the parent

☐ Non-controlling interest describes shares in the subsidiary not held by the parent

☐ 20% of Swing's consolidated retained earnings will be allocated to the non-controlling interest

☐ 20% of Cat's profit after tax will be allocated to the non-controlling interest

(2 marks)

Task 5

Complete the following to determine consolidated retained earnings

	Swing $'000	Cat $'000	
Per question			
Adjustment			Add/subtract
Pre-acquisition retained earnings			Add/subtract
Total			
Group share of Cat			
Group retained earnings			

(5 marks)

25.2 Black and Bury

The following are the financial statements relating to Black, a limited liability company, and its subsidiary company Bury.

STATEMENTS OF PROFIT OR LOSS
FOR THE YEAR ENDED 31 OCTOBER 20X5

	Black $'000	Bury $'000
Sales revenue	245,000	95,000
Cost of sales	(140,000)	(52,000)
Gross profit	105,000	43,000
Distribution costs	(12,000)	(10,000)
Administrative expenses	(55,000)	(13,000)
Dividend income from Bury	7,000	–
Profit before tax	45,000	20,000
Tax	(13,250)	(5,000)
Profit for the year	31,750	15,000

STATEMENTS OF FINANCIAL POSITION
AS AT 31 OCTOBER 20X5

	Black $'000	Black $'000	Bury $'000	Bury $'000
Assets				
Non-current assets				
Property, plant and equipment		110,000		40,000
Investments				
21,000,000 $1 ordinary shares in Bury at cost		21,000		–
		131,000		40,000
Current assets				
Inventory, at cost	13,360		3,890	
Trade receivables and dividend receivable	14,640		6,280	
Bank	3,500		2,570	
Total assets		31,500		12,740
		162,500		52,740
Equity and liabilities				
Equity				
$1 Ordinary shares		100,000		30,000
Retained earnings		33,500		10,280
		133,500		40,280
Current liabilities				
Payables	9,000		2,460	
Dividend	20,000		10,000	
Total equity and liabilities		29,000		12,460
		162,500		52,740

Additional information

(1) Black purchased its $1 ordinary shares in Bury on 1 November 20X0. At that date the balance on Bury's retained earnings was $2 million. The fair value of the non-controlling interest at the date of acquisition was $11,800,000. Goodwill on acquisition was $800,000.

(2) During the year ended 31 October 20X5 Black sold goods which originally cost $12 million to Bury. Black invoiced Bury at cost plus 40%. Bury still has 30% of these goods in inventory at 31 October 20X5.

(3) Bury owed Black $1.5 million at 31 October 20X5 for some of the goods Black supplied during the year.

Task 1

Black purchased its shares in Bury on 1 November 20X0. Goodwill on acquisition was $800,000.

What was the amount paid by Black to acquire the shares? (see the information in note 1)

$ [   ]

(3 marks)

Task 2

The dividend due to Black from Bury will be:

O   Included in consolidated profit for the year
O   Added to the total of non-controlling interest
O   Included in consolidated current liabilities
O   Eliminated on consolidation

The dividend payable by Black will be:

O   Deducted from consolidated profit for the year
O   Deducted from consolidated current assets
O   Included in consolidated current liabilities
O   Eliminated on consolidation

(4 marks)

Task 3

What is the amount of the unrealised profit on the intragroup sale?

$ [   ]

Show how this is posted:

	DR	CR
Inventory	O	O
Retained earnings	O	O

(3 marks)

Task 4

Bury owed Black $1.5 million for goods supplied. How will this be accounted for in the consolidated financial statements?

	DR	CR
Payables	O	O
Receivables	O	O

(1 marks)

Task 5

Non-controlling interest will appear in both the consolidated statement of profit or loss (SPL) and the consolidated statement of financial position (SFP).

The amount of non-controlling interest in the consolidated SPL is $ [   ]

Fill in the blanks to calculate the amount of non-controlling interest in the consolidated SFP

	$	
Fair value at acquisition		
Share of post-acquisition retained earnings		Add / subtract
Total		

(4 marks)

25.3 Prestend

Prestend is the parent company of Northon. The following are the statements of financial position for both companies as at 31 October 20X7.

	Prestend		Northon	
	$'000	$'000	$'000	$'000
Assets				
Non-current assets				
Property, plant and equipment		4,200		3,300
Investments: shares in Northon at cost		3,345		–
Current assets				
Inventory	1,500		800	
Receivables	1,800		750	
Bank	600		350	
		3,900		1,900
Total assets		11,445		5,200
Equity and liabilities				
Equity				
$1 ordinary shares		9,000		4,000
Retained earnings		525		200
		9,525		4,200
Current liabilities				
Payables		1,220		200
Tax		700		800
Total equity and liabilities		11,445		5,200

The following information is also available.

(a) Prestend purchased 2,800,000 shares in Northon a year ago when Northon had retained earnings of $60,000. The fair value of the non-controlling interest at the date of acquisition was $1,415,000.

(b) During the year Prestend sold goods with an invoice value of $240,000 to Northon. These goods were invoiced at cost plus 20%. Half of the goods are still in Northon's inventory at the year end.

(c) Northon owes Prestend $30,000 at 31 October 20X7 for goods it purchased during the year.

Task 1

Complete the following to determine goodwill at acquisition:

Fair value of consideration transferred

Fair value of non-controlling interest at acquisition   Add / Subtract

Total A

Fair value of net assets acquired:

Ordinary share capital

Retained earnings

Total B

Select the correct formula for goodwill:

O   A minus 100% B
O   A minus 70% B
O   A plus 100% B
O   A plus 70% B   **(5 marks)**

Task 2

What is the unrealised profit on intragroup sales?

O $40,000
O $48,000
O $20,000
O $24,000   **(2 marks)**

Task 3

A parent-subsidiary relationship is based on **control**.

Which **TWO** of the following would signify that one entity controls another?

☐ Ownership of more than 50% of equity shares

☐ Ownership of 40% of equity shares and 80% of preference shares

☐ Ability to exert significant influence over policies

☐ Power to appoint or remove the majority of board members   **(2 marks)**

Task 4

Fill in the gaps to complete the working for group retained earnings

	Prestend $'000		Northon $'000	
Per question				
Adjustment for unrealised profit		OR		Add / Subtract
Pre-acquisition retained earnings		OR		Add / Subtract
Total Northon				
Group share of Northon				
Group retained earnings				

(6 marks)

25.4 Liverton and Everpool

The summarised statements of profit or loss of two companies, Liverton and Everpool, for the year ended 31 May 20X6 are provided below. Liverton acquired 3,000,000 ordinary shares in Everpool for $3,500,000 on 1 June 20X4. At that time, the retained earnings of Everpool were $200,000 and the fair value of the non-controlling interest in Everpool was $1,000,000.

STATEMENTS OF PROFIT OR LOSS FOR THE YEAR ENDED 31 MAY 20X6

	Liverton $'000	Everpool $'000
Sales revenue	6,400	2,600
Cost of sales	(3,700)	(1,450)
Gross profit	2,700	1,150
Distribution costs	(1,100)	(490)
Administrative expenses	(700)	(320)
Profit from operations	900	340
Dividends received from Everpool	150	–
Profit before tax	1,050	340
Tax	(400)	(80)
Profit for the year	650	260

The following information is also available.

(a)   Everpool's total share capital consists of 4,000,000 ordinary shares of $1 each.

(b)   During the year ended 31 May 20X6 Liverton sold goods costing $120,000 to Everpool for $200,000. At 31 May 20X6, 60% of these goods remained in Everpool's inventory.

Task 1

Complete the following to determine goodwill on acquisition of Everpool.

$

Fair value of consideration transferred

Fair value of non-controlling interest

Total

Fair value of net assets acquired:

Share capital

Retained earnings

Total

Goodwill

(3 marks)

Task 2

Calculate the unrealised profit on Liverton's sales to Everpool

$

(2 marks)

Task 3

Complete the consolidated statement of profit or loss

$

Sales revenue

Cost of sales

Gross profit

Distribution costs

Administrative expenses

Profit before tax

Income tax expense

Profit for the year

Profit attributable to:

Owners of the parent

Non-controlling interest

(10 marks)

(Total = 60 marks)

26 Consolidated financial statements

65 mins

The following information is relevant for Questions 26.1 to 26.3.

On 1 January 20X0 Alpha Co purchased 90,000 ordinary $1 shares in Beta Co for $270,000. At that date Beta Co's retained earnings amounted to $90,000 and the fair values of Beta Co's assets at acquisition were equal to their book values.

Three years later, on 31 December 20X2, the statements of financial position of the two companies were:

	Alpha Co $	Beta Co $
Sundry net assets	230,000	260,000
Shares in Beta	180,000	–
	410,000	260,000
Share capital		
Ordinary shares of $1 each	200,000	100,000
Retained earnings	210,000	160,000
	410,000	260,000

The share capital of Beta Co has remained unchanged since 1 January 20X0. The fair value of the non-controlling interest at acquisition was $42,000.

26.1 What amount should appear in the group's consolidated statement of financial position at 31 December 20X2 for goodwill?

    A $52,000
    B $80,000
    C $122,000
    D $212,000   **(2 marks)**

26.2 What amount should appear in the group's consolidated statement of financial position at 31 December 20X2 for non-controlling interest?

    A $49,000
    B $58,000
    C $51,000
    D $42,000   **(2 marks)**

26.3 What should the figure for retained earnings be in the group's consolidated statement of financial position at 31 December 20X2?

    $_____   **(2 marks)**

26.4 Which of the following companies are subsidiaries of Gamma Co?

Zeta Co: Gamma Co owns 51% of the non-voting preference shares of Zeta Co

Iota Co: Gamma Co has three representatives on the board of directors of Iota Co. Each director can cast 10 votes each out of the total of 40 votes at board meetings.

Kappa Co: Gamma Co owns 75% of the ordinary share capital of Kappa Co, however Kappa Co is located overseas and is subject to tax in that country.

    A   Zeta Co, Iota Co and Kappa Co
    B   Zeta Co and Kappa Co
    C   Iota Co and Kappa Co
    D   Zeta Co and Iota Co   **(2 marks)**

The following information is relevant for Questions 26.5 and 26.6.

Hilton Co acquired 80% of the share capital of Shrew Co on 1 January 20X3 for $280,000.

The statements of financial position of the two companies at 31 December 20X3 were as follows:

STATEMENTS OF FINANCIAL POSITION

	Hilton Co $	Shrew Co $
Sundry assets	660,000	290,000
Investment in Shrew	280,000	–
	940,000	290,000
Issued share capital	400,000	140,000
Share premium account	320,000	50,000
Retained earnings		
As at 1 Jan 20X3	140,000	60,000
Profit for 20X3	80,000	40,000
	940,000	290,000

There have been no changes in the share capital or share premium account of either company since 1 January 20X3. The fair value of the non-controlling interest on acquisition was $65,000.

26.5 What figure for goodwill on consolidation should appear in the consolidated statement of financial position of the Hilton group at 31 December 20X3?

    A $30,000
    B $55,000
    C $95,000
    D $(10,000)   **(2 marks)**

26.6 What figure for non-controlling interest should appear in the consolidated statement of financial position of the Hilton group at 31 December 20X3?

    A $77,000
    B $85,000
    C $73,000
    D $105,000   **(2 marks)**

26.7 Fanta Co acquired 100% of the ordinary share capital of Tizer Co on 1 October 20X7.

    On 31 December 20X7 the share capital and retained earnings of Tizer Co were as follows:

	$'000
Ordinary shares of $1 each	400
Retained earnings at 1 January 20X7	100
Retained profit for the year ended 31 December 20X7	80
	580

    The profits of Tizer Co have accrued evenly throughout 20X7. Goodwill arising on the acquisition of Tizer Co was $30,000.

    What was the cost of the investment in Tizer Co?

    A $400,000
    B $580,000
    C $610,000
    D $590,000   **(2 marks)**

26.8 Evergreen Co owns 35% of the ordinary shares of Deciduous. What is the correct accounting treatment of the revenues and costs of Deciduous for reporting period in the consolidated statement of profit or loss of the Evergreen group?

A   The revenues and costs of Deciduous are added to the revenues and costs of Evergreen on a line by line basis.

B   35% of the profit after tax of Deciduous should be added to Evergreen's consolidated profit before tax.

C   35% of the revenues and costs of Deciduous are added to the revenues and costs of Evergreen on a line by line basis.

D   The revenues and costs of Deciduous are added to the revenues and costs of Evergreen Co on a line by line basis, then 65% of the profit after tax is deducted so that only Evergreen Co's share remains in the consolidated financial statements.   **(2 marks)**

26.9 Mercedes Co has owned 100% of Benz Co since incorporation. At 31 March 20X9 extracts from their individual statements of financial position were as follows.

	Mercedes Co	Benz Co
	$	$
Share capital	100,000	50,000
Retained earnings	450,000	120,000
	550,000	170,000

During the year ended 31 March 20X9, Benz Co had sold goods to Mercedes Co for $50,000. Mercedes Co still had these goods in inventory at the year end. Benz Co uses a 25% mark up on all goods.

What were the consolidated retained earnings of Mercedes Group at 31 March 20X9?

A $560,000
B $580,000
C $570,000
D $557,500   **(2 marks)**

26.10 Micro Co acquired 90% of the $100,000 ordinary share capital of Minnie Co for $300,000 on 1 January 20X9 when the retained earnings of Minnie Co were $156,000. At the date of acquisition the fair value of plant held by Minnie Co was $20,000 higher than its carrying amount. The fair value of the non-controlling interest at the date of acquisition was $75,000.

What is the goodwill arising on the acquisition of Minnie Co?

A $119,000
B $99,000
C $139,000
D $24,000   **(2 marks)**

26.11 On 1 April 20X7 Possum Co acquired 60% of the share capital of Koala Co for $120,000. During the year Possum Co sold goods to Koala Co for $30,000, including a profit margin of 25%. 40% of these goods were still in inventory at the year end.

The following extract was taken from the financial statements of Possum Co and Koala Co at 31 March 20X8.

	Possum Co	Koala Co
	$'000	$'000
Revenue	750	400
Cost of sales	(420)	(100)
Gross profit	330	300

What is the consolidated gross profit of the Possum group at 31 March 20X8?

A $627,600
B $633,000
C $622,500
D $627,000   **(2 marks)**

26.12 Which **TWO** of the following statements are correct?

    A   Aye Co owns 25% of the ordinary share capital of Bee Co, which means that Bee Co is an associate of Aye Co.

    B   Cee Co can appoint 4 out of 6 directors to the board of Dee Co, which means that Cee Co has control over Dee Co.

    C   Ear Co has the power to govern the financial and operating policies of Fef Co, which means that Fef Co is an associate of Ear Co.

    D   Gee Co owns 19% of the share capital of Hay Co, but by agreement with the majority shareholder, has control over the financial and operating policies of Hay Co, so Hay Co is an associate of Gee Co.

(2 marks)

26.13 Clementine Co has owned 21% of the ordinary shares of Tangerine Co for several years. Clementine Co does not have any investments in any other companies, and chooses to account for the investment at cost.

How should the investment in Tangerine Co be reflected in the financial statements of Clementine Co?

    A   The revenues and costs and assets and liabilities of Tangerine Co are added to the revenues and costs and assets and liabilities of Clementine Co on a line by line basis.

    B   An amount is shown in the statement of financial position for 'investment in associate' being the original cost paid for the investment plus Clementine Co's share of the profit after tax of Tangerine Co. 21% of the profit after tax of Tangerine Co should be added to Clementine Co's profit before tax in the statement of profit or loss each year.

    C   An amount is shown in the statement of financial position under 'investments' being the original cost paid for the investment, this amount does not change. Dividends received from Tangerine are recognised in the statement of profit or loss of Clementine Co.

    D   An amount is shown in the statement of financial position under 'investments' being the original cost paid for the investment, this amount does not change. 21% of the profit after tax of Tangerine Co should be added to Clementine Co's profit after tax in the statement of profit or loss each year. **(2 marks)**

26.14 Which of the following statements relating to parent companies and subsidiaries are correct?

    1   A parent company could consolidate a company in which it holds less than 50% of the ordinary share capital in certain circumstances.

    2   Goodwill on consolidation will appear as an item in the parent company's individual statement of financial position.

    3   Consolidated financial statements ignore the legal form of the relationship between parents and subsidiaries and present the results and position of the group as if it was a single entity.

    A   1 and 2 only
    B   1 and 3 only
    C   2 and 3 only
    D   3 only
(2 marks)

26.15 P Co, the parent company of a group, owns shares in three other companies. P Co's holdings are:

Q   Shares giving control of 60% of the voting rights in Q Co

R   Shares giving control of 20% of the voting rights in R Co. P Co also has the right to appoint or remove all the directors of R Co

S   Shares giving control of 10% of the voting rights in S Co, plus 90% of the non-voting preference shares

Which of these companies are subsidiaries of P Co?

A   Q Co, R Co and S Co
B   Q Co and S Co only
C   R Co and S Co only
D   Q Co and R Co only   (2 marks)

26.16 Which of the following should be accounted for in the consolidated financial statements of Company A using equity accounting?

1   An investment in 51% of the ordinary shares of W Co

2   An investment in 20% of the preference (non-voting) shares of X Co

3   An investment in 33% of the ordinary shares of Y Co

4   An investment in 20% of the ordinary shares of Z Co, and an agreement with other shareholders to appoint the majority of the directors to the board of Z Co

A   1 and 4 only
B   2 only
C   3 only
D   3 and 4 only   (2 marks)

26.17 Breakspear Co purchased 600,000 of the voting equity shares of Fleet Co when the value of the non-controlling interest in Fleet Co is $150,000.

The following information relates to Fleet at the acquisition date.

	At acquisition $'000
Share capital, $0.5 ordinary shares	500
Retained earnings	150
Revaluation surplus	50
	700

The goodwill arising on acquisition is $70,000. What was the consideration paid by Breakspear Co for the investment in Fleet Co?

A $420,000
B $770,000
C $620,000
D $570,000   (2 marks)

26.18 Date Co owns 100% of the ordinary share capital of Prune Co. The following balances relate to Prune Co.

	At acquisition $'000	At 31.12.X8 $'000
Tangible non-current assets		
Freehold land	500	500
Plant and equipment	350	450
	850	950

At acquisition, the fair value of Prune Co's land was $50,000 more than shown in the financial statements of Prune Co. At 31 December 20X8, Date Co's financial statements show a total tangible non-current asset balance of $1,250,000.

What amount should be included in the consolidated financial statements of the Date group at 31 December 20X8 for tangible non-current assets?

A $2,250,000
B $1,000,000
C $1,850,000
D $2,200,000   **(2 marks)**

26.19 Six Co owns 80% of the equity share capital of Seven Co. At 31 December 20X4, the trade receivables and trade payables of the two companies were as follows:

	Six Co	Seven Co
Trade receivables	$64,000	$39,000
Trade payables	$37,000	$48,000

These figures include $30,000 that is owed by Seven Co to Six Co for the purchase of goods, for which Six Co has not yet paid. These goods were sold by Six Co for a profit of $15,000 and 50% of them were still held as inventory by Seven Co at 31 December 20X4.

What should be the amounts for trade receivables and trade payables in the consolidated statement of financial position as at 31 December 20X4?

A   Trade receivables $73,000, Trade payables $55,000
B   Trade receivables $88,000, Trade payables $70,000
C   Trade receivables $95,000, Trade payables $77,000
D   Trade receivables $103,000, Trade payables $85,000   **(2 marks)**

26.20 Donna Co acquired 80% of the equity share capital of Blitsen Co on 1 January 20X4 when the retained earnings of Blitsen Co were $40,000. The fair value of the non-controlling interest at this date was $25,000. At 31 December 20X4, the equity capital of Blitsen Co was as follows:

	$'000
Share capital	40
Share premium	10
Retained earnings	60
	110

During the year Blitsen Co sold goods to Donna Co for $20,000. This price included a mark-up of $12,000 for profit. At 31 December 20X4, 50% of these goods remained unsold in the inventory of Donna Co.

What is the value of the non-controlling interest in the Donna Group at 31 December 20X4, for the purpose of preparing the consolidated statement of financial position?

$_____   **(2 marks)**

26.21 Volcano Co acquired 75% of the equity share capital of Lava Co on 1 September 20X3. The retained profits of the two individual companies at the beginning and end of their financial year were as follows.

	Volcano Co $'000	Lava Co $'000
Retained earnings at 1 January 20X3	596	264
Retained earnings at 31 December 20X3	650	336

What is the parent company's share of consolidated retained earnings that should be reported in the consolidated statement of financial position of the Volcano Group at 31 December 20X3?

A $668,000
B $674,000
C $704,000
D $722,000

(2 marks)

26.22 Tin Co acquired 90% of the equity share capital of Drum Co on 1 April 20X3. The following information relates to the financial year to 31 December 20X3 for each company.

	Tin Co $'000	Drum Co $'000
Retained earnings at 1 January 20X3	840	170
Profit for the year	70	60
Retained earnings at 31 December 20X3	910	230

Neither company paid any dividends during the year.

What profit is attributable to the parent company in the consolidated statement of profit or loss of the Tin Group for the year to 31 December 20X3?

A $83,500
B $110,500
C $115,000
D $124,000

(2 marks)

26.23 Sand Co acquired 80% of the equity share capital of Sun Co several years ago. In the year to 31 December 20X4, Sand Co made a profit after taxation of $120,000 and Sun Co made a profit after taxation of $35,000. During the year Sun Co sold goods to Sand Co at a price of $40,000. The profit mark-up was 40% on the sales price. At 31 December 20X4, 25% of these goods were still held in the inventory of Sand Co.

What profit is attributable to the parent company in the consolidated statement of profit or loss of the Sand Group for the year to 31 December 20X4?

A $144,000
B $148,000
C $144,800
D $151,000

(2 marks)

26.24 On 1 August 20X7 Patronic purchased 18 million of the 24 million $1 equity shares of Sardonic. The acquisition was through a share exchange of two shares in Patronic for every three shares in Sardonic. The market price of a share in Patronic at 1 August 20X7 was $5.75.

What is the fair value of the consideration transferred for the acquisition of Sardonic?

A $103.5 million
B $69 million
C $155.25 million
D $92 million

(2 marks)

26.25 X Co acquired 80% of the equity share capital in Y Co on 31 July 20X6. Extracts from the two companies' statements of profit or loss for the year ended 30 September 20X6 were as follows:

	X Co $'000	Y Co $'000
Revenue	3 400	2 400
Cost of sales	1 500	1 800

During the year ended 30 September 20X6, Y Co sold goods for $5 000 each month to X Co, at a mark up of 25%. At the end of the year X Co had 50% of these goods left in inventory.

What is the group gross profit for the year ended 30 September 20X6?

A $1,901,000
B $1,999,000
C $2,004,000
D $1,904,000

(2 marks)

26.26 WX acquired 75% of the equity share capital of YZ several years ago. At 31 March 20X6 WX had goods in inventory valued at cost of $60,000, that had been purchased from YZ at a mark-up of 20%.

What is the effect on the profit attributable to the non-controlling interest, and the profit attributable to the parent company for the year ended 31 March 20X6?

	Profit attributable to non-controlling interest	Profit attributable to WX
A	no effect	decrease by $5,000
B	no effect	decrease by $12,000
C	decrease by $3,000	decrease by $9,000
D	decrease by $2,500	decrease by $7,500

(2 marks)

26.27 P owns 80% of the equity share capital of S The profit after tax of S for the year ended 31 December 20X6 was $60 million. During 20X6, P sold goods to S for $4 million at cost plus 20%. At the year end 50% of these goods were left in the inventory of S.

What is non-controlling interest share of the after-tax profit of S for the year ended 31 December 20X6?

A $11.36 million
B $11.6 million
C $11.68 million
D $12 million

(2 marks)

(Total = 54 marks)

Do you know? – Interpretation of financial statements

Check that you can fill in the blanks in the statements below before you attempt any questions. If in doubt, you should go back to your BPP Interactive Text and revise first.

- Users of financial statements can gain a better understanding of the **s**.............. of the information in financial statements by comparing it with other **r**.............. information.

- Ratios provide information through ....

- **P**.................. ratios include:
  - Return on capital employed
  - Net .... as a percentage of sales
  - .... turnover ratio
  - **G**........ profit as a percentage of sales

- Liquidity and working capital ratios include:
  - .... ratio
  - .... ratio
  - Accounts .... collection period
  - Accounts .... payment period
  - .... inventory .... period

- Debt and **g**.................. /leverage ratios include:
  - Debt ratios
  - **G**................ ratio/leverage
  - **I**.................. cover

Did you know? – Interpretation of financial statements

Could you fill in the blanks? The answers are in bold. Use this page for revision purposes as you approach the exam.

- Users of financial statements can gain a better understanding of the **significance** of the information in financial statements by comparing it with other **relevant** information.

- Ratios provide information through **comparison**.

- **Profitability** ratios include:

    - Return on capital employed
    - Net **profit** as a percentage of sales
    - **Asset** turnover ratio
    - **Gross** profit as a percentage of sales

- Liquidity and working capital ratios include:

    - **Current** ratio
    - **Quick** ratio
    - Accounts **receivable** collection period
    - Accounts **payable** payment period
    - **Average** inventory **turnover** period

- Debt and **gearing**/leverage ratios include:

    - Debt ratios
    - **Gearing** ratio/leverage
    - **Interest** cover

27 15 mark question: interpretation of financial statements   18 mins

27.1 Binky and Smokey

Two companies Binky and Smokey trade in the same market. Their financial statements for the year ended 31 October 20X6 are summarised below:

STATEMENTS OF PROFIT OR LOSS FOR THE YEAR ENDED 31 OCTOBER 20X6

	Binky		Smokey	
	$'000	$'000	$'000	$'000
Sales revenue		284		305
Cost of sales		(155)		(151)
Gross profit		129		154
Expenses				
Administrative	24		37	
Selling and distribution	35		53	
Depreciation	9		12	
Loan note interest	–		5	
		(68)		(107)
Net profit		61		47

STATEMENTS OF FINANCIAL POSITION AS AT 31 OCTOBER 20X6

	Binky		Smokey	
Assets	$'000	$'000	$'000	$'000
Non-current assets				
At cost	320		515	
Accumulated depreciation	(75)		(96)	
		245		419
Current assets				
Inventory	91		293	
Receivables	46		75	
Bank	64		15	
		201		383
		446		802
Equity and liabilities				
Share capital and reserves				
Share capital		150		250
Retained earnings		108		177
10% Loan note		–		50
Current liabilities		188		325
Total equity and liabilities		446		802

Task 1

Complete the following table to show the main ratios for Binky and Smokey

Ratio	Formula	Binky	Smokey
Gross profit %			
Net profit %			
Asset turnover			
Current ratio			
Quick ratio			
Receivables collection period			

(9 marks)

Task 2

Fill in the blanks to complete this short comment on the performance of Binkey and Smokey:

Of the two companies [   ] has the higher net profit percentage. This is due to (higher/lower) [   ].

Both companies have low quick ratios. In Smokey's case this is because much of its working capital is tied up in [   ]. This has given rise to [   ] problems.

[   ] needs to improve credit control.

The [   ] ratio shows that Binky is making better use of its working capital than Smokey.

(6 marks)

(Total = 15 marks)

28 Interpretation of financial statements   26 mins

28.1 Which one of the following would help a company with high gearing to reduce its gearing ratio?

A   Making a rights issue of equity shares
B   Issuing further long-term loan notes
C   Making a bonus issue of shares
D   Paying dividends on its equity shares   **(2 marks)**

28.2 A company's gross profit as a percentage of sales increased from 24% in the year ended 31 December 20X1 to 27% in the year ended 31 December 20X2.

Which of the following events is most likely to have caused the increase?

A   An increase in sales volume
B   A purchase in December 20X1 mistakenly being recorded as happening in January 20X2
C   Overstatement of the closing inventory at 31 December 20X1
D   Understatement of the closing inventory at 31 December 20X1   **(2 marks)**

28.3 Which of the following transactions would result in an increase in capital employed?

A   Selling inventory at a profit
B   Writing off a bad debt
C   Paying a payable in cash
D   Increasing the bank overdraft to purchase a non-current asset   **(2 marks)**

28.4 From the following information regarding the year to 31 August 20X6, what is the accounts payable payment period? You should calculate the ratio using purchases as the denominator.

	$
Sales	43,000
Cost of sales	32,500
Opening inventory	6,000
Closing inventory	3,800
Trade accounts payable at 31 August 20X6	4,750

A   40 days
B   50 days
C   53 days
D   57 days   **(2 marks)**

The following information is relevant for Questions 28.5 to 28.7.

Quality Co is analysing its financial performance. An extract from its draft statement of financial position at 31 March 20X8 is set out below.

	$	$
Non-current assets		450
Current assets: Inventory	65	
Receivables	110	
Prepayments	30	
	205	
Current liabilities: Payables	30	
Bank overdraft (Note)	50	
	80	
		125
		575
Non-current liability: Loan		(75)
		500
Ordinary share capital		400
Statement of profit or loss		100
		500

Note. The bank overdraft first occurred on 30 September 20X7.

In the analysis of the financial and liquidity position of Quality Co, its gearing, current and quick ratios are calculated.

From the list of tokens below, match the correct token to the relevant ratio. You should calculate gearing using the capital employed as the denominator.

TOKEN		Question 28.5	Question 28.6	Question 28.7
13%		**Gearing**	**Quick ratio**	**Current ratio**
16%				
20%				
24%				
1.75				
2.56				
2.88				
3.20				

(2 marks each, Total 6 marks)

28.8 Which of the following is a ratio which is used to measure how much a business owes in relation to its size?

    A   Asset turnover
    B   Profit margin
    C   Gearing
    D   Return on capital employed   **(2 marks)**

28.9 A business operates on a gross profit margin of $33\frac{1}{3}\%$. Gross profit on a sale was $800, and expenses were $680.

What is the net profit margin?

    A   3.75%
    B   5%
    C   11.25%
    D   22.67%   **(2 marks)**

28.10 A company has the following details extracted from its statement of financial position:

	$'000
Inventories	1,900
Receivables	1,000
Bank overdraft	100
Payables	1,000

The industry the company operates in has a current ratio norm of 1.8. Companies who manage liquidity well in this industry have a current ratio lower than the norm.

Which of the following statements accurately describes the company's liquidity position?

A   Liquidity appears to be well managed as the bank overdraft is relatively low

B   Liquidity appears to be poorly-controlled as shown by the large payables balance

C   Liquidity appears to be poorly-controlled as shown by the company's relatively high current ratio

D   Liquidity appears to be poorly-controlled as shown by the existence of a bank overdraft

(2 marks)

28.11 Why is analysis of financial statements carried out?

A   So that the analyst can determine a company's accounting policies

B   So that the significance of financial statements can be better understood through comparisons with historical performance and with other companies

C   To get back to the 'real' underlying figures, without the numbers being skewed by the requirements of International Financial Reporting Standards

D   To produce a report that can replace the financial statements, so that the financial statements no longer need to be looked at   **(2 marks)**

(Total = 22 marks)

29   Mixed bank 1   46 mins

29.1   The following information is available for a sole trader who keeps no accounting records:

	$
Net business assets at 1 July 20X4	186,000
Net business assets at 30 June 20X5	274,000

During the year ended 30 June 20X5:

	$
Cash drawings by proprietor	68,000
Additional capital introduced by proprietor	50,000
Business cash used to buy a car for the proprietor's wife, who takes no part in the business	20,000

Using this information, what is the trader's profit for the year ended 30 June 20X5?

$_____   **(2 marks)**

29.2 Evon, a limited liability company, issued 1,000,000 ordinary shares of 25 cents each at a price of $1.10 per share, all received in cash.

What should be the accounting entries to record this issue?

A	Debit:	Cash	$1,100,000
	Credit:	Share capital	$250,000
	Credit:	Share premium	$850,000
B	Debit:	Share capital	$250,000
	Debit:	Share premium	$850,000
	Credit:	Cash	$1,100,000
C	Debit:	Cash	$1,100,000
	Credit:	Share capital	$1,100,000
D	Debit:	Cash	$1,100,000
	Credit:	Share capital	$250,000
	Credit:	Retained earnings	$850,000

(2 marks)

29.3 Which of the following statements apply when producing a consolidated statement of financial position?

(1) All intra-group balances should be eliminated.
(2) Intra-group profit in year-end inventory should be eliminated.
(3) Closing inventory held by subsidiaries needs to be included at fair value.

A (1) only
B (1), (2) and (3)
C (1) and (2) only
D (3) only

(2 marks)

29.4 At 1 July 20X4 a limited liability company's capital structure was as follows:

	$
Share capital 1,000,000 shares of 50c each	500,000
Share premium account	400,000

In the year ended 30 June 20X5 the company made the following share issues:

1 January 20X5:

A bonus issue of one share for every four in issue at that date, using the share premium account.

1 April 20X5

A rights issue of one share for every ten in issue at that date, at $1.50 per share.

What will be the balances on the company's share capital and share premium accounts at 30 June 20X5 as a result of these issues?

	Share capital $	Share premium account $
A	687,500	650,000
B	675,000	375,000
C	687,500	150,000
D	687,500	400,000

(2 marks)

29.5 The receivables ledger control account below contains several incorrect entries.

RECEIVABLES LEDGER CONTROL ACCOUNT

	$		$
Opening balance	138,400	Credit sales	80,660
		Contras against credit balances	
		in payables ledger	1,000
Cash received from credit customers	78,420	Irrecoverable debts written off	4,950
		Dishonoured cheques from credit	
		customers	850
		Closing balance	129,360
	216,820		216,820

What should the closing balance be when all the errors are corrected?

A $133,840
B $135,540
C $137,740
D $139,840   (2 marks)

29.6 A limited liability company's trial balance does not balance. The totals are:

Debit $384,030
Credit $398,580

A suspense account is opened for the difference.

Which of the following pairs of errors could clear the balance on the suspense account when corrected?

A   Debit side of cash book undercast by $10,000; $6,160 paid for rent correctly entered in the cash book but entered in the rent account as $1,610.

B   Debit side of cash book overcast by $10,000; $1,610 paid for rent correctly entered in the cash book but entered in the rent account as $6,160.

C   Debit side of cash book undercast by $10,000; $1,610 paid for rent correctly entered in the cash book but entered in the rent account as $6,160.

D   Debit side of cash book overcast by $10,000; $6,160 paid for rent correctly entered in the cash book but entered in the rent account as $1,610.   (2 marks)

29.7 Which **TWO** of the following items could appear in a company's statement of cash flows?

A   Surplus on revaluation of non-current assets
B   Repayment of long-term borrowing
C   Bonus issue of shares
D   Interest received   (2 marks)

29.8 The following information is available for Orset, a sole trader who does not keep full accounting records:

	$
Inventory 1 July 20X4	138,600
30 June 20X5	149,100
Purchases made for year ended 30 June 20X5	716,100

Orset makes a standard gross profit of 30 percent on sales.

Based on these figures, what is Orset's sales figure for the year ended 30 June 20X5?

A $2,352,000
B $1,038,000
C $917,280
D $1,008,000   (2 marks)

29.9 At 1 July 20X4 a company had prepaid insurance of $8,200. On 1 January 20X5 the company paid $38,000 for insurance for the year to 30 September 20X5.

What figures should appear for insurance in the company's financial statements for the year ended 30 June 20X5?

	Statement of Profit or Loss	Statement of Financial Position
A	$27,200	Prepayment $19,000
B	$39,300	Prepayment $9,500
C	$36,700	Prepayment $9,500
D	$55,700	Prepayment $9,500

(2 marks)

29.10 Which of the following statements are correct?

(i)   A liability is a present obligation, arising from past events, the settlement of which is expected to result in an outflow of economic resources.

(ii)   An uncertain liability may be called a provision.

(iii)   A contingent liability should be disclosed in the notes to the financial statements.

A   (i) only
B   (i) and (ii) only
C   (ii) and (iii) only
D   (i), (ii) and (iii)   **(2 marks)**

29.11 Alpha buys goods from Beta. At 30 June 20X5 Beta's account in Alpha's records showed $5,700 owing to Beta. Beta submitted a statement to Alpha as at the same date showing a balance due of $5,200.

Which one of the following could account fully for the difference?

A   Alpha has sent a cheque to Beta for $500 which has not yet been received by Beta.
B   The credit side of Beta's account in Alpha's records has been undercast by $500.
C   An invoice for $250 from Beta has been treated in Alpha's records as if it had been a credit note.
D   Beta has issued a credit note for $500 to Alpha which Alpha has not yet received.   **(2 marks)**

29.12 Which of the following statements about intangible assets are correct?

1   If certain criteria are met, research expenditure must be recognised as an intangible asset.

2   The notes to the financial statements should disclose the gross carrying amount and the accumulated amortisation at the beginning and the end of the period for each class of intangible asset.

3   Intangible assets must be amortised over their useful life.

A   2 and 3 only
B   1 and 3 only
C   1 and 2 only
D   All three statements are correct.   **(2 marks)**

29.13 Which of the following material events that took place after the reporting date, but before the financial statements were approved, are non-adjusting when applying IAS 10 *Events after the reporting period*?

(i)   Inventory held at the reporting date was sold for less than cost.

(ii)   Capital raised by issuing shares at a premium.

(iii)   A company reorganisation which results in discontinuing a line of activity producing 25% of its profit.

(iv)   The settlement of a claim for compensation from a former employee wrongly dismissed just before the reporting date.

A   (i) and (ii)
B   (i), (iii) and (iv)
C   (i) and (iii) only
D   (ii) and (iii)   **(2 marks)**

29.14 A company sublets part of its office accommodation. In the year ended 30 June 20X5 cash received from tenants was $83,700.

Details of rent in arrears and in advance at the beginning and end of the year were:

	In arrears	In advance
	$	$
1 July 20X4	3,800	2,400
30 June 20X5	4,700	3,000

All arrears of rent were subsequently received.

What figure should be included for rental income in the company's statement of profit or loss for the year ended 30 June 20X5?

$_____   (2 marks)

29.15 At 30 June 20X4 a company's allowance for receivables was $39,000. At 30 June 20X5 trade receivables totalled $517,000. It was decided to write off debts totalling $37,000. The allowance for receivables was to be adjusted to the equivalent of 5 per cent of the trade receivables.

What figure should appear in the statement of profit or loss for these items?

A $61,000
B $22,000
C $24,000
D $23,850   (2 marks)

29.16 IAS 2 *Inventories* defines the extent to which overheads are included in the cost of inventories of finished goods.

Which of the following statements about the IAS 2 requirements in this area are correct?

1   Finished goods inventories may be valued on the basis of labour and materials cost only, without including overheads.

2   Carriage inwards, but not carriage outwards, should be included in overheads when valuing inventories of finished goods.

3   Factory management costs should be included in fixed overheads allocated to inventories of finished goods.

A   All three statements are correct
B   1 and 2 only
C   1 and 3 only
D   2 and 3 only   (2 marks)

29.17 A limited liability company sold a building at a profit.

How will this transaction be treated in the company's statement of cash flows?

	Proceeds of sale	*Profit on sale*
A	Cash inflow under financing activities	Add to profit in calculating cash flow from operating activities
B	Cash inflow under investing activities	Deducted from profit in calculating cash flow from operating activities
C	Cash inflow under investing activities	Added to profit in calculating cash flow from operating activities
D	Cash inflow under financing activities	Deducted from profit in calculating cash flow from operating activities

(2 marks)

29.18 Which of the following items may appear in a company's statement of changes in equity, according to IAS 1 *Presentation of financial statements*?

    1   Unrealised revaluation gains
    2   Dividends paid
    3   Proceeds of equity share issue
    4   Profit for the period

    A   2, 3 and 4 only
    B   1, 3 and 4 only
    C   All four items
    D   1, 2 and 4 only   **(2 marks)**

29.19 Sigma's bank statement shows an overdrawn balance of $38,600 at 30 June 20X5. A check against the company's cash book revealed the following differences:

    1   Bank charges of $200 have not been entered in the cash book.

    2   Lodgements recorded on 30 June 20X5 but credited by the bank on 2 July $14,700.

    3   Cheque repayments entered in cash book but not presented for payment at 30 June 20X5 $27,800.

    4   A cheque payment to a supplier of $4,200 charged to the account in June 20X5 recorded in the cash book as a receipt.

Based on this information, what was the cash book balance **before** any adjustments?

    A $43,100 overdrawn
    B $16,900 overdrawn
    C $60,300 overdrawn
    D $34,100 overdrawn   **(2 marks)**

(Total = 38 marks)

30   Mixed bank 2   48 mins

30.1 The plant and machinery cost account of a company is shown below. The company's policy is to charge depreciation at 20% on the straight line basis, with proportionate depreciation in years of acquisition and disposal.

PLANT AND MACHINERY – COST

20X5	$	20X5		$
1 Jan Balance b/f	280,000	30 June	Transfer disposal	14,000
1 Apr Cash	48,000			
1 Sept Cash	36,000	31 Dec	Balance c/f	350,000
	364,000			364,000

What should be the depreciation charge for the year ended 31 December 20X5?

    A $67,000
    B $70,000
    C $64,200
    D $68,600   **(2 marks)**

30.2 Which of the following are correct?

1   The statement of financial position value of inventory should be as close as possible to net realisable value.

2   The valuation of finished goods inventory must include production overheads.

3   Production overheads included in valuing inventory should be calculated by reference to the company's normal level of production during the period.

4   In assessing net realisable value, inventory items must be considered separately, or in groups of similar items, not by taking the inventory value as a whole.

A   1 and 2 only
B   3 and 4 only
C   1 and 3 only
D   2, 3 and 4   (2 marks)

30.3 A business sublets part of its office accommodation.

The rent is received quarterly in advance on 1 January, 1 April, 1 July and 1 October. The annual rent has been $24,000 for some years, but it was increased to $30,000 from 1 July 20X5.

What amounts for this rent should appear in the company's financial statements for the year ended 31 January 20X6?

	Profit or Loss	Financial Position
A	$27,500	$5,000 in accrued income
B	$27,000	$2,500 in accrued income
C	$27,000	$2,500 in deferred income
D	$27,500	$5,000 in deferred income

(2 marks)

30.4 The figures shown in the table below are an extract from the financial statements of Ridgeway (capital employed is $1.5m).

	$
Revenue	1,000,000
Cost of sales	400,000
Gross profit	600,000
Distribution expenses and administration cost	300,000
Profit before interest and tax	300,000
Finance cost	50,000
Profit before tax	250,000
Income tax expense	100,000
Profit after tax	150,000

What is the return on capital employed (ROCE)?

A   7%
B   10%
C   40%
D   20%   (2 marks)

30.5 Which of the following events after the reporting period would normally qualify as adjusting events according to IAS 10 *Events after the reporting period*?

1   The bankruptcy of a credit customer with a balance outstanding at the end of the reporting period
2   A decline in the market value of investments
3   The declaration of an ordinary dividend
4   The determination of the cost of assets purchased before the end of the reporting period

A   1, 3, and 4
B   1 and 2 only
C   2 and 3 only
D   1 and 4 only   (2 marks)

30.6 Ordan received a statement from one of its suppliers, Alta, showing a balance due of $3,980. The amount due according to the payables ledger account of Alta in Ordan's records was only $230. Comparison of the statement and the ledger account revealed the following differences:

1 A cheque sent by Ordan for $270 has not been allowed for in Alta's statement.

2 Alta has not allowed for goods returned by Ordan $180.

3 Ordan made a contra entry, reducing the amount due to Alta by $3,200, for a balance due from Alta in Ordan's receivables ledger. No such entry has been made in Alta's records.

What is the remaining difference between the two companies' records after adjusting for these items?

$_____   (2 marks)

30.7 A company's trial balance failed to agree, and a suspense account was opened for the difference.

Subsequent checking revealed that sales returns of $130 had been credited to the purchases returns account and an entry on the credit side of the cash book for the purchase of some machinery $18,000 had not been posted to the plant and machinery account.

Which **TWO** of the following journal entries would correct the errors?

		Debit $	Credit $
A	Sales returns	130	
	Purchases returns		130
B	Sales returns	130	
	Purchases returns	130	
	Suspense account		260
C	Suspense account	260	
	Sales returns		130
	Purchases returns		130
D	Plant and machinery	18,000	
	Suspense account		18,000
E	Suspense account	18,000	
	Plant and machinery		18,000

(2 marks)

The following information is relevant for Questions 30.8 and 30.9.

A company's draft financial statements for 20X5 showed a profit of $630,000. However, the trial balance did not agree, and a suspense account appeared in the company's draft statement of financial position. Subsequent checking revealed the following errors:

(1) The cost of an item of plant $48,000 had been entered in the cash book and in the plant register as $4,800. Depreciation at the rate of 10% per year ($480) had been charged.

(2) Bank charges of $440 appeared in the bank statement in December 20X5 but had not been entered in the company's records.

(3) One of the directors of the company paid $800 due to a supplier in the company's payables ledger by a personal cheque. The bookkeeper recorded a debit in the supplier's ledger account but did not complete the double entry for the transaction. (The company does not maintain a payables ledger control account).

(4) The payments side of the cash book had been understated by $10,000.

30.8 Which of the above items would require an entry to the suspense account in correcting them?

A All four items
B 3 and 4 only
C 2 and 3 only
D 1, 2 and 4 only   (2 marks)

30.9 What will the company's profit be after the correction of the above errors?

    A $634,760

    B $624,760

    C $624,440

    D $625,240   **(2 marks)**

30.10 Which of the following statements are correct?

    1   A company might make a rights issue if it wished to raise more equity capital.

    2   A rights issue might increase the share premium account whereas a bonus issue is likely to reduce it.

    3   A bonus issue will generate cash for a company.

    4   A rights issue will always increase the number of shareholders in a company whereas a bonus issue will not.

    A   1 and 2

    B   1 and 3

    C   2 and 3

    D   2 and 4   **(2 marks)**

30.11 Which of the following statements are correct?

    1   Contingent assets are included as assets in financial statements if it is probable that they will arise.

    2   Contingent liabilities must be provided for in financial statements if it is probable that they will arise.

    3   Material non-adjusting events are disclosed by note in the financial statements.

    A   1 only

    B   1 and 3

    C   2 and 3

    D   3 only   **(2 marks)**

30.12 At 1 January 20X5 a company had an allowance for receivables of $18,000

At 31 December 20X5 the company's trade receivables were $458,000.

It was decided:

(a)   To write off debts totalling $28,000 as irrecoverable

(b)   To adjust the allowance for receivables to the equivalent of 5% of the remaining receivables

What figure should appear in the company's statement of profit or loss for the total of debts written off as irrecoverable and the movement in the allowance for receivables for the year ended 31 December 20X5?

    A $49,500

    B $31,500

    C $32,900

    D $50,900   **(2 marks)**

30.13 The following payables ledger control account contains some errors. All goods are purchased on credit.

PAYABLES LEDGER CONTROL ACCOUNT

	$		$
Purchases	963,200	Opening balance	384,600
Discounts received	12,600	Purchases returns	17,400
Contras with amounts		Cash paid to suppliers	988,400
receivable in receivables ledger	4,200		
Closing balance	410,400		
	1,390,400		1,390,400

What should the closing balance be when the errors have been corrected?

A $325,200
B $350,400
C $358,800
D $376,800   **(2 marks)**

30.14 Which one of the following journal entries is required to record goods taken from inventory by the owner of a business?

A   Debit Drawings
     Credit Purchases

B   Debit Sales
     Credit Drawings

C   Debit Drawings
     Credit Inventory

D   Debit Purchases
     Credit Drawings   **(2 marks)**

30.15 The following information is available about the transactions of Razil, a sole trader who does not keep proper accounting records:

	$
Opening inventory	77,000
Closing inventory	84,000
Purchases	763,000
Gross profit as a percentage of sales	30%

Based on this information, what is Razil's sales revenue for the year?

A $982,800
B $1,090,000
C $2,520,000
D $1,080,000   **(2 marks)**

30.16 Which of the following statements are correct?

1   All non-current assets must be depreciated.

2   If property accounted for in accordance with *IAS 16 Property, plant and equipment* is revalued, the gain on revaluation is shown in the statement of profit or loss.

3   If a tangible non-current asset is revalued, all tangible assets of the same class should be revalued.

4   In a company's published statement of financial position, tangible assets and intangible assets must be shown separately.

A   1 and 2
B   2 and 3
C   3 and 4
D   1 and 4   **(2 marks)**

30.17 The following bank reconciliation statement has been prepared by a trainee accountant at 31 December 20X5.

	$
Balance per bank statement (overdrawn)	38,640
Add: lodgements not credited	19,270
	57,910
Less: unpresented cheques	14,260
Balance per cash book	43,650

What should the final cash book balance be when all the above items have been properly dealt with?

A $43,650   overdrawn
B $33,630   overdrawn
C $5,110   overdrawn
D $72,170   overdrawn
                                                                                     (2 marks)

30.18 On 1 January 20X5 a company purchased some plant.

The invoice showed

	$
Cost of plant	48,000
Delivery to factory	400
One year warranty covering breakdown during 20X5	800
	49,200

Modifications to the factory building costing $2,200 were necessary to enable the plant to be installed.

What amount should be capitalised for the plant in the company's records?

A $51,400
B $48,000
C $50,600
D $48,400   **(2 marks)**

30.19 A business had an opening inventory of $180,000 and a closing inventory of $220,000 in its financial statements for the year ended 31 December 20X5.

Which of the following entries for these opening and closing inventory figures are made when completing the financial records of the business?

		Debit $	Credit $
A	Inventory account	180,000	
	Statement of profit or loss (SPL)		180,000
	Statement of profit or loss (SPL)	220,000	
	Inventory account		220,000
B	Statement of profit or loss (SPL)	180,000	
	Inventory account		180,000
	Inventory account	220,000	
	Statement of profit or loss (SPL)		220,000
C	Inventory account	40,000	
	Purchases account		40,000
D	Purchases account	40,000	
	Inventory account		40,000

(2 marks)

30.20 Tinsel Co has 5 million $1 issued ordinary shares. At 1 May 20X0 Fairy Co purchased 60% of Tinsel Co's $1 ordinary shares for $4,000,000. At that date Tinsel Co had net assets with a fair value of $4,750,000 and a share price of $1.10. Fairy Co valued the non-controlling interest in Tinsel Co at acquisition as $2,200,000.

What is the total goodwill on acquisition at 1 May 20X0?

A $1,150,000
B $1,750,000
C $ 750,000
D $1,450,000

(2 marks)

(Total = 40 marks)

31 Mixed bank 3 — 46 mins

31.1 On 1 September 20X6, a business had inventory of $380,000. During the month, sales totalled $650,000 and purchases $480,000. On 30 September 20X6 a fire destroyed some of the inventory. The undamaged goods in inventory were valued at $220,000. The business operates with a standard gross profit margin of 30%.

Based on this information, what is the cost of the inventory destroyed in the fire?

A $185,000
B $140,000
C $405,000
D $360,000

(2 marks)

31.2 Which of the following should appear as separate items in a company's statement of changes in equity?

1 Profit for the financial year
2 Income from investments
3 Dividends paid on redeemable preference shares
4 Dividends paid on equity shares

A 1, 3 and 4
B 1 and 4 only
C 2 and 3 only
D 1, 2 and 3 **(2 marks)**

31.3 The following information is available about a company's dividends:

		$
20X5		
Sept.	Final dividend for the year ended 30 June 20X5 paid (declared August 20X5)	100,000
20X6		
March	Interim dividend for the year ended 30 June 20X6 paid	40,000
Sept.	Final dividend for the year ended 30 June 20X6 paid (declared August 20X6)	120,000

What figures, if any, should be disclosed in the company's statement of profit or loss and other comprehensive income (SPLOCI) for the year ended 30 June 20X6 and its statement of financial position (SOFP) as at that date?

	SPLOCI for the period	*SOFP liability*
A	$160,000 deduction	$120,000
B	$140,000 deduction	nil
C	nil	$120,000
D	nil	nil	**(2 marks)**

31.4 Goose Co has a 49% shareholding in each of the following three companies.

1 Turkey Co: Goose Co has the right to appoint or remove a majority of the directors of Turkey Co.

2 Duck Co: Goose Co has more than half the voting rights in Duck Co as a result of an agreement with other investors.

3 Partridge Co: Goose Co has the power to govern the financial and operating policies of Partridge Co.

Which of these companies are subsidiaries of Goose Co for financial reporting purposes?

A Turkey Co and Duck Co only
B Partridge Co and Duck Co only
C Partridge Co and Turkey Co only
D Partridge Co, Turkey Co and Duck Co **(2 marks)**

31.5 At 1 July 20X5 a company's allowance for receivables was $48,000.

At 30 June 20X6, trade receivables amounted to $838,000. It was decided to write off $72,000 of these debts and adjust the allowance for receivables to $60,000.

What are the final amounts for inclusion in the company's statement of financial position at 30 June 20X6?

	Trade receivables	*Allowance for receivables*	*Net balance*
	$	$	$
A	838,000	60,000	778,000
B	766,000	60,000	706,000
C	766,000	108,000	658,000
D	838,000	108,000	730,000	**(2 marks)**

31.6 Which **TWO** of the following statements about inventory valuation for statement of financial position purposes are correct?

A   According to IAS 2 *Inventories*, average cost and FIFO (first in, first out) are both acceptable methods of arriving at the cost of inventories.

B   Inventories of finished goods may be valued at labour and materials cost only, without including overheads.

C   Inventories should be valued at the lowest of cost, net realisable value and replacement cost.

D   It may be acceptable for inventories to be valued at selling price less estimated profit margin.

(2 marks)

31.7 A business received a delivery of goods on 29 June 20X6, which was included in inventory at 30 June 20X6. The invoice for the goods was recorded in July 20X6.

What effect will this have on the business?

1   Profit for the year ended 30 June 20X6 will be overstated.
2   Inventory at 30 June 20X6 will be understated.
3   Profit for the year ending 30 June 20X7 will be overstated.
4   Inventory at 30 June 20X6 will be overstated.

A   1 and 2
B   2 and 3
C   1 only
D   1 and 4

(2 marks)

31.8 Based on the information below, what is the acid test ratio for Edward Co?

EDWARD CO TRIAL BALANCE (EXTRACT)

	$
Receivables	176,000
Inventories	20,000
Trade payables	61,000
Bank overdraft	79,000
Long term loan	10,000
Retained earnings	5,000

A   1.13:1
B   1.40:1
C   1.35:1
D   1.26:1

(2 marks)

31.9 Which of the following characteristics of financial information are included in the IASB's *Conceptual Framework for Financial Reporting*?

1   Comparability
2   Relevance
3   Timeliness
4   Faithful representation

A   All four items
B   1, 2 and 3 only
C   1, 2 and 4 only
D   2, 3 and 4 only

(2 marks)

31.10 Details of a company's insurance policy are shown below:

Premium for year ended 31 March 20X6 paid April 20X5 $10,800
Premium for year ending 31 March 20X7 paid April 20X6 $12,000

What figures should be included in the company's financial statements for the year ended 30 June 20X6?

	Profit or Loss SPL $	Financial position SOFP $
A	11,100	9,000 prepayment (Dr)
B	11,700	9,000 prepayment (Dr)
C	11,100	9,000 accrual (Cr)
D	11,700	9,000 accrual (Cr)

(2 marks)

31.11 Which of the following statements about bank reconciliations are correct?

1   In preparing a bank reconciliation, unpresented cheques must be deducted from a balance of cash at bank shown in the bank statement.

2   A cheque from a customer paid into the bank but dishonoured must be corrected by making a debit entry in the cash book.

3   An error by the bank must be corrected by an entry in the cash book.

4   An overdraft is a debit balance in the bank statement.

A   1 and 3
B   2 and 3
C   1 and 4
D   2 and 4

(2 marks)

31.12 At 30 June 20X5 the capital and reserves of Meredith, a limited liability company, were:

	$m
Share capital	
Ordinary shares of $1 each	100
Share premium account	80

During the year ended 30 June 2006, the following transactions took place:

1 September 20X5   A bonus issue of one ordinary share for every two held, using the share premium account.

1 January 20X6   A fully subscribed rights issue of two ordinary shares for every five held at that date, at $1.50 per share.

What would the balances on each account be at 30 June 20X6?

	Share capital $m	Share premium $m
A	210	110
B	210	60
C	240	30
D	240	80

(2 marks)

31.13 Which of the following statements about the requirements of IAS 37 *Provisions, Contingent Liabilities and Contingent Assets* are correct?

1   Contingent assets and liabilities should not be recognised in the financial statements.

2   A contingent asset should only be disclosed in the notes to a financial statement where an inflow of economic benefits is probable.

3   A contingent liability may be ignored if the possibility of the transfer of economic benefits is remote.

A   All three statements are correct
B   1 and 2 only
C   1 and 3 only
D   2 and 3 only   **(2 marks)**

31.14 Which of the following errors would cause a trial balance not to balance?

1   An error in the addition in the cash book.

2   Failure to record a transaction at all.

3   Cost of a motor vehicle debited to motor expenses account. The cash entry was correctly made.

4   Goods taken by the proprietor of a business recorded by debiting purchases and crediting drawings account.

A   1 only
B   1 and 2 only
C   3 and 4 only
D   All four items   **(2 marks)**

31.15 Manchester has 10 million $1 issued ordinary shares. At 1 May 20X9 Bristol purchased 70% of Manchester's $1 ordinary shares for $8,000,000. At that date Manchester had net assets with a fair value of $8,750,000 and its share price was $1.20. The non-controlling interest is valued using the share price at the date of acquisition.

What was the total goodwill arising on acquisition at 1 May 20X9?

$_____   **(2 marks)**

31.16 All the sales made by a retailer are for cash, and her sale prices are fixed by doubling cost. Details recorded of her transactions for September 20X6 are as follows:

		$
1 Sept	Inventories	40,000
30 Sept	Purchases for month	60,000
	Cash banked for sales for month	95,000
	Inventories	50,000

Which **TWO** of the following conclusions could separately be drawn from this information?

1    $5,000 cash has been stolen from the sales revenue prior to banking.
2   Goods costing $5,000 have been stolen.
3   Goods costing $2,500 have been stolen.
4   Some goods costing $2,500 had been sold at cost price.

A   1 and 2
B   1 and 3
C   2 and 4
D   3 and 4   **(2 marks)**

31.17 A company owns a number of properties which are rented to tenants. The following information is available for the year ended 30 June 20X6:

	Rent in advance $	Rent in arrears $
1 July 20X5	134,600	4,800
30 June 20X6	144,400	8,700

Cash received from tenants in the year ended 30 June 20X6 was $834,600.

All rent in arrears was subsequently received.

What figure should appear in the company's statement of profit or loss for rent receivable in the year ended 30 June 20X6?

A $840,500
B $1,100,100
C $569,100
D $828,700 **(2 marks)**

31.18 The following receivables ledger control account has been prepared by a trainee accountant:

		$			$
20X3			*20X3*		
1 Jan	Balance	284,680	31 Dec	Cash received from credit customers	179,790
31 Dec	Credit sales	189,120		Contras against amounts owing by company in	
	Irrecoverable debts written off	5,460		payables ledger	800
	Sales returns	4,920		Balance	303,590
		484,180			484,180

What should the closing balance on the account be when the errors in it are corrected?

A $290,150
B $286,430
C $282,830
D $284,430 **(2 marks)**

31.19 The carrying amount of a company's non-current assets was $200,000 at 1 August 20X0. During the year ended 31 July 20X1, the company sold non current assets for $25,000 on which it made a loss of $5,000. The depreciation charge of the year was $20,000. What was the carrying amount of non-current assets at 31 July 20X1?

A $150,000
B $155,000
C $170,000
D $175,000 **(2 marks)**

(Total = 38 marks)

32 Mixed bank 4   43 mins

32.1 A company issued one million ordinary $1 shares at a premium of 50c per share. The proceeds were correctly recorded in the cash book, but were incorrectly credited to the sales account.

Which one of the following journal entries will correct the error?

		Debit $	Credit $
A	Sales	1,500,000	
	Share capital		1,000,000
	Share premium		500,000
B	Share capital	1,000,000	
	Share premium		500,000
	Sales		1,500,000
C	Sales	1,500,000	
	Share capital		1,500,000
D	Share capital	1,500,000	
	Sales		1,500,000

(2 marks)

32.2 After proposing a final dividend, Kenilworth Co has a current ratio of 2.0 and a quick ratio of 0.8.

If the company now uses its positive cash balance to pay that final dividend, what will be the effect upon these two ratios?

A   Increase current ratio and decrease quick ratio
B   Increase current ratio and increase quick ratio
C   Decrease current ratio and decrease quick ratio
D   Decrease current ratio and increase quick ratio   **(2 marks)**

32.3 A property company received cash for rent totalling $838,600 in the year ended 31 December 20X6.

Figures for rent in advance and in arrears at the beginning and end of the year were:

	1 January 20X6 $	31 December 20X6 $
Rent received in advance	102,600	88,700
Rent in arrears (all subsequently received)	42,300	48,400

What amount should appear in the company's statement of profit or loss for the year ended 31 December 20X6 for rental income?

A $818,600
B $738,000
C $939,200
D $858,600   **(2 marks)**

32.4 Which one of the following journal entries is correct according to its narrative?

		Debit $	Credit $
A	Mr Smith personal account	100,000	
	Directors' remuneration		100,000

Bonus allocated to account of managing director (Mr Smith)

		Debit $	Credit $
B	Purchases	14,000	
	Wages	24,000	
	Repairs to buildings		38,000

Transferring cost of repairs to buildings carried out by company's own employees, using materials from inventory.

		Debit $	Credit $
C	Sales returns	2,800	
	Purchases returns		2,800

Correction of error: sales returns incorrectly debited to purchases returns account

		Debit $	Credit $
D	Suspense account	20,000	
	Rent receivable		10,000
	Rent payable		10,000

Correction of error: rent received credited in error to rent payable account. **(2 marks)**

32.5 IAS 37 *Provisions, Contingent Liabilities and Contingent Assets* deals with accounting for contingencies. What is the correct accounting treatment for the following?

1 A probable loss (a constructive obligation exists, for which the amount can be reliably estimated)

2 A probable gain

	Probable loss	Probable gain
A	Accrued	Disclosed
B	Accrued	Not disclosed
C	Disclosed, but not accrued	Disclosed
D	Disclosed, but not accrued	Not disclosed

(2 marks)

32.6 A company has occupied rented premises for some years, paying an annual rent of $120,000. From 1 April 20X6 the rent was increased to $144,000 per year. Rent is paid quarterly in advance on 1 January, 1 April, 1 July and 1 October each year.

What figures should appear for rent in the company's financial statements for the year ended 30 November 20X6?

	SPLOCI $		SOFP $
A	136,000	Prepayment	12,000
B	136,000	Prepayment	24,000
C	138,000		Nil
D	136,000	Accrual	12,000

(2 marks)

32.7 At 1 January 20X6 a company had an allowance for receivables of $49,000.

At 31 December 20X6 the company's trade receivables were $863,000 and it was decided to write off balances totalling $23,000. The allowance for receivables was to be adjusted to the equivalent of 5% of the remaining receivables.

What total figure should appear in the company's statement of profit or loss for receivables expense?

A $16,000
B $65,000
C $30,000
D $16,150   (2 marks)

32.8 At 1 January 20X6, a company's capital structure was as follows:

	$
Ordinary share capital	
2,000,000 shares of 50c each	1,000,000
Share premium account	1,400,000

In January 20X6 the company issued 1,000,000 shares at $1·40 each.

In September 20X6 the company made a bonus issue of one share for every three held using the share premium account.

What were the balances on the company's share capital and share premium accounts after these transactions?

	Share capital	Share premium
	$	$
A	4,000,000	800,000
B	3,200,000	600,000
C	2,000,000	1,800,000
D	2,000,000	1,300,000

(2 marks)

32.9 Which of the following statements about the treatment of inventory and work in progress in financial statements are correct?

1   Inventory should be valued at the lowest of cost, net realisable value and replacement cost.

2   In valuing work in progress, materials costs, labour costs and variable and fixed production overheads must be included.

3   Inventory items can be valued using either first in, first out (FIFO) or weighted average cost.

4   A company's financial statements must disclose the accounting policies used in measuring inventories.

A   All four statements are correct.
B   1, 2 and 3 only
C   2, 3 and 4 only
D   1 and 4 only   (2 marks)

32.10 The plant and equipment account in the records of a company for the year ended 31 December 20X6 is shown below.

PLANT AND EQUIPMENT – COST

20X6	$	20X6	$
1 Jan Balance	960,000		
1 July Cash	48,000	30 Sept Transfer disposal account	84,000
		31 Dec Balance	924,000
	1,008,000		1,008,000

The company's policy is to charge depreciation on the straight line basis at 20% per year, with proportionate depreciation in the years of purchase and sale.

What should be the charge for depreciation in the company's statement of profit or loss for the year ended 31 December 20X6?

$_____   (2 marks)

32.11 The trial balance of a company did not balance, and a suspense account was opened for the difference.

Which **TWO** of the following errors would require an entry to the suspense account in correcting them?

A   A cash payment to purchase a motor van had been correctly entered in the cash book but had been debited to the motor expenses account.

B   The debit side of the wages account had been undercast.

C   Sales returns had been credited to the purchases returns account.

D   A cash refund to a customer had been recorded by debiting the cash book and crediting the customer's account. **(2 marks)**

32.12 A trader took goods that had cost $2,000 from inventory for personal use.

Which one of the following journal entries would correctly record this?

		Debit $	Credit $
A	Drawings	2,000	
	Inventory		2,000
B	Purchases	2,000	
	Drawings		2,000
C	Sales	2,000	
	Drawings		2,000
D	Drawings	2,000	
	Purchases		2,000

(2 marks)

32.13 Nasty is a wholly owned subsidiary of Ugly. Inventories in their individual statements of financial position at the year end are shown as:

Ugly $40,000
Nasty $20,000

Sales by Ugly to Nasty during the year were invoiced at $15,000 which included a profit by Ugly of 25% on cost. Two thirds of these goods were included in inventories at the year end.

At what value should inventories appear in the consolidated statement of financial position?

A $50,000
B $57,000
C $57,500
D $58,000 **(2 marks)**

32.14 Where in the financial statements should tax on profit for the current period, and profit for the period, be separately disclosed?

	Statement of profit or loss and other comprehensive income	Statement of changes in equity
A	Tax on profit and profit for the period	Tax on profit
B	Profit for the period	Tax on profit and profit for the period
C	Tax on profit	Profit for the period
D	Tax on profit and profit for the period	Profit for the period

(2 marks)

32.15 When is the reducing balance method of depreciating non-current assets more appropriate than the straight-line method?

A　When the expected life of the asset is short

B　When the asset is expected to decrease in value by a fixed percentage of cost each year

C　When the expected life of the asset is not capable of being estimated accurately

D　When the asset is expected to decrease in value less in later years than in the early years of its life　　　　**(2 marks)**

32.16 A draft statement of cash flows contains the following:

	$m
Profit before tax	22
Depreciation	8
Increase in inventories	(4)
Decrease in receivables	(3)
Increase in payables	(2)
Net cash inflow from operating activities	21

Which of the following corrections need to be made to the calculation?

1　Depreciation should be deducted, not added
2　Increase in inventories should be added, not deducted
3　Decrease in receivables should be added, not deducted
4　Increase in payables should be added, not deducted

A　1 and 2
B　1 and 3
C　2 and 4
D　3 and 4　　　　**(2 marks)**

32.17 Your inexperienced colleague, Paul Jones, has attempted to extract and total the individual balances in the receivables ledger. He provides you with the following listing which he has prepared.

	$
Bury Inc	7,500
P Fox & Son (Swindon) Co	2,000
Frank Wrendlebury & Co	4,297
D Richardson & Co	6,847
Ultra Co	783
Lawrenson Co	3,765
Walkers Inc	4,091
P Fox & Son (Swindon) Co	2,000
Whitchurch Co	8,112
Ron Bradbury & Co	5,910
Anderson Co	1,442
	46,747

Subsequent to the drawing up of the list, the following errors have so far been found.

(a)　A sales invoice for $267 sent to Whitchurch Co had been correctly entered in the day book but had not then been posted to the account for Whitchurch Co in the receivables ledger.

(b)　One of the errors made by Paul Jones was to omit the $2,435 balance of Rectofon Co from the list.

(c)　A credit note for $95 sent to Bury Co had been correctly entered in the day book but was entered in the account in the receivables ledger as $75.

What is the revised balance of the receivables ledger after correcting these errors?

A　$45,665
B　$47,449
C　$47,429
D　$45,645　　　　**(2 marks)**

(Total = 34 marks)

33 Mixed bank 5

33.1 A firm has the following transactions with its product R.

1 January 20X1	Opening inventory: nil
1 February 20X1	Buys 10 units at $300 per unit
11 February 20X1	Buys 12 units at $250 per unit
1 April 20X1	Sells 8 units at $400 per unit
1 August 20X1	Buys 6 units at $200 per unit
1 December 20X1	Sells 12 units at $400 per unit

The firm uses FIFO to value its inventory. What is the inventory value at the end of the year?

A $nil
B $1,700
C $2,400
D $2,007.20

(2 marks)

33.2 Which of the following provides advice to the International Accounting Standards Board (IASB) as well as informing the IASB of the implications of proposed standards for users and preparers of financial statements?

A   The IFRS Advisory Council
B   The IFRS Interpretations Committee
C   The IFRS Foundation
D   The Trustees of the IFRS

(2 marks)

33.3 Samantha has extracted a trial balance and created a suspense account with a credit balance of $759 to make it balance.

Samantha found the following:

1   A sales invoice for $4,569 has not been entered in the accounting records.

2   A payment of $1,512 has been posted correctly to the payables control account but no other entry has been made.

3   A credit sale of $131 has only been credited to the sales account.

What is the remaining balance on the suspense account after these errors have been corrected?

A $3,810 debit
B $2,140 credit
C $890 credit
D $622 debit

(2 marks)

33.4 Which of the following errors should be identified by performing a receivables control account reconciliation?

A   A sales invoice of $500 has been omitted from the sales daybook.

B   A sales return of $45 was entered as $54 in the sales returns daybook.

C   Purchases of $72 were entered as sales returns in the sales returns daybook and the individual account.

D   The total of the sales daybook was miscast by $200.

(2 marks)

33.5 Carol had receivables of $598,600 at 30 November 20X8. Her allowance for receivables at 1 December 20X7 was $12,460. She wished to change it to the equivalent of 2% of receivables at 30 November 20X8. On 29 November 20X8 she received $635 in full settlement of a debt that she had written off in the year ended 30 November 20X7.

What total amount should be recognised for receivables in the statement of profit or loss for the year ended 30 November 20X8?

A $488 credit
B $11,972 debit
C $1,123 credit
D $147 debit   (2 marks)

33.6 Joanna has prepared her draft financial statements for the year ended 30 April 20X8, and needs to adjust them for the following items:

1 Rent of $10,500 was paid and recorded on 2 January 20X7 for the period 1 January to 31 December 20X7. The landlord has advised that the annual rent for 20X8 will be $12,000 although it has not been invoiced or paid yet.

2 Property and contents insurance is paid annually on 1 March. Joanna paid and recorded $6,000 on 1 March 20X8 for the year from 1 March 20X8 to 28 February 20X9.

What should the net effect on profit be in the draft financial statements for the year ended 30 April 20X8 of adjusting for the above items?

A $1,000 decrease
B $1,500 increase
C $1,000 increase
D $1,500 decrease   (2 marks)

33.7 Carter, a limited liability company, has non-current assets with a carrying amount of $2,500,000 on 1 December 20X7.

During the year ended 30 November 20X8, the following occurred:

– Depreciation of $75,000 was charged to the statement of profit or loss.
– Land and buildings with a carrying amount of $1,200,000 were revalued to $1,700,000.
– An asset with a carrying amount of $120,000 was disposed of for $150,000.
– The carrying amount of non-current assets at 30 November 20X8 was $4,200,000.

In accordance with IAS7 *Statement of Cash Flows*, what are the net cash flows from the above transactions to be included in 'net cash flows from investing activities' for the year ended 30 November 20X8?

A $(1,395,000)
B $(1,365,000)
C $150,000
D $(1,245,000)   (2 marks)

33.8 Steven's receivables ledger control account does not agree with the total of the receivables ledger. He discovered the following errors:

1 A sales invoice has been entered into the sales day book as $895 rather than $859.
2 The receivables column of the cash received day book has been undercast by $600.
3 A contra of $400 against the purchase ledger has only been entered in the control account.

Which of the above errors would cause a difference between the receivables control account and the total of the receivables ledger?

A 2 and 3 only
B 1 and 3 only
C 1 and 2 only
D 1, 2 and 3   (2 marks)

33.9 Luis sold goods to Pedro in May 20X9 with a list price of $98,000. Luis allowed a trade discount of 10%. Pedro returned goods with a list price of $3,000 on 31 May and returned a further $5,000 of goods at list price on 6 June as they were found to be unsuitable.

How much should Luis record in the sales returns account at 31 May?

A $2,700
B $3,000
C $8,000
D $7,200   (2 marks)

33.10 A newly-registered company is considering the accounting policies it should adopt.

Policies under consideration are:

1   Research and development expenditure should be capitalised and amortised over the years in which the resultant product is sold or used.

2   Inventory should be valued at the lower of cost and net realisable value.

3   Goodwill arising in a business combination should be written off immediately to the statement of profit or loss.

Which of these possible accounting policies would, if adopted, contravene International Financial Reporting Standards?

A   1 and 2 only
B   2 and 3 only
C   1 and 3 only
D   1, 2 and 3   (2 marks)

33.11 You have recently been appointed as assistant accountant of PQR Co. You have assisted in preparing a forecast set of financial statements for the company whose year end is 31 December 20X7. The forecast shows that the company is expected to make a loss during the year to 31 December 20X7.

The managing director is concerned that the company's shareholders would be unhappy to hear that the company had made a loss. He is determined to avoid making a loss if at all possible. He has made the following suggestions in order to remedy the situation.

1   Value inventory using the LIFO basis as prices are rising so this will reduce inventory costs in the statement of profit or loss.

2   Create a provision against future losses in case this happens again in the future.

3   Stop amortising all capitalised development expenditure.

Which of these suggestions do you agree with?

A   1 and 2 only
B   3 only
C   2 only
D   None of the statements   (2 marks)

33.12 Which of the following journal entries may be accepted as being correct according to their narratives?

		DR $	CR $
1	Wages account	38,000	
	Purchases account	49,000	
	Buildings account		87,000

Labour and materials used in construction of extension to factory

			DR $	CR $
2	Directors' personal accounts:	A	30,000	
		B	40,000	
	Directors' remuneration			70,000

Directors' bonuses transferred to their accounts

		DR $	CR $
3	Suspense account	10,000	
	Sales account		10,000

Correction of error in addition – total of credit side of sales account $10,000 understated

A 1 and 3
B 1 and 2
C 3 only
D 2 and 3 **(2 marks)**

33.13 Which of the following costs should be included in valuing inventories of finished goods held by a manufacturing company, according to IAS 2 *Inventories*?

1 Carriage inwards
2 Carriage outwards
3 Depreciation of factory plant
4 Accounts department costs relating to wages for production employees

A All four items
B 2 and 3 only
C 1, 3 and 4 only
D 1 and 4 only **(2 marks)**

33.14 Frog acquired 100% of the ordinary share capital of Toad on 1 October 20X7.

On 31 December 20X7 retained earnings of Toad and Frog were as follows:

	Frog $'000	Toad $'000
Retained earnings at 1 January 20X7	500	100
Retained profit for the year ended 31 December 20X7	150	60
	650	160

The profits of Toad have accrued evenly throughout 20X7.

What figure for retained earnings should be included in the consolidated financial statements of the Frog group at 31 December 20X7?

A $150,000
B $175,000
C $665,000
D $810,000 **(2 marks)**

33.15 The following extract is from the statement of profit or loss of Gearing Co for the year ended 30 April 20X8.

	$
Profit before tax	68,000
Tax	(32,000)
Profit for the year	36,000

In addition to the profit above:

1 Gearing Co paid a dividend of $21,000 during the year.
2 A gain on revaluation of land resulted in a surplus of $18,000.

What total amount will be added to retained earnings at the end of the financial year?

A $36,000
B $33,000
C $47,000
D $15,000

(2 marks)

33.16 What does an increase in the allowance for receivables result in?

A A decrease in current liabilities
B An increase in net profit
C An increase in working capital
D A decrease in working capital

(2 marks)

33.17 A company's telephone bill consists of two elements. One is a quarterly rental charge, payable in advance; the other is a quarterly charge for calls made, payable in arrears. At 1 April 20X9, the previous bill dated 1 March 20X9 had included line rental of $90. Estimated call charges during March 20X9 were $80.

During the following 12 months, bills totalling $2,145 were received on 1 June, 1 September, 1 December 20X9 and 1 March 20Y0, each containing rental of $90 as well as call charges. Estimated call charges for March 20Y0 were $120.

What is the amount to be charged to the statement of profit or loss for the year ended 31 March 20Y0?

A $2,185
B $2,205
C $2,155
D $2,215

(2 marks)

33.18 Which THREE of the following sets of items all appear on the same side of the trial balance?

1 Sales, interest received and accruals
2 Receivables, drawings and discount received
3 Non current assets, cost of sales and carriage outwards
4 Capital, trade payables and other operating expenses
5 Sundry expenses, prepayments and purchases

A 1, 4 and 5
B 1, 3 and 5
C 1, 2 and 3
D 3, 4 and 5

(2 marks)

33.19 A sole trader's accounts show an increase in net assets over a year of $173,000. Drawings were $77,000 and capital introduced was $45,000.

What was the net profit for the year?

$_____

(2 marks)

33.20 Capital introduced is $50. Profits brought forward at the beginning of the year amount to $100 and liabilities are $70. Assets are $90.

What is the retained profit for the year?

A $130 profit
B $130 loss
C $10 profit
D $10 loss   **(2 marks)**

(Total = 40 marks)

---

34   Mixed bank 6   41 mins

34.1 If there is a debit balance of $1,250 on X's account in the books of Y, what does this mean?

A   X owes $1,250 to Y
B   Y owes $1,250 to X
C   X has returned goods worth $1,250 to Y
D   X is owed $1,250 by Y   **(2 marks)**

34.2 You are an employee of Exelan Co and have been asked to help prepare the end of year statements for the period ended 30 November 20X9 by agreeing the figure for the total receivables.

The following figures, relating to the financial year, have been obtained from the books of original entry.

	$
Purchases for the year	361,947
Sales	472,185
Returns inwards	41,226
Returns outwards	16,979
Irrecoverable debts written off	4,586
Discounts received	1,864
Cheques paid to suppliers	342,791
Cheques received from customers	429,811
Customer cheques dishonoured	626

You discover that at the close of business on 30 November 20X8 the total of the receivables amounted to $50,241. What is the balance on the receivables ledger control account at 30 November 20X9?

A $47,429
B $56,601
C $46,177
D $71,676   **(2 marks)**

34.3 Sandilands Co uses a computer package to maintain its accounting records. A printout of its cash book for the month of May 20X3 was extracted on 31 May and is summarised below.

	$		$
Balance b/d	546	Payments	5,966
Receipts	6,293	Balance c/d	873
	6,839		6,839

The company's chief accountant provides you with the following information.

(a) Bank charges of $630 shown on the bank statement have not been entered in the company's cash book.

(b) Three standing orders entered on the bank statement have not been recorded in the company's cash book: a subscription for trade journals of $52, an insurance premium of $360 and a business rates payment of $2,172.

(c) A cheque drawn by Sandilands Co for $693 and presented to the bank on 26 May has been incorrectly entered in the cash book as $936.

After correcting the errors above, what is the revised balance on the cash book?

A $2,098 debit
B $2,584 debit
C $3,868 credit
D $3,382 credit   **(2 marks)**

34.4 A company purchases a machine with an expected useful life of six years for $9,000. After two years of use, management revised the expected useful life to eight years. The machine is to be depreciated at 30% per annum on the reducing balance basis. A full year's depreciation is charged in the year of purchase, with none in the year of sale. During Year 4, it is sold for $3,000.

What is the profit or loss on disposal?

A $1,000 profit
B $87 loss
C $1,410 profit
D $840 profit   **(2 marks)**

34.5 Which one of the following does a business aim to ensure by charging depreciation in the financial statements?

A   The cost of non-current assets is spread over the accounting periods which benefit from their use.
B   There are sufficient funds set aside to replace the assets when necessary.
C   Profits are not understated.
D   Assets are shown at their realisable value.   **(2 marks)**

34.6 A business purchased an asset on 1 January 20X1 at a cost of $160,000. The asset had an expected life of eight years and a residual value of $40,000. The straight-line method is used to measure depreciation. The financial year ends on 31 December.

At 31 December 20X3, the estimated remaining life of the asset from that date is now expected to be only three more years, but the residual value is unchanged.

What will be the net book value of the asset as at 31 December 20X3, for inclusion in the statement of financial position?

A $97,500
B $100,000
C $107,500
D $115,000   **(2 marks)**

34.7 The debit side of a trial balance totals $400 more than the credit side.

Which one of the following errors would fully account for the difference?

A $200 paid for building repairs has been correctly entered in the cashbook and credited to the building non-current asset account.

B   Purchases returns of $200 were debited to the sales returns account.

C   A receipt of $400 for commission receivable has been omitted from the records.

D   An invoice for $400 has been entered into the sales day book but omitted from the receivables ledger. **(2 marks)**

34.8 Under IAS 1 *Presentation of financial statements*, which of the following **must** be disclosed on the **face** of the statement of profit or loss and other comprehensive income?

A   Profit before tax
B   Gross profit
C   Revenue
D   Dividends **(2 marks)**

34.9 The following bank reconciliation has been prepared:

	$
Balance per bank statement (overdrawn)	73,680
Add: Outstanding lodgements	102,480
Less: Unpresented cheques	(87,240)
Balance per cash book (credit)	88,920

Assuming the amounts stated for items other than the cash book balance are correct, what should the cash book balance be?

A $88,920 credit (as currently stated)
B $120,040 credit
C $58,440 debit
D $58,440 credit **(2 marks)**

34.10 In relation to statements of cash flows, which, if any, of the following are correct?

1   The direct method of calculating net cash from operating activities leads to a different figure from that produced by the indirect method, but this is balanced elsewhere in the statement of cash flows.

2   A company making high profits must necessarily have a net cash inflow from operating activities.

3   Profits and losses on disposals of non-current assets appear as items under cash flows from investing activities in the statement of cash flows or a note to it.

A   Item 1 only
B   Items 2 and 3 only
C   None of the items
D   All of the items **(2 marks)**

34.11 Which of the following items could appear on the credit side of a sales ledger control account?

1   Cash received from customers
2   Irrecoverable debts written off
3   Increase in the allowance for receivables
4   Sales
5   Credits for goods returned by customers
6   Cash refunds to customers

A   1, 2 and 5
B   1, 2 and 6
C   3, 4 and 5
D   3, 4, 5 and 6 **(2 marks)**

34.12 A business has compiled the following information for the year ended 31 October 20X2:

	$
Opening inventories	386,200
Purchases	989,000
Closing inventories	422,700

The gross profit percentage of sales is 40%

What is the sales revenue for the year?

A $1,333,500
B $1,587,500
C $2,381,250
D   The sales revenue is impossible to calculate from this information.   **(2 marks)**

34.13 On 30 September 20X1 part of the inventory of a company was completely destroyed by fire.

The following information is available:

–   Inventory at 1 September 20X1 at cost $49,800
–   Purchases for September 20X1 $88,600
–   Sales for September 20X1 $130,000
–   Inventory at 30 September 20X1 – undamaged items $32,000
–   Standard gross profit percentage on sales 30%

Based on this information, what is the cost of the inventory destroyed?

A $17,800
B $47,400
C $15,400
D $6,400   **(2 marks)**

34.14 Catt sells goods at a margin of 50%. During the year to 31 March 20X3 the business made purchases totalling $134,025 and sales totalling $240,000. Inventories in hand at 31 March 20X3, valued at cost, was $11,385 higher than the corresponding figure at 1 April 20X2.

What was the cost of the goods Catt had drawn out?

A $2,640
B $14,590
C $25,410
D $37,360   **(2 marks)**

34.15 Thatch plc's current ratio this year is 1.33:1 compared to that of 1.25:1 last year. Which of the following would be possible explanations?

1   Thatch made an unusually large sale immediately prior to the year end.

2   Thatch paid its payables earlier than usual out of a bank overdraft.

3   Thatch made an unusually large purchase of goods for cash immediately prior to the year end and these goods remain in inventory.

4   Thatch paid its payables earlier than usual out of a positive cash balance.

A   1 and 2 only
B   2 and 3 only
C   1 and 3 only
D   1 and 4 only   **(2 marks)**

34.16 Lexus has owns 60% of voting equity of Nexus. The following information relates to the results of Lexus and Nexus for the year.

	Lexus $'000	Nexus $'000
Revenue	350	150
Cost of sales	200	60
Gross profit	150	90

During the year, Nexus sold goods to Lexus for $50,000. Lexus still had 40% of these goods in inventory at the year end. Nexus uses a 25% mark up on all goods.

What were the consolidated sales and cost of sales of the Lexus group at the year end?

	Sales	Cost of sales
A	$500,000	$210,000
B	$500,000	$214,000
C	$450,000	$210,000
D	$450,000	$214,000

(2 marks)

34.17 At 1 July 20X0 the share capital and share premium account of a company were as follows:

	$
Share capital – 300,000 ordinary shares of 25c each	75,000
Share premium account	200,000

During the year ended 30 June 20X1 the following events took place:

1   On 1 January 20X1 the company made a rights issue of one share for every five held, at $1.20 per share.

2   On 1 April 20X1 the company made a bonus (capitalisation) issue of one share for every three in issue at that time, using the share premium account to do so.

What are the correct balances on the company's share capital and share premium accounts at 30 June 20X1?

	Share capital	Share premium account
A	$460,000	$287,000
B	$480,000	$137,000
C	$120,000	$137,000
D	$120,000	$227,000

(2 marks)

34.18 A statement of cash flows prepared in accordance with IAS 7 *Statement of Cash Flows* opens with the calculation of cash flows from operating activities from the net profit before taxation.

Which of the following lists of items consists only of items that would be **added** to net profit before taxation in that calculation?

A   Decrease in inventories, depreciation, profit on sale of non-current assets
B   Increase in trade payables, decrease in trade receivables, profit on sale of non-current assets
C   Loss on sale of non-current assets, depreciation, increase in trade receivables
D   Decrease in trade receivables, increase in trade payables, loss on sale of non-current assets

(2 marks)

(Total = 36 marks)

35 Mixed bank 7

43 mins

35.1 The following information was disclosed in the financial statements of Highfield Co for the year ended 31/12/20X2

	20X1	20X2
	$	$
Plant & Equipment cost	255,000	235,000
Accumulated depreciation	(100,000)	(110,000)

During 20X2, the following occurred in respect of Plant & Equipment:

	$
Purchases of plant and equipment	10,000
Depreciation charged on plant and equipment	25,000
Loss on disposal of plant and equipment	8,000

What were the sales proceeds received on disposal of the plant and equipment?

A $7,000
B $15,000
C $25,000
D $8,000

(2 marks)

35.2 The issued share capital of Maelstrom Co is as follows:

Ordinary shares of 10c each	$1,000,000
8% Preferred shares of 50c each (redeemable)	$500,000

In the year ended 31 October 20X2, the company has paid the preferred dividend for the year and an interim dividend of 2c per share on the ordinary shares. A final ordinary dividend of 3c per share is declared on 30 October 20X2.

What is the total amount of dividends recognised in the financial statements relating to the year ended 31 October 20X2?

A $580,000
B $90,000
C $130,000
D $500,000

(2 marks)

35.3 When a company makes a rights issue of equity shares which of the following effects will the issue have?

1 Working capital is increased
2 Liabilities are increased
3 Share premium account is reduced
4 Investments are increased

A 1 only
B 1 and 2
C 3 only
D 1 and 4

(2 marks)

35.4 Which of the following may appear as current liabilities in a company's statement of financial position?

1 A revaluation surplus
2 Loan due for repayment within 1 year
3 Income tax payable
4 Preferred dividends payable on redeemable preference shares

A 1,2 and 3
B 1,2 and 4
C 1,3 and 4
D 2,3 and 4

(2 marks)

35.5 If a trial balance does not balance, which of the following errors might have caused this?

(i) The discounts received column of the cash payments book was overcast.
(ii) Cash paid for the purchase of office furniture was debited to the general expenses account.
(iii) Returns inwards were included on the credit side of the trial balance.

A (i) only
B (i) and (ii)
C (iii) only
D (ii) and (iii) **(2 marks)**

35.6 The following information is available about a company's dividends:

$

20X5
Sept Final dividend for the year ended
30 June 20X5 paid (declared August 20X5) 100,000
20X6
March Interim dividend for the year ended
30 June 20X6 paid 40,000
Sept Final dividend for the year ended
30 June 20X6 paid (declared August 20X6) 20,000

What figures, if any, should be disclosed in the company's statement of profit or loss and other comprehensive income for the year ended 30 June 20X6 and its statement of financial position as at that date?

	SPLOCI for the period	SOFP liability
A	$160,000 deduction	$120,000
B	$140,000 deduction	nil
C	nil	$120,000
D	nil	nil

(2 marks)

35.7 Which, if any, of the following statements about intangible assets are correct?

1 Deferred development expenditure must be amortised over a period not exceeding five years.

2 If the conditions specified in IAS 38 *Intangible assets* are met, development expenditure may be capitalised, if the directors decide to do so.

3 Trade investments must appear in a company's statement of financial position under the heading of intangible assets.

A 1 and 2
B 2 and 3
C 1 and 3
D None of the statements is correct **(2 marks)**

35.8 A company owns a number of properties which are rented to tenants. The following information is available for the year ended 30 June 20X6:

	Rent in advance	Rent in arrears
	$	$
30 June 2005	134,600	4,800
30 June 2006	144,400	8,700

The rent income recognised in the company's statement of profit and loss for the year ended 30 June 20X6 was $828,700.

All rent in arrears was subsequently received.

What was the cash received from tenants in the year ended 30 June 2006?

$_____ **(2 marks)**

35.9 Which of the following transactions is a capital transaction?

A   Depreciation of plant and equipment
B   Expenditure on rent
C   Payment of interest on loan stock
D   Buying shares as an investment   **(2 marks)**

35.10 Which of the following transactions is revenue expenditure?

A   Expenditure resulting in improvements to property
B   Expenditure on heat and light
C   Purchasing non-current assets
D   Repaying a bank overdraft   **(2 marks)**

35.11 The payables ledger control account below contains a number of errors:

PAYABLES LEDGER CONTROL ACCOUNT

	$		$
Opening balance (amounts owed to suppliers)	318,600	Purchases	1,268,600
Cash paid to suppliers	1,364,300	Contras against debt balances in receivables ledger	48,000
Purchases returns	41,200	Discounts received	8,200
Refunds received from suppliers	2,700	Closing balance	402,000
	1,726,800		1,726,800

All items relate to credit purchases.

What should the closing balance be when all the errors are corrected?

A $128,200
B $509,000
C $224,200
D $144,600   **(2 marks)**

35.12 What are the journal entries for an accrual of rent expenses of $500?

A   Debit prepayments $500, credit rent $500
B   Debit accrual $500, credit rent $500
C   Debit rent $500, credit accruals $500
D   Debit rent $500, credit prepayments $500   **(2 marks)**

35.13 An electrical store and a cake shop both have the same mark up on cost. However, the gross profit margin of the electrical store is significantly higher than that of the cake shop.

Which of the following is a possible reason for this?

A   The cake shop has a higher turnover of inventory than the electrical store.
B   The electrical store takes advantage of trade-discounts for bulk buying.
C   The cake shop has a higher level of wastage of inventory than the electrical store.
D   The cake shop's revenue is increasing, while that of the electrical store is decreasing.   **(2 marks)**

35.14 Analysis of the statement of financial position of Charon for the year ended 20X9 reveals the following relationships:

Current ratio	2:1
Sales: current assets	5:1
Acid test ratio	1.5:1

If the sales for the year were $30 million, what is the value of inventory that will appear in the statement of financial position?

A $1.5m
B $10.5m
C $3.0m
D $4.5m   **(2 marks)**

35.15 Which of the following statements are correct?

1   If company A has an investment in company B that gives it control over the company B, then company B is classified as a subsidiary in the consolidated financial statements of company A.

2   If a company has associates, but not subsidiaries, it will not prepare consolidated financial statements.

3   If a company has a 21% investment in the voting equity of another company, it will account for its investment using the equity method in the consolidated financial statements.

A   1 and 2
B   2 and 3
C   All three statements are correct
D   None of the statements are correct   **(2 marks)**

35.16 XYX Co's non-current assets had carrying amounts of $368,400 and $485,000 at the beginning and end of the year respectively. Depreciation for the year was $48,600. Assets originally costing $35,000, with a carrying amount of $18,100 were sold in the year for $15,000.

What were the additions to non-current assets in the year?

A $183,300
B $200,200
C $49,900
D $180,200   **(2 marks)**

35.17 At 1 November 20X9, Telway Co had an allowance for receivables of $90,000. At 31 October 20X0, its trade receivables were $1,232,000 of which $60,000 was identified as unrecoverable and was written off. Telway Co's allowance for receivables has now been adjusted to the equivalent of 5% of remaining trade receivables.

What amount should be recorded in the statement of profit or loss for the receivables expense for the year ended 31 October 20X0?

A $58,600 debit
B $28,600 debit
C $31,400 credit
D $118,600 debit   **(2 marks)**

35.18 Why do we prepare a trial balance?

A   To test the accuracy of the double entry bookkeeping records
B   To prepare management accounts
C   To prepare financial statements
D   To clear the suspense account   **(2 marks)**

(Total = 36 marks)

Answers

1 The context and purpose of financial reporting

1.1 C The role of the IASB is to develop and publish International Financial Reporting Standards.

1.2 B A sole trader does not have any shareholders. The financial statements are unlikely to be of interest to a financial analyst, they are more usually interested in the financial statements of public companies.

1.3 The correct answers are:

(1) A supplier of goods on credit is interested only in the statement of financial position, ie an indication of the current state of affairs.		**False**
(2) The objective of financial statements is to provide information about the financial position, performance and changes in financial position of an entity that is useful to a wide range of users in making economic decisions.	**True**	

(1) is false – although the supplier needs to know the current situation, the supplier also needs to be able to assess future prospects to ensure the entity has the ability to pay and to support an ongoing relationship.

(2) is the IASB's *Conceptual framework* description of the purpose of financial statements, and is therefore true.

1.4 A (2) is incorrect – shareholders are only liable for the debts of the business up to the amount they have invested in shares, whereas sole traders are liable for all of the debts of the business.

1.5 B Corporate governance is the system by which companies and other entities are directed and controlled.

1.6 A The responsibility of the financial statements rests with the directors, whether or not those financial statements are audited. Some of the duties of directors are statutory duties, laid down in law, including the duty to act within their powers, promote the success of the company and exercise reasonable skill and care.

1.7 B The Statement of Financial Position contains a list of all the assets owned and all the liabilities owed by a business.

1.8 C The Statement of Profit or Loss contains a record of income generated and expenditure incurred over a given period.

1.9 C Unless a partnership is a limited liability partnership, the partners' individual exposure to debt is not limited because the partnership is not a separate legal entity from the partners themselves. Financial records must be maintained by a partnership, but there is no requirement to make them publicly available unless the partnership is a limited liability partnership.

1.10 C All three statements are true.

1.11 D The IFRS Advisory Council is a forum for the IASB to consult with the outside world. The IASB produces IFRSs and is overseen by the IFRS Foundation.

1.12 B The role of the IASB is to develop and publish international financial reporting standards.

1.13 C The IFRS Foundation does not focus primarily on the needs of global, multi-national organisations. One of the objectives of the foundation is to take account of the financial reporting needs of emerging economies and small and medium-sized entities (SMEs).

1.14 A   One of the ways IFRSs are used is as an international benchmark for those countries which develop their own requirements.

2 The qualitative characteristics of financial information

2.1 D   The business entity concept.

2.2 C   The accruals concept.

2.3 C   The materiality concept.

2.4 C   Information has the quality of faithful representation when it is complete, neutral and free from material error.

2.5 D   Consistency. To maintain consistency, the presentation and classification of items in the financial statements should stay the same from one period to the next, unless a change is required by an IFRS or unless there is a significant change in the nature of operations or a review of the accounts indicates a more appropriate presentation.

2.6 D   Relevance and faithful representation.

2.7 D   Financial information should be complete, neutral and free from error.

2.8 A   Statement (1) only is correct

   (2)   Materiality concerns whether an item in the financial statements can influence users' decisions.

   (3)   Information should be a faithful representation of the economic phenomena it purports to represent. This includes being neutral, ie without bias in the selection or presentation of the financial information. Therefore information must not be manipulated in any way in order to influence the decisions of the users.

2.9 C   Statement (2) only is correct. Information is material if its omission or misstatement could influence the economic decisions of users taken on the basis of the financial statements. Statement (1) describes the opposite of the accruals concept. Statement (3) is also incorrect, faithful representation does not prevent estimates being made.

2.10 A   Relevance, Faithful representation, Comparability, Verifiability, Timeliness and Understandability.

2.11 D   The accruals concept is not a qualitative characteristic of financial information.

2.12 D   Providing information regarding the financial position and performance of a business are primary objectives of financial statements. All classes of users require information for decision making.

2.13   The correct answers are:

(1) Companies should never change the presentation or classification of items in their financial statements, even if there is a significant change in the nature of operations.		**Incorrect**
(2) Companies should create provisions in times of company growth to be utilised in more difficult times, to smooth profits.		**Incorrect**

   (1) is incorrect. The presentation or classification can be changed if there is a significant change in the nature of operations, if an IFRS requires it, or if a review of the accounts indicates a more appropriate presentation.

   (2) is incorrect. Companies should not make provisions in order to smooth profits. Provisions should only be made in accordance with IAS 37.

3 Double entry bookkeeping I

3.1 C Assets – liabilities = opening capital + profits – drawings

Therefore, assets – liabilities – opening capital + drawings = profit

3.2 B Closing capital – opening capital = increase in net assets.

This is the correct form of the accounting equation.

3.3 D Increase in net assets = profit + new capital – drawings
= $(72,500 + 8,000 – 2,200)
= $78,300

Therefore, closing net assets = $(101,700 + 78,300) = $180,000.

3.4 $55,500

Increase in net assets = profit + new capital – drawings
= $(35,400 + 10,200 – 6,000)
= $39,600

Opening capital = opening net assets = $(95,100 – 39,600) = $55,500.

3.5 B The selling price is not relevant to this adjustment.

3.6 C This will mean less cash coming into the bank.

3.7 A Increase in net assets = Capital introduced + profit – drawings

184,000 – 128,000 = 50,000 + profit – 48,000

Profit = 56,000 – 50,000 + 48,000

= $54,000

3.8 C Dr Purchases $400
Dr Trade Payables $250
Cr Cash $650

A payment is a credit to the cash account. The payment to J Bloggs is a cash purchase and so the double entry is Dr Purchases, Cr Cash. Remember that the purchase from J Doe has already been recorded as Dr Purchases, Cr Trade Payables, so the payment of cash to clear the invoice should now be recorded as Dr Trade Payables, Cr Cash.

3.9 A Dr Receivables $150
Dr Sales Returns $300
Cr Sales $150
Cr Cash $300

The double entry for the sale of goods on credit is Dr Receivables, Cr Sales $150. The return of goods previously sold for cash is Dr Sales Returns, Cr Cash $300.

3.10 A A debit note is sent to a supplier with a return of goods. A debit note is in effect a request for a credit note.

3.11 A The journal, cash book and sales day book are books of prime entry. The purchases day book is the book of prime entry for purchases, not the purchase ledger.

3.12 C Debit notes sent to suppliers are recorded in the purchase returns day book.

3.13 D Balance carried down from previous period shows debits exceed credits and so it is a debit balance brought down for the new period.

3.14 B The opening balance on the ledger is $14,000 CR, this is the amount that would have appeared in the trial balance at 1 October 20X0.

3.15 B Cash received is recorded in the cash book. Credit notes received are to do with returned purchases (not sales). Trade discounts are not recorded, as they are deducted on the sales invoices and only the net sale is recorded.

3.16   The correct answers are:

A debit records an increase in liabilities.		**False**
A debit records a decrease in assets.		**False**
A credit records an increase in liabilities.	**True**	
A credit records an decrease in capital.		**False**

A debit records an increase in assets or a decrease in liabilities. A credit records an increase in liabilities and/or capital. Therefore only the third statement is true.

3.17   D   Remember that only credit purchases are listed in the purchases daybook.

3.18   D   An imprest system for petty cash helps with management of small cash expenditures and reduces the risk of fraud. The amount paid in to replenish petty cash at the beginning of each period should be the amount of petty cash spending in the previous period, which is the total of expenditures shown by petty cash vouchers for the previous period. The amount of petty cash at any time is the maximum petty cash balance minus the value of the petty cash vouchers for the period.

3.19   A   The petty cash voucher is a record that cash has been issued for an approved item of expense. The receipt is evidence of the amount of the expense. The petty cash book is used to record the transaction in the book-keeping system.

4   Double entry bookkeeping II

4.1 $534

SALES DAY BOOK

20X9		$
1 May	P Dixon	160
4 May	M Maguire ($80 × 87.5%)	70
5 May	M Donald	304
		534

4.2 $823

PURCHASES BOOK

20X9		$
2 May	A Clarke (W1)	323
4 May	D Daley	400
6 May	G Perkins	100
		823

W1 $380 × $\dfrac{85}{100}$ = $323

4.3   C   Dr Purchases $450
            Dr Trade Payables $250
            Cr Purchase Returns $700

The purchase of goods on credit is recorded as Dr Purchases, Cr Trade payables $450. The return of goods which were purchased on credit is recorded as Dr Trade Payables, Cr Purchase Returns, combining both entries gives the answer above.

4.4   B   Dr Cash

Cr Sales

Cr Trade Receivables

Cash received is a debit to the cash account. The cash received from R Singh is offset against the trade receivable balance due from R Singh: Dr Cash, Cr Trade Receivables. The cash received from S Kalu is a cash sale: Dr Cash, Cr Sales.

4.5   D   Remember the receivables account is a memorandum account.

4.6   The correct answers are:

A debit entry in the cash book will increase an overdraft in the accounts.		**False**
A debit entry in the cash book will increase a bank balance in the accounts.	**True**	

When cash is received by a business, a debit entry is made in the cashbook. A receipt of cash decreases an overdraft and increases a bank balance.

4.7   C

TRADE PAYABLES ACCOUNT

	$		$
Cash at bank	100,750	Balance b/d	250,225
Balance c/d	474,485	Purchases	325,010
	575,235		575,235

4.8   C   Credit sales = $80,000 – $10,000 + $9,000 = $79,000.

4.9   C   A is incorrect as the debits and credits don't equal each other, B is incorrect as the debits and credits are the wrong way round and D are incorrect as the credit purchase has been ignored.

4.10

TOKEN		DEBIT ENTRY	CREDIT ENTRY
		Receivables $250	
			Sales $250
Purchases $250			
Payables $250			
Cash $250			

You are recording the transaction in Steel Co's books – Steel Co is the seller, so the double entry is Dr receivables, Cr sales.

4.11   A $22,000

	$	$
Sales		40,000
Returns inwards		(2,000)
		38,000
Opening inventory	3,000	
Purchases	20,000	
Returns outwards	(4,000)	
Closing inventory	(3,000)	
		(16,000)
Gross profit		22,000

4.12   A   The receivables allowance is deducted from trade receivables and the net figure of $71,192 ($75,943 – $4,751) is reported in the statement of financial position.

4.13 B   Assets are represented by debit balances.

4.14 C   The two balances must be separately disclosed.

4.15 D   The debits are as follows:

	$
Opening inventory	9,649
Purchases	142,958
Expenses	34,835
Non-current assets	63,960
Receivables	31,746
Cash at bank	1,783
	284,931

4.16 A   (5,754 + 11,745 + 150)

4.17 C   No system can prevent a transaction being processed inaccurately, for example being posted to an incorrect but valid account code (although an effective system can reduce the likelihood of this).

4.18 B   Cash purchases are recorded in the cash book. The sales day book lists invoices sent to customers, not invoices received from suppliers.

5 Sales tax

5.1 D   A, B and C could all be reasons why the output tax does not equal 20% of sales. D is incorrect as it makes no difference whether the customer is registered for sales tax or not.

5.2 $11,910

SALES TAX CONTROL ACCOUNT

	$		$
		b/d	4,540
Purchases ($64,000 × 15%)	9,600	Sales ($109,250 × 15%/115%)	14,250
∴ Cash	11,910	c/d	2,720
	21,510		21,510

5.3 D   Dr Purchases $575 and Cr Payables $575.

Alana is not registered for sales tax purposes and therefore cannot reclaim the input sales tax of $75.

5.4 A $7,000

SALES TAX CONTROL ACCOUNT

	$		$
Purchases ($65,000 × 20%)	13,000	Sales ($120,000 × 20% / 120%)	20,000
∴ Paid to tax authority	7,000		
	20,000		20,000

5.5 D

	$
Assets	
Opening cash	1,000
Cash received $(1,000 + 200 sales tax)	1,200
Closing cash	2,200
Inventory $(800 – 400)	400
	2,600
Liabilities	
Opening liabilities	–
Sales tax payable $(200 – 160)	40
Purchase inventory $(800 + 160 sales tax)	960
Closing liabilities	1,000
Capital	
Opening capital	1,000
Profit on sale of inventory $(1,000 – 400)	600
Closing capital	1,600

5.6 A Receivables and payables include sales tax where applicable.

5.7 B The sales tax element of the invoices will go to the sales tax account in the statement of financial position.

5.8 B

	$
Output sales tax $27,612.50 $\times \dfrac{17.5}{117.5}$	4,112.50
Input sales tax $18,000 $\times \dfrac{17.5}{100}$	3,150.00
$\therefore$ Balance on sales tax a/c (credit)	962.50

6 Inventory

6.1 $952,750

950,000 – 11,750 + 1,500 + (14,950 × 100/115) = $952,750

6.2 C Carriage outwards and storage are distribution costs.

6.3 B

	$
Original value	284,700
Coats – Cost 400 × $80	(32,000)
– NRV ($75 × 95%) × 400	28,500
	281,200

At 31 January 20X3 the skirts were correctly valued at costs incurred to date of $20 per skirt which was lower than the NRV of $22. Therefore no adjustment is required for the value of the skirts.

6.4 A

	$
50 @ $190	9,500
500 @ $220	110,000
300 @ $230	69,000
	188,500

6.5   The correct answers are:

(1) Inventory items are normally to be valued at the higher of cost and net realisable value.		**Incorrect**
(2) The cost of goods manufactured by an entity will include materials and labour only. Overhead costs cannot be included.		**Incorrect**
(3) LIFO (last in, first out) cannot be used to value inventory.	**Correct**	
(4) Selling price less estimated profit margin may be used to arrive at cost if this gives a reasonable approximation to actual cost.	**Correct**	

Statement (1) is incorrect because inventory should be valued at the lower of cost and NRV, not the higher.
Statement (2) is incorrect because production overheads based on a normal level of production should be included.

6.6   D

	$
Inventory check balance	483,700
Less: goods from suppliers	(38,400)
Add: goods sold	14,800
Less: goods returned	(400)
Add: goods returned to supplier	1,800
	461,500

6.7   C   If closing inventory is understated, cost of sales will be overstated. Next year opening inventory will be understated and cost of sales will be understated.

6.8   C

	$
Inventory count, 4 January 20X2	527,300
Purchases since end of year	(7,900)
Cost of sales since end of year (15,000 × 60%)	9,000
Purchase returns since end of year	800
Inventory at 31 December 20X1	529,200

6.9   A   IAS 2 emphasises that production overheads must be allocated to items of inventory on the basis of the normal capacity of the production facilities. Although trade discounts should be deducted, selling costs must not be included in the cost of inventories. IAS 2 does not allow the use of LIFO. Production overheads are part of the costs of conversion of finished goods, and so do form part of the valuation.

6.10   B

	$
Original inventory valuation	41,875
Cost of damaged items	(1,960)
NRV of damaged items (1,200 – 360)	840
	40,755

6.11   B

	Cost	Net realisable value	Lower of cost & NRV	Units	Value
	$	$	$		$
Basic	6	8	6	200	1,200
Super	9	8	8	250	2,000
Luxury	18	10	10	150	1,500
					4,700

6.12 C $2,950 (10 units @$45 and 50 units @$50)

6.13 C   Carriage outwards (in Options A and D) is a selling expense, so should not be included in the cost of the inventory.

IAS2 states that storage costs should not be included in the cost of inventory unless they are necessary in the production process before a further production stage. As such, storage of finished goods (in Option B) should not be included in the cost of inventory.

6.14 C

	$
	116,400
Line 1: (400 × $3) – $200	1,000
Line 2: (200 × $35) – $300 – $1,200	5,500
	122,900

6.15 A

	$
Inventory count value	836,200
Less: purchases	(8,600)
Add: sales (14,000 × 70/100)	9,800
Add: goods returned	700
Inventory figure	838,100

6.16 B   The cost of materials used should be based on opening and closing valuations of inventory at AVCO.

	$
Opening inventory	56,200
Purchases	136,500
	192,700
Less: Closing inventory	(59,800)
Cost of materials used	132,900

6.17 C   Continuous inventory reduces the need for physical inventory counts, but in practice periodic counts are needed to ensure that the recorded quantities of inventory match the physical quantities that are held (and, for example, there have not been significant losses of inventory due to theft).

6.18 B

Date	Units	Unit cost	Cost of issues $	Balance in inventory $
1 March	50	$40		2,000
17 March	50	$50		2,500
	100	$45*		4,500
31 March	(60)	$45	2,700	
	40	$45		1,800

* 4,500 / 100

6.19 $2,057.12

Price per unit under periodic weighted average cost (AVCO):

= Total cost /(opening quantity + total quantity received)

= ($300 × 10)+($250 × 12)+($200 × 6)/(0+10+12+6)

= $257.14 per unit.

Valuation of closing inventory of 8 units (10+12–8+6–12) × $257.14 = $2,057.12

7 Tangible non-current assets I

7.1   A   It is **never** B as funds are not set aside, nor C, this is revaluation, nor D – depreciation has nothing to do with the wearing out of assets, depreciation is an application of the matching concept and allocates the cost of the asset over the accounting periods expected to benefit from its use.

7.2   C   An internal control to ensure information relating to non-current assets in the nominal ledger and the financial statements is correct.

7.3 $62,210

	$
Balance b/d	67,460
Less: Carrying amount of non-current asset sold	
(4,000 + 1,250)	5,250
	62,210

7.4   A   If disposal proceeds were $15,000 and profit on disposal is $5,000, then carrying amount must be $10,000, the difference between the asset register figure and the non-current asset account in the nominal ledger.

7.5   A   An expense has been posted as a non-current asset.

7.6   B   Assets which are intended to be used by the business on a continuing basis, including both tangible and intangible assets that do not meet the IASB definition of a current asset.

7.7   C

	$
Valuation	210,000
Carrying amount (170,000 × 16/20)	(136,000)
Revaluation surplus	74,000

7.8   A

	$
Repairs cost overstated	20,000
Depreciation understated ((20,000 − 4,000) × 20% × 6/12)	(1,600)
Profit understated	18,400

7.9   A

	$
Plant held all year (200,000 − 40,000) × 20%	32,000
Disposal 40,000 × 20% × 9/12	6,000
Additions 50,000 × 20% × 6/12	5,000
	43,000

7.10   D

	$
Plant held all year (240,000 − 60,000) × 20%	36,000
Addition 160,000 × 20% × 6/12	16,000
Disposal 60,000 × 20% × 3/12	3,000
	55,000

7.11   C   Cost less 4 months depreciation = 25,500 − 2,125 = $23,375

7.12 $86,000

	$
Purchase price of machine	80,000
Installation	5,000
Testing	1,000
	86,000

Staff training cannot be capitalised as part of the cost of the asset.

7.13   C   Dr Non-current assets – cost, Cr Payables

7.14 A   Using T accounts:

PLANT AND MACHINERY ACCOUNT

	$		$
Balance b/d	100,000	Plant and machinery disposals a/c	100,000

PLANT AND MACHINERY ACCUMULATED DEPRECIATION

	$		$
Plant and machinery disposals	35,000	Balance b/d	35,000

PLANT AND MACHINERY DISPOSALS

	$		$
Plant and machinery account	100,000	Accumulated depreciation	35,000
		Cash	50,000
		SPL (loss on sale)	15,000
	100,000		100,000

7.15   The correct answers are:

IAS 16 *Property, plant and equipment* requires entities to disclose the purchase date of each asset.		**False**
The carrying amount of a non-current asset is the cost or valuation of that asset less accumulated depreciation.	**True**	
IAS 16 *Property, plant and equipment* permits entities to make a transfer from the revaluation surplus to retained earnings for excess depreciation on revalued assets.	**True**	
Once decided, the useful life of a non-current asset should not be changed.		**False**

IAS 16 does not require the purchase date of each asset to be disclosed. The carrying amount of an asset = cost/valuation – accumulated depreciation. The useful life of an asset is determined upon acquisition and should be reviewed at least annually and depreciation rates adjusted for the current and future periods if expectations vary significantly from the original estimates. When an asset is revalued, IAS 16 permits entities to make a transfer from the revaluation surplus to retained earnings of the excess depreciation arising due to the revaluation.

7.16 B   The depreciation charge is calculated based on the remaining useful life at the date of the revaluation: 1,000,000/20 years = $50,000

7.17

TOKEN		DEBIT	CREDIT
		Revaluation surplus $20,000	
			Retained earnings $20,000
Revaluation surplus $12,500			
Retained earnings $12,500			

The excess deprecation is the new depreciation amount of $50,000 less the old depreciation charge of $30,000 ($750,000/25 years) which is $20,000. This amount should be debited from the revaluation surplus and credited to retained earnings each year. Remember that both retained earnings and the revaluations surplus are credit balances in the trial balance.

7.18 C The disclosure requirements in IAS 16 are comprehensive, particularly in relation to revalued assets.

7.19 B In this question the consequence of the revaluation to $432,000 is a higher annual depreciation charge. The difference between the new depreciation charge based on the revalued carrying amount and the old depreciation charge based on £400,000 original cost is known as the excess depreciation.

IAS16 allows entities to transfer an amount equal to the excess depreciation from the revaluation surplus to retained earnings in the equity section of the statement of financial position. As X Co wishes to make the transfer, the calculations are as follows:

Old depreciation = $400,000/40 years = $10,000 New depreciation = $432,000/36 years = $12,000

Excess depreciation = $12,000 – $10,000 = $2,000

An amount of $2,000 which represents the excess depreciation can be transferred each year from the revaluation surplus to retained earnings.

The correct accounting entries would be:

Debit Revaluation surplus $2,000 Credit Retained earnings $2,000

8 Tangible non-current assets II

8.1 $781 profit

	$
Cost	10,000
20X0 Depreciation (25% reducing balance)	2,500
	7,500
20X1 Depreciation	1,875
	5,625
20X2 Depreciation	1,406
	4,219
20X3 Part exchange	5,000
Profit	781

Note. The road tax is an expense. It does not form part of the cost of the car.

8.2 A

	$	$
Carrying amount at 01 August 20X0		200,000
Less depreciation		(20,000)
Proceeds	25,000	
Loss	5,000	
Therefore carrying amount		(30,000)
		150,000

8.3 B

DEBIT	Property, plant and equipment	$38,000	
CREDIT	Plant repairs		$38,000
DEBIT	Dep'n expense	$1,900	
CREDIT	Accumulated dep'n		$1,900

Profit is understated by $38,000 – $1,900 = $36,100

8.4 B $\dfrac{\$30,000 - \$6,000}{4 \text{ years}} \times \dfrac{5 \text{ months}}{12 \text{ months}} = \$2,500$

8.5   B   Revaluation surplus – (1,000,000 – (800,000 – (800,000 × 2% × 10))) = $360,000
          Depreciation charge – (1,000,000/40) = $25,000

8.6   D   Improvements are capital expenditure, repairs and maintenance are not.

8.7   C   An illuminated sign advertising the business name will provide long-term benefits for the business
          and is therefore a non-current asset, ie capital expenditure. A replacement for a broken window is
          a repair, so it is revenue expenditure. Repainting the restaurant is a repair and renewal expense
          so it would be likely to be treated as revenue expenditure. Cleaning of the kitchen floors is a
          maintenance cost and therefore is revenue expenditure.

8.8   A   Number plates, stereo and delivery costs are included in the capital cost of acquiring the car.
          Road tax is an annual charge against revenue.

8.9   B

	$
Water treatment equipment	39,800
Delivery	1,100
	40,900

8.10 C   A is a receivable, B and D are inventory.

8.11 C   Items (i) and (ii) are non-current assets. Only item (iii) is a current asset.

8.12 C   Assets which are expected to be converted into cash in the short term.

8.13 C   To record the purchase of the asset:
          Dr Non-current assets – cost $15,000
          Cr Payables $15,000
          Depreciation charge is 15,000 × 15% × 2/12 = $375

8.14 D $585,000

          The revaluation surplus at 30 June 20Y8 was $600,000 ($1,600k – $1,000k). The old
          deprecation charge was $25,000 ($1,250,000/50 years) per year. The new depreciation charge
          is $40,000 ($1,600,000/40 years), so the excess depreciation is $15,000 per year. The
          balance on the revaluation surplus is therefore $600,000 – $15,000 = $585,000 at
          30 June 20Y9.

8.15 D

	$
Carrying amount at disposal (15,000 – 10,000)	5,000
Trade-in allowance	5,500
Profit on disposal	500

8.16 B $52,500

          Carrying amount at 1.1.X3 = 100,000 – (100,000 × 2/5) = $60,000
          New depreciation charge = Carrying amount/Revised useful life = $60,000/8 years = $7,500
          Carrying amount at 31.12.X3 = $60,000 – $7,500 = $52,500

8.17 A $7,000

          Carrying amount at 1.10.X8: 34,000 – ((34,000 – 4,000) × 3/5) = $16,000

          Revised depreciation charge: (Carrying amount – revised residual value)/remaining useful life

          = (16,000 – 2,000)/2 = $7,000.

8.18 A   Dr Depreciation charge $6,000
          Cr Accumulated depreciation $6,000

8.19 $792,000

          In the 5 years to 31 December 20X5, accumulated depreciation on the building is
          $1,600,000 × 2% × 5 years = $160,000.

On revaluation on 1 January 20X6:

	Debit $	Credit $
Building (2,250,000 – 1,600,000)	650,000	
Accumulated depreciation	160,000	
Revaluation surplus		810,000

The annual depreciation charge from 1 January 20X6 = $2,250,000/45 years remaining = $50,000. This is $18,000 more than the annual depreciation charge based on the historical cost of the asset.

This excess depreciation charge is transferred each year from revaluation surplus to retained earnings, and the revaluation surplus at 31 December 20X6 = $810,000 – $18,000 = $792,000.

8.20 A Annual depreciation was initially $1,000,000/50 years = $20,000.

After revaluation, annual depreciation is $1,200,000/48 years = $25,000.

		$
Valuation, 1 January 20X5		1,200,000
Accumulated depreciation to 30 June 20X5	(6/12 × $25,000)	12,500
Carrying amount at 30 June 20X5		1,187,500
Sale/disposal price		1,195,000
Profit on disposal in statement of profit or loss		7,500

Note. The balance on the revaluation surplus at 30 June will be transferred to realised profits (retained profits reserve), but this will not be reported as profit in the statement of profit or loss.

9 Intangible non-current assets

9.1 The correct answers are:

Research expenditure, other than capital expenditure on research facilities, should be recognised as an expense as incurred.	**True**	
In deciding whether development expenditure qualifies to be recognised as an asset, it is necessary to consider whether there will be adequate finance available to complete the project.	**True**	
Development expenditure recognised as an asset must be amortised over a period not exceeding five years.		**False**

There is no requirement that development expenditure should be amortised over a period not exceeding five years.

9.2 C (1) Development expenditure must be capitalised if the criteria are met.
(3) There is no time scale given by IAS 38 for amortisation.

9.3 C Development costs are amortised over the useful life of the project. This is not confined to five years.

9.4   A   (3) only.

The other statements are incorrect:

There is no requirement that development expenditure should be amortised over a period not exceeding five years.

Development expenditure must be capitalised if the criteria are met.

Amortisation is recognised as an expense in the statement of profit and loss.

9.5   B   A factory is a tangible asset as it has physical form. The others are intangible assets.

9.6   A   Research expenditure is never capitalised.

9.7   B   Amortisation of development expenditure should reflect the period over which the economic benefits from the development are recognised. IAS 38 does not specify that this period cannot exceed five years.

9.8   A   Research expenditure is never capitalised, development expenditure is capitalised if it meets certain conditions per IAS 38. Intangible assets are amortised over their useful life, if the life of the asset is indefinite, then it does not have to be amortised.

9.9 $25,000

The patent should be amortised over its useful life of 10 years. (250,000 / 10) = $25,000

9.10   B   The amortisation charge is $15,000/3 years = $5,000 per annum. The double entry to record the amortisation is Dr expenses, Cr accumulated amortisation.

9.11   A   Amortisation is an application of the matching concept and allocates the cost of the intangible asset over its useful life (over the accounting periods expected to benefit from its use).

9.12   D   A patent has no physical substance and provides future economic benefits; it is therefore an intangible non-current asset.

Computer hardware is a tangible non-current asset as it is physical in substance and provides future economic benefits.

Operating software that operates the computer hardware on first glance may appear to be an intangible non-current asset. However, since it is an integral part of the computer hardware (which could not function without it), it is classed as part of the computer hardware.

A building extension has physical substance and provides future economic benefits and is therefore a tangible non-current asset.

10   Accruals and prepayments

10.1   C

	$
Receipt	
1 October 20X1 ($7,500 × 1/3)	2,500
30 December 20X1	7,500
4 April 20X2	9,000
1 July 20X2	9,000
1 October 20X2 (9,000 × 2/3)	6,000 (3,000 Credit; rent in advance)
Credit to statement of profit or loss	34,000

10.2   B

	$
February to March 20X2 (22,500 × 2/3)	15,000
April to June	22,500
July to September	22,500
October to December	30,000
January 20X3 (30,000 × 1/3)	10,000
Rent for the year	100,000

Accrual 30,000 × 1/3 = 10,000

10.3 $33,100

	$
Payments made	34,600
Add: opening balance	8,200
Less: opening accrual	(3,600)
Less: closing balance	(9,300)
Add: closing accrual	3,200
	33,100

10.4 B

	$
Statement of profit or loss	
December to June 8,400 × 7/12	4,900
July to November 12,000 × 5/12	5,000
	9,900

Sundry payables 12,000 × 1/12 = 1,000 (December rent received in advance)

10.5 C

	$
August to September 60,000 × 2/12	10,000
October to July 72,000 × 10/12	60,000
	70,000

10.6 A $87,700

Diesel fuel payable account

	$
Balance b/fwd	(1,700)
Payments	85,400
Balance c/fwd	1,300
Purchases	85,000

Cost of fuel used

	$
Opening inventory	12,500
Purchases	85,000
Closing inventory	(9,800)
Transfer to SPL	87,700

10.7 C

ELECTRICITY ACCOUNT

		$			$
			Balance b/fwd		300
20X0:					
1 August	Paid bank	600			
1 November	Paid bank	720			
20X1:					
1 February	Paid bank	900			
30 June	Paid bank	840			
30 June	Accrual c/d				
	$840 × 2/3	560	SPL		3,320
		3,620			3,620

10.8 A

GAS SUPPLIER ACCOUNT

	$			$
Balance b/fwd	200			
Bank $600 × 12	7,200	28 February	invoice	1,300
		31 May	invoice	1,400
		31 August	invoice	2,100
		30 November	invoice	2,000
		30 November	bal. c/d	600
	7,400			7,400

GAS ACCOUNT

		$			$
28 February	invoice	1,300			
31 May	invoice	1,400			
31 August	invoice	2,100			
30 November	invoice	2,000	30 November	SPL	6,800
		6,800			6,800

10.9 A $\dfrac{5 \text{ months}}{12 \text{ months}} \times \$24,000 = \$10,000$

$\dfrac{7 \text{ months}}{12 \text{ months}} \times \$30,000 = \$17,500$

Total rent: $10,000 + $17,500 = $27,500

10.10 $316,200   RENTAL INCOME ACCOUNT

	$		$
Opening rent owing	16,900	Opening rent in advance	24,600
Rent income (balancing figure)	316,200	Cash received	318,600
Closing rent in advance	28,400	Closing rent owing	18,300
	361,500		361,500

10.11 A   Statement of profit or loss and other comprehensive income = $60,000 × 12/18 = $40,000

Statement of financial position = $60,000 × 3/18 prepayment = $10,000

10.12 A   An accrual should be made for $10,000 ($30,000/3 months). The double entry to record the accrual in the accounts is:

Dr Expenses (SPL) $10,000
Cr Accruals (SOFP) $10,000
This reduces profit from $25,000 to $15,000

An accrual is a liability and so will reduce the net asset position, from $275,000 to $265,000. Remember that net assets = assets – liabilities.

10.13 B

	$
Original loss	(1,486)
Accrual	(1,625)
Prepayment	834
Revised loss	(2,277)

10.14 C   The double entry to record the accrual in the accounts is:

Dr Expenses (SPL) $50,000
Cr Accruals (SOFP) $50,000

This reduces profit from $125,000 to $75,000 and the net asset position from $375,000 to $325,000.

10.15 A   This question is designed to test whether candidates understand prepayments and accruals. The best way to approach the question is to prepare a simple working for the heat and light expenses. Prepayment are those expenses that have already been paid but relate to a future accounting period and accruals are expenses that relate to the current accounting period but have not yet been paid for. Using all the information available in the question, the working would look like:

Heat and light expenses for the year ended 31 March 2017

	$
Gas prepayment 1 April 2016	1,000
Electricity accrual 1 April 2016	(500)
Gas paid during year	5,000
Electricity paid during year	7,800
Gas accrual 1 April 2017	2,000
Electricity prepayment 1 April 2017	(1,200)
Total expense	14,100

11   Receivables and payables

11.1   The correct answers are:

Payables represent money the business owes.	True	
Payables are an asset.		False
Receivables represent money owed to the business.	True	

Payables are a liability, so the second statement is false.

11.2 D

	$
Closing allowance (400,000 – 38,000) × 10%	36,200
Opening allowance	50,000
Decrease in allowance	(13,800)
Irrecoverable debts written off	38,000
Statement of profit or loss charge	24,200

11.3 A

	$
Irrecoverable debts written off	14,600
Reduction in allowance	(2,000)
	12,600

11.4 $32,500

	$
Irrecoverable debt written off	28,500
Increase in allowance ((868,500 – 28,500) × 5% – 38,000)	4,000
	32,500

11.5 C $146,000 + ($218,000 – $83,000) = $281,000

11.6 B   Because the debt has been previously written off, there is no receivable for which to offset the cash, therefore the double entry is Dr Cash, Cr Irrecoverable debts expense.

11.7 B

	$
Allowance required 5% × (864,000 – 13,000)	42,550
Existing allowance	(48,000)
Reduction in allowance	(5,450)
Irrecoverable debts written off	13,000
Statement of profit or loss charge	7,550

Net trade receivables = $864,000 – 13,000 – 42,550
= $808,450

11.8 D   A decrease in the allowance is written back to profit or loss.

11.9 C   The debt needs to be fully written out of the books. An allowance was already made, so the SPL has already been charged ie:

Dr Irrecoverable debts (SPL)   X
Cr Allowance for receivables (SOFP)   X

Therefore you only need to clear the balances from Receivables and Allowances for receivables, which Option C will do.

11.10 C   An increase in the allowance for receivables will reduce profits and receivables. Gross profit will not be affected since allowances for receivables are dealt with in the net profit section.

11.11 $1,800 credit

	$	SPL charge $
Receivables allowance at 31.12.X1 (15% of $20,000)	1,000	
Receivables allowance at 1.1.X1	3,000	
Decrease in allowance		2,000
Irrecoverable debts written off		(1,000)
Debt recovered		800
Total credit to statement of profit or loss		1,800

11.12 A   When a business first establishes an allowance for receivables the full amount of the allowance should be debited to Irrecoverable debts (statement of profit or loss) and credited to Allowance for receivables (statement of financial position).

11.13 C

	$	SPL charge $
Receivables allowance at year end	1,000	
Receivables allowance at beginning of year	850	
Increase in allowance		(150)
Irrecoverable debts written off		(500)
Total charge to statement of profit or loss		650

11.14 A, C   An aged receivables analysis shows the outstanding balances owed by each customer analysed by how long they have been outstanding, usually 30, 60 and 90+ days. The receivables allowance is deducted from the receivables balance in the statement of financial position.

A credit limit is set by the credit control department of the business and is the maximum amount of credit each customer of that business can have. Credit limits are not applied to cash sales.

11.15 A   The trade payables are due to be paid within 12 months, the overdraft is repayable on demand.

11.16 D   Offering credit facilities will not reduce the level of irrecoverable debts.

11.17 D   Dr Payables control account, Cr Discounts received (income).

11.18 D   Statement (4) only is correct.

A payable is a person or institution to whom a business owes money.
Statements (1) to (3) are examples of where money is owed to the business from others, so these are receivables. In the case of (2), if a company makes a loan or advance to an employee, this creates a receivable, being the repayment due from the employee.

Statement (4) is an example of where money is owed by the business to others, so this is a payable.

11.19 C   Statements (2) only is correct.

A payable is a person or institution to whom a business owes money eg, a supplier. The amount of money owed will be known exactly as it will have been billed or invoiced by the supplier. Therefore the liability of $500 for invoiced goods (2) is a payable.

The amount owed to the tax authorities (1) is an accrual rather than a payable. An accrual or accrued expense is an expense which is charged against the profit or loss for a particular period, with a corresponding liability, even though it has not yet been paid for. The amount and timing of money owed will not be known exactly as it will not yet have been billed or invoiced. However timing is virtually certain and a close estimate is usually known. This is recorded as the accrual.

The amount owed for the warranty claims (3) is a provision rather than a payable. A provision is a liability of uncertain timing or amount. The timing and/or amount are less certain than for an accrual – as is the estimate for the warranty claim.

11.20 C The reconciling items are (3) and (6).

The supplier statement reconciliation would read as follows with items (3) and (6) as reconciling items. All the other transactions appear both in the ledger and the supplier statement.

Balance per supplier's statement 31 March 20X1	520
Less reconciling items:	
Payment (30 March) not on statement (3)	(385)
Invoice (#533) on statement, not on payables ledger (6)	(35)
Balance per payables ledger 31 March 20X1	100

Invoice #533 would then need to be investigated with the supplier to ensure it is not an error on their part. Once it is established it is a valid invoice, the ledger should be corrected to record this invoice.

12 Provisions and contingencies

12.1 The correct answers are:

A company should disclose details of the change in carrying amount of a provision from the beginning to the end of the year.	**True**	
Contingent assets must be recognised in the financial statements in accordance with the prudence concept.		**False**
Contingent liabilities must be treated as actual liabilities and provided for if it is probable that they will arise.	**True**	

Contingent assets should not be recognised in the financial statements. However, they should be disclosed if it is probable that the economic benefits associated with the asset will flow to the entity. If it becomes probable that the a transfer of economic benefits associated with a contingent liability will happen, then the contingent liability is no longer contingent and a liability should be recognised in the financial statements.

12.2 A A possible transfer of economic benefits should be disclosed. Where transfer is probable a provision should be made.

12.3 C As the claim is unlikely to succeed, the potential settlement of $500,000 should be disclosed as a contingent liability note. However, given that the legal costs of $50,000 must be paid whether the claim is successful or not, this amount should be provided for in the company's financial statements.

12.4 A A provision is required for the warranties sold, it should be calculated using the expected value approach. (2) is a contingent liability because it is possible that the company will have to pay out, if it was probable, then a provision would be required. If it was remote, no disclosure would be needed.

12.5 A All three statements are correct.

12.6 C   The provision should be increased by $1,086, the double entry is therefore Dr Expenses, Cr Provision.

12.7 B   Doggard Co needs to reduce the provision by $500 ie a credit to the statement of profit or loss.

12.8 A   A provision is a liability of uncertain timing or amount. A contingent liability is a **possible** obligation of uncertain timing or amount.

12.9 C   The statement is the definition of a contingent liability.

12.10 $3,000

          Montague should include a provision of $3,000 in his year-end financial statements as this is the best estimate of the amount he will probably have to pay out.

12.11 D   Mobiles Co should provide on the basis of the expected cost. The expected cost would be calculated as $(2.5\% \times 100,000 \times \$50) + (2.5\% \times 100,000 \times \$10) = \$125,000 + \$25,000 = \$150,000$.

12.12 B   The expected value approach to calculating a provision takes each possible outcome (ie the amount of money that will need to be paid under each circumstance) and weights it according to the probability of that outcome happening. The total amount of each weighted value is the provision.

12.13 C

	$'000
Provision required at 31.12.X1 = $(0.05 \times 150) + (0.20 \times 25) + (0.75 \times 60)$	57.5
Provision b/f at 31.12.X0	64
Utilised during year	(25)
Increase required – charge to SPL	18.5
Provision c/f at 31.12.X1	57.5

13 Capital structure and finance costs

13.1 $200,000

          Paid ordinary dividend only: 10m × 2c = $200,000. The dividend paid on the redeemable preference shares will be recognised in the financial statements as a finance cost. Note: the Ordinary shares are 10c shares, not $1 each. Therefore Alpha's share capital of $1,000,000 means it has $10 million shares in issue (at 10 cents each).

          The proposed ordinary dividend will not be recognised in the financial statements, as this arose after the reporting date, and does not provide further evidence of conditions that existed at the reporting date. However, it should be disclosed in the notes to the financial statements.

          Only the paid interim ordinary dividend will be recognised as a deduction from equity reserves in the statement of financial position.

13.2 A   A rights issue will increase cash and therefore assets. Retained earnings remain the same and the share premium account will be increased.

13.3 B   Share capital will be credited with the nominal value of the shares – the balance goes to share premium.

13.4 B

	$
Ordinary shares at start of year	50,000
Add: bonus issue 50,000 × 50c	25,000
Add: new issue 60,000 × 50c	30,000
	105,000
Share premium at start of year	180,000
Less: bonus issue 50,000 × 50c	(25,000)
Add: new issue 60,000 × 30c	18,000
	173,000

13.5 B $9,000 is payable (SPL), but only $6,000 has been paid (April and July).

13.6   The correct answers are:

Dividends paid on ordinary shares should be included in the statement of profit or loss and other comprehensive income.		**False**
Dividends paid on redeemable preference shares are treated in the same way as dividends paid on ordinary shares.		**False**
The statement of profit or loss and other comprehensive income shows the gain on revaluation of non-current assets for the period.	**True**	

Dividends paid on ordinary shares are included in the statement of changes in equity, not the statement of profit or loss and other comprehensive income. Dividends paid on redeemable preference shares are treated like interest on loans and are shown in the statement of profit or loss and other comprehensive income as a finance charge. The gain on revaluation of non-current assets is shown in the statement of profit or loss and other comprehensive income, as other comprehensive income.

13.7   C

		$
Ordinary shares		
Opening balance		125,000
Rights issue	250,000 × 25c	62,500
Bonus issue	150,000 × 25c	37,500
		225,000
Share premium		
Opening balance		100,000
Rights issue	250,000 × 75c	187,500
Bonus issue	150,000 × 25c	(37,500)
		250,000

13.8 $73,750

		$
July – September	1,000,000 × 8% × 3/12	20,000
October – March	750,000 × 8% × 6/12	30,000
April – June	750,000 × 8% × 3/12	15,000
	500,000 × 7% × 3/12	8,750
		73,750

13.9   B   This is the transfer of the premium to the share premium account.

13.10 C   A bonus issue does not involve cash but can be financed from the share premium account.

13.11 D   A bonus issue does not raise any funds, instead other reserves are capitalised and reclassified as share capital. A rights issue is an issue of shares for cash, the right to buy the shares are initially offered to existing shareholders. If the existing shareholders do not take up their right to buy the shares, then their shareholding will be diluted.

13.12 C

	$
Share capital @ 1.1.20X0	500,000
Issue on 1.4.20X0 (200,000 @ 50c)	100,000
Bonus issue (1.2m ÷ 4) @ 50c	150,000
Share capital as at 31.12.20X0	750,000
Share premium @ 1.1.20X0	300,000
1.4.20X0 200,000 shares @ (130c – 50c)	160,000
Bonus issue (as above)	(150,000)
	310,000

13.13 B   The statement of changes in equity.

13.14 B   From the information given we can see that Yellow has a credit against Dividends of $5,000 and a debit against Bank, which means that the company has received dividend income. The options for the correct answer are therefore narrowed down to B or C. We can now calculate the return from the investment in Blue as follows:

$5,000 Dividend / 50,000 shares = 10c Dividend per share

10c Dividend/ 50c Share = 20% return

14   15 mark question: trial balance

14.1 Mr Yousef

Task 1

	$	DR	CR
Sales	138,078		O
Purchases	82,350	O	
Carriage	5,144	O	
Drawings	7,800	O	
Rent and insurance	6,622	O	
Postage and stationery	3,001	O	
Advertising	1,330	O	
Salaries and wages	26,420	O	
Irrecoverable debts	877	O	
Allowance for receivables	130		O
Receivables	12,120	O	
Payables	6,471		O
Cash on hand	177	O	
Cash at bank	1,002	O	
Inventory as at 1 June 20X5	11,927	O	
Equipment at cost	58,000	O	
Accumulated depreciation	19,000		O
Capital at 1 June 20X5	53,091		O

Task 2

Cost of sales is $82,937

	$
Opening inventory	11,927
Purchases	82,350
Carriage inwards	2,211
Closing inventory	(13,551)
	82,937

Task 3

Profit for the year will be **decreased** by the rent accrual and **increased** by the insurance prepayment.

Task 4

Capital at 31 May 20X6 will be $51,179

	$
Capital at 1 June 20X5	53,091
Profit for the year	5,888
Drawings	(7,800)
	51,179

Task 5

The carrying amount of equipment at 31 May 20X6 will be $30,300

	$
Equipment at cost	58,000
Accumulated depreciation at 1 June 20X5	(19,000)
Depreciation for the year (58,000 × 15%)	(8,700)
	30,300

15 Control accounts

15.1 $79,000

Credit sales = $80,000* – $10,000 + $9,000 = $79,000.

*Total receipts of $85,000 include $5,000 in relation to cash sales. Therefore receipts in relation to credit sales are $80,000.

15.2 B A, C and D would make the supplier's statement $150 **higher**.

15.3 A

	$
Opening balance	34,500
Credit purchases	78,400
Discounts	(1,200)
Payments	(68,900)
Purchase returns	(4,700)
	38,100

15.4 A $8,500 – (2 × $400) = $7,700.

15.5 A Sales and refunds are posted on the **debit** side, changes in the allowance for receivables do not appear in the control account.

15.6 B

RECEIVABLES LEDGER CONTROL ACCOUNT

	$		$
Opening balance	180,000	Cash from credit customers	232,200
Credit sales	190,000	Irrecoverable debts written off	1,500
Cash refunds	3,300	Sales returns	8,000
		Contras	2,400
		Closing balance	129,200
	373,300		373,300

15.7 A

PAYABLES LEDGER CONTROL ACCOUNT

	$		$
Purchases returns	41,200	Bal b/f	318,600
Cash paid	1,364,300	Purchases	1,268,600
Discounts received	8,200	Refunds	2,700
Contras	48,000		
Bal c/f	128,200		
	1,589,900		1,589,900

15.8 $307,100

RECEIVABLES LEDGER CONTROL ACCOUNT

	$		$
Opening balance	308,600	Cash received	148,600
Credit sales	154,200	Contra	4,600
Interest charged	2,400	Irrecoverable debts	4,900
		Closing balance	307,100
	465,200		465,200

15.9 A

RECEIVABLES LEDGER CONTROL ACCOUNT

	$		$
Opening balance	614,000	Cash from customers	311,000
Credit sales	301,000	Irrecoverable debts written off	35,400
Interest charged on overdue		Contras	8,650
accounts	1,600	Closing balance	561,550
	916,600		916,600

15.10 A

	Debit	Credit	$
Sales price			800
Less: 20% trade discount			120
Less: 5% settlement discount			32
Sale	PQ Co	Sales	608
Cash payment	Bank	PQ Co	608
			608

Goods are sold with a trade discount of 20% ($120) so this is deducted from the sales price. Therefore $640 ($800 – $120) is invoiced to the customer.

The invoice also offers a settlement discount of 5% of the invoiced amount ($32) for early payment. Although it is uncertain if the customer will take advantage of this, you expect that they will, and so the settlement discount must be reflected in the amount recognised as revenue when recording the sale. Therefore $608 ($640 – $32) is recorded in sales, with a corresponding amount for trade receivables.

Since the customer did pay the discounted amount of $608, this amount is debited to bank and credited to the trade receivables.

B represents a situation where the customer was not expected to take up the discount at the time of the sale (and so revenue was recorded at the full invoiced amount), and did not take up the discount when they paid.

C represents a situation where the customer was expected to take up the discount at the time of the sale (and so revenue was recorded at the discounted invoiced amount), but did not take up the discount when they paid (and so the discount not taken was credited to revenue).

D represents a situation where the customer was not expected to take up the discount at the time of the sale (and so revenue was recorded at the full invoiced amount), but did take up the discount when they paid (and so the discount taken was debited to revenue).

15.11 B   A receivables ledger control account does not ensure the trial balance balances.

15.12 A

15.13 C

RECEIVABLES LEDGER CONTROL ACCOUNT

	$		$
Opening balance	318,650	Cash from customers	181,140
Credit sales	163,010	Irrecoverable debts written off	1,390
Interest on overdue accounts	280	Sales returns	3,990
		Closing balance	295,420
	481,940		481,940

15.14 A $130,585

PAYABLES LEDGER CONTROL ACCOUNT

	$		$
Returns outwards	27,490	Balance b/f	142,320
Payments to payables	196,360	Credit purchases (183,800 × 1.175)	215,965
Discount received	1,430		
Contra	2,420		
Balance c/f	130,585		
	358,285		358,285
		Balance b/f	130,585

15.15 C

Balance per ledger	$31,554	Cr
Discount	$53	Dr
Invoice	$622	Cr
Corrected balance	$32,123	

15.16 D

	Control account $	List of balances $
Balance/total	68,566	68,538
Credit balance omitted	–	127
Undercasting of day book	99	–
	68,665	68,665

15.17 D Trade payables are a current liability

15.18 B *Sales invoices:*

Invoices amounting to $2,000 should be recorded net of the 5% settlement discount (ie, $1,900), since Y Ltd expects X to take the discount on these. The remaining $3,000 of invoices should be recorded at the full amount.

Therefore, sales = ($1,900 + $3,000) = $4,900, with a corresponding amount for receivables.

Payment received:

Y Ltd did not expect Z to take the settlement discount on invoices of $3,000, so these would have been originally recorded in sales and receivables at the full amount of $3,000.

However Customer Z has paid £2,850 against receivables of $3,000. The difference of $150 is debited to sales and credited to receivables, thereby accounting for the discount.

15.19 C The invoice offers a settlement discount of 5% of the invoiced amount ($50) for early payment. Although it is uncertain if the customer will take advantage of this, you expect that they will not, therefore the full sales amount must be recognised as revenue when recording the sale, ie, $1,000.

As the customer did pay the discounted amount of $950, this amount is debited to bank, however this is against a receivable of $1,000, so the difference of $50 is debited to sales, to account for the fact that revenue has been reduced by the discount.

A represents a situation where the customer was expected to take up the discount at the time of the sale (and so revenue was recorded at the discounted invoiced amount), and took up the discount when they paid.

In B, the entry for the sale is correct. However, the entry for the payment is incorrect as the discount (which was not accounted for at the time of the sale) has still not been accounted for.

In D, the entry for the payment is correct. However, the entry for the sale is incorrect as it records the sale at the discounted amount, even though the customer was not expected to take the discount at the time of the sale.

16 Bank reconciliations

16.1 B $(565)o/d – $92 dishonoured cheque = $(657) o/d

16.2 $6,450 overdrawn

	$
Balance b/d	5,675 o/d
Less duplicated standing order	(125)
Add dishonoured cheque (450 × 2)	900
	6,450 o/d

16.3 A

	$
Opening bank balance	2,500
Payment ($1,000 – $200) × 90%	(720)
Receipt ($200 – $10)	190
Closing bank balance	1,970

16.4 B

	$
Balance per bank statement	(800)
Unpresented cheque	(80)
Dishonoured cheque (affects cash book only)	–
	(880)

16.5 B $11,200 overdrawn

Cash book	$	Bank statement	$
Balance	(8,970)	Balance b/f (bal fig)	(11,200)
Bank charges	(550)	Credit in error	(425)
		Unpresented cheques	(3,275)
		Outstanding deposits	5,380
	(9,520)		(9,520)

16.6 D

	$
Bank statement	(36,840)
Deposits credited after date	51,240
Unpresented cheques	(43,620)
Balance per cash book (o/d)	(29,220)

16.7 A, C   Dishonoured cheques and bank charges must be entered in the cash book.

16.8 B   Bank charges, direct debits and dishonoured cheques will all be written into the cash book.

16.9 B

	$
Overdraft	(3,860)
Unpresented cheques	(9,160)
	(13,020)
Outstanding lodgements	16,690
Cash at bank	3,670

16.10 A   Bank charges not entered in the cash book can be entered, and the cash book balance adjusted.

16.11 $11,200 overdrawn

Cash book	$	Bank statement	$
Balance	(8,970)	Balance	(11,200)
Bank charges	(550)	Credit in error	(425)
		Unpresented cheques	(3,275)
		Outstanding lodgements	5,380
	(9,520)		(9,520)

16.12 C   The bank is overdrawn.

	$
Overdraft	(38,600)
Outstanding lodgements	41,200
	2,600
Unpresented cheques	(3,300)
Overdraft	(700)

16.13 A   The other two items are part of the bank reconciliation.

16.14 B

	$
Overdraft per bank statement	39,800
Less: deposits credited after date	(64,100)
Add: unpresented cheques	44,200
Overdraft per cash book	19,900

16.15 B   Cash book 3, 5: bank reconciliation 1, 2, 4

17 Correction of errors

17.1 B   The credit note should have been **credited** to trade receivables, so the effect is doubled.

17.2 B   Start by posting the adjustment in full:

	Debit $	Credit $
Sales returns	384	296
Purchases returns	384	296
Suspense account		176

17.3 D   Returns outwards are returns to suppliers, which should therefore reduce the purchases balance – ie it should be a credit balance.
Option A would result in credits being higher than debits in the trial balance. Options B and C would not cause an imbalance.

17.4 A   B and C would make the credit side $50 higher. D would have no effect.

17.5 B   This has debited a non-current asset to cost of sales which is an error of principle as it has broken the principles of accounting – ie that non-current assets should be capitalised.

17.6 C   A transaction has been posted to the wrong account, but not the wrong class of account.

17.7 B   This is an error of original entry.

17.8 $97,100

	$
Draft net profit	83,600
Add: purchase price	18,000
Less: additional depreciation (18,000 × 25%)	(4,500)
Adjusted profit	97,100

17.9 B   The cash book was credited with $210 reimbursement of petty cash. However, the nominal ledger was posted with only $200 of expenditure (debits). Therefore the credits are $10 higher than the debits.

17.10 D $10,200 + $3,000 + $1,400 = $14,600.

17.11 A   Both errors will affect cost of sales and therefore gross profit, making a net effect of $40,000. Net profit will be further reduced by $10,000 missing from stationery expense.

17.12 D   Debits will exceed credits by 2 × $48 = $96

17.13 D   Errors of principle, such as recording a capital expenditure transaction as revenue expenditure, would not be revealed by a trial balance because it would not create an inequality between total debits and total credits. Transposition errors are errors where figures (digits) are written in the wrong order in either a credit or a debit entry. This would create an imbalance between credits and debits, and so the error would be indicated by extracting a trial balance.

17.14 C

	Debit $	Credit $
Non-current assets	85,000	
Receivables	7,000	
Trade payables		3,000
Bank loan		15,000
Allowance for depreciation, non-current assets		15,000
Inventory	4,000	
Accruals		1,000
Prepayments	2,000	
Bank overdraft		2,000
	98,000	36,000

17.15 $46,000

Debit balances	$	$
Purchases	160,000	
Non-current assets	120,000	
Receivables	33,000	
Other expenses	110,000	
Bank	18,000	
		441,000
Credit balances		
Payables	27,000	
Capital	66,000	
Sales	300,000	
Purchase returns	2,000	
		395,000
Bank loan (credit balance)		46,000

17.16 B $600,000 – $50,000 = $600,000. $150,000 – $50,000 = $100,000.

17.17 A   Statement of financial position $560, Statement of profit or loss $3,320.

ELECTRICITY ACCOUNT

		$		$
Balance b/fwd		300		
20X9:				
1 August	Paid bank	600		
1 November	Paid bank	720		
20Y0:				
1 February	Paid bank	900		
30 June	Paid bank	840		
30 June	Accrual c/d $840 × $^2/_3$	560	SPL	3,320
		3,620		3,620

17.18 D   This question tests whether candidates understand the nature of the errors and where the corrections need to be recorded.

Item 1 – there has been a transposition error recorded in the individual ledger, therefore the adjustment must be made in the receivables ledger.

Item 2 – This transaction is a cash sale, therefore it should not have been posted to individual receivables ledger and needs to be removed.

18 Suspense accounts

18.1 D   Error (5) will not cause a trial balance imbalance.

18.2 A

SUSPENSE ACCOUNT

	$		$
Share capital	3,000	Opening balance	3,460
Motor vehicles	9,000	Plant asset (2,800 × 2)	5,600
		Petty cash (TB)	500
		Closing balance	2,440
	12,000		12,000

18.3 B   This results in a debit to the suspense account therefore reducing the balance.

Option A results in a credit to the suspense account and Options C and D do not affect the suspense account at all.

18.4 B   (1)   This entry has been correctly debited but to the wrong account – no effect on trial balance
          (4)   Double entry has been carried out although the wrong way round – no effect on trial balance

18.5   A

SUSPENSE ACCOUNT

	$		$
Balance b/d	210	Gas bill[2] (420 – 240)	180
Interest[1]	70	Sales invoice[3] (2 × 50)	100
	280		280

[1] error of omission
[2] transposition error
[3] error of commission

18.6 C   The $25,000 currently held in the Suspense account needs to be posted to Plant and machinery.

18.7 $1,500 credit
          Suspense account

	$	
Opening balance	16,500	credit
Discount received (credit discount received)	(5,100)	debit
Transposition of cash received (credit RLCA)	(9,900)	debit
Balance remaining	1,500	credit

18.8 A, C   Only errors (A) and (C) involve a suspense account entry to correct them.

18.9 D   A and B will only affect the personal ledgers, C will cause an incorrect double entry.

18.10 B   A would give a debit balance of $130, C would have no effect and D would not cause a trial balance imbalance.

18.11 B   The initial step in correcting the error of commission would be to make a credit entry of $1,400 in the suspense account as follows:

DEBIT   Suspense account $1,400
CREDIT   Receivables control $1,400

The receivables control account and the suspense account would appear as follows:

RECEIVABLES CONTROL ACCOUNT

	$		$
Discounts allowed incorrectly debited	700	Suspense A/c Error corrected	1,400
Balance c/d	700		
	1,400		1,400

SUSPENSE ACCOUNT

	$		$
Receivables Con A/c Error corrected	1,400	Balance b/f	560
		(Remaining) Balance c/d	840
	1,400		1,400

The remaining balance on the suspense account is $840.

19 15 mark questions: preparing financial statements

19.1 Shuswap

Task 1

The correct answer is:

Inventory should be credited with $140,000

The sale was made after the year end but provides evidence that inventory was overvalued at the year end.

Task 2

There is $100,000 loss on disposal.

	$'000
Carrying amount	700
Proceeds (5,000,000 – (4,000,000 × $1.10))	(600)
Loss	100

The depreciation adjustment is $350,000 (1,400,000 × 25%)

Task 3

	DR	CR	Neither DR nor CR
Issued share capital		O	
Share premium		O	
Cash			O
Plant and equipment – cost			O
Plant and equipment – disposal account		O	
Suspense account	O		

Balances after the suspense account has been cleared will be:

Share capital $8,000,000 (6,000,000 + (4,000,000 × 50c))

Share premium $2,400,000 (4,000,000 × 60c)

Task 4

	DR	CR	Neither DR nor CR
Irrecoverable debts	O		
Depreciation adjustment (Task 2)		O	
Inventory adjustment (Task 1)	O		

19.2 Malright

Task 1

	On SFP	Not on SFP
Buildings at cost	O	
Buildings, accumulated depreciation, 1 November 20X6		O
Plant at cost	O	
Plant, accumulated depreciation, 1 November 20X6		O
Bank balance	O	
Revenue		O
Purchases		O

	On SFP	Not on SFP
Inventory at 1 November 20X6		O
Cash	O	
Trade payables	O	
Trade receivables	O	
Administrative expenses		O
Allowance for receivables, at 1 November 20X6		O
Retained earnings at 1 November 20X6		O
$1 ordinary shares	O	
Share premium account	O	

Task 2

	DR	CR	Neither DR nor CR
Trade receivable			O
Administrative expenses	O		
Allowance for receivables		O	
Revenue			O

The amount included in the statement of profit or loss after the allowance is increased to 5% of trade receivables is $6,000. ((320,000 × 5%) − 10,000)

Task 3

	DR	CR	Neither DR nor CR
Administrative expenses			O
Cost of sales	O		
Buildings cost			O
Plant cost			O
Buildings accumulated depreciation		O	
Plant accumulated depreciation		O	

Depreciation charge for the year ended 31 October 20X7:

Buildings $37,000 (740,000 × 5%)

Plant $22,000 ((220,000 − 110,000) × 20%)

Task 4

Cost of sales for the year is $1,225,000

	$'000
Opening inventory	160
Purchases	1,140
Closing inventory	(75)
	1,225

Task 5

The double entry to post the year end adjustments for energy costs is:

	DR	CR
Accrual		O
Administrative expenses	O	

The amount to be posted within the year end adjustment double entry above is $10,000 (15,000 × 2/3)

19.3 **Tonson**

Task 1

	P/L	Not P/L
Inventory at 1 November 20X5		O
Administrative expenses	O	
Share premium account		O
Retained earnings at 1 November 20X5		O
Allowance for receivables at 1 November 20X5		O
Sales revenue	O	
Bank		O
Returns inward	O	
Trade payables		O
Loan note interest	O	
Trade receivables		O
Purchases	O	
7% loan notes		O
Irrecoverable debts	O	
$1 ordinary shares		O
Accumulated depreciation at 1 November 20X5		
Buildings		O
Motor Vehicles		O
Furniture and equipment		O
Land at cost		O
Buildings at cost		O
Motor vehicles at cost		O
Furniture and equipment at cost		O

Task 2

Carrying amount in the financial statements at 31 October 20X6

Land $740,000
Buildings $1,065,000 (1,500 – 360 – (1,500 × 5%))
Motor vehicles $128,000 (240 – 80 – ((240 – 80) × 20%))
Furniture and equipment $540,000 (1,200 – 420 – (1,200 × 20%))

Task 3

	Debit	Credit
Inventory valuation adjustment	O	
Administrative expenses relating to November 20X6		O
Increase in allowance for receivables	O	
Outstanding wages and salaries	O	

Task 4

The bonus issue will not affect Tonson's cash balance.

Balances following the bonus issue:

Share capital $1,980,000 (1,800 + 180)
Share premium $20,000 (200 – 180)

19.4 **Emma**

EMMA
STATEMENT OF CASH FLOWS FOR THE YEAR ENDED 31 DECEMBER 20X2 (extract)

	$'000	
Cash flows from operating activities		
Net profit before taxation	350	
Adjustments for:		
Depreciation	90	Add
Loss on sale of non-current assets	13	Add
Profit on sale of non-current asset investments	(5)	Subtract
Increase in inventories	(48)	Subtract
Increase in receivables	(75)	Subtract
Increase in payables	8	Add
Income taxes paid	(190)	Subtract
Cash flows from investing activities		
Purchase of intangible non-current assets	(50)	Subtract
Purchase of tangible non-current assets	(201)	Subtract
Receipts from sale of non-current assets	62	Add
Cash flows from financing activities		
Proceeds from issue of share capital	60	Add
Long-term loan	100	Add

Workings

1   *Depreciation charge*

	$'000	$'000
Depreciation at 31 December 20X2		340
Depreciation 31 December 20X1	290	
Depreciation on assets sold (85 – 45)	40	
		250
Charge for the year		90

2   *Tax paid*

INCOME TAX

	$'000		$'000
Tax paid	190	1.1.X2 balance b/d	240
31.12.X2 balance c/d	290	Statement of profit or loss	240
	480		480

3   *Purchase of tangible non-current assets*

TANGIBLE NON-CURRENT ASSETS

	$'000		$'000
1.1.X2 Balance b/d	595	Disposals	85
Revaluation (100 – 91)	9		
Purchases (bal fig)	201	31.12.X2 Balance c/d	720
	805		805

19.5 **Sioux**

SIOUX
STATEMENT OF CASH FLOWS FOR THE YEAR ENDED 31 DECEMBER 20X4

	$'000	
Net profit before tax	2,350	Before tax
Add: depreciation (W)	1,250	Add
Less: profit on disposal (500 – 350)	(150)	Subtract
Decrease in inventories	400	Add
Increase in receivables	(900)	Subtract
Increase in payables	500	Add
Tax paid	(600)	Subtract
Cash flows from investing activities		
Payments to acquire non-current assets (W)	(3,300)	Subtract
Proceeds from sale of non-current assets	500	Add
Cash flows from financing activities		
Proceeds from issue of loan notes (3,000 – 2,000)	1,000	Add
Dividends paid	(750)	Subtract
Net increase in cash	300	
Cash at 1 January 20X4	100	
Cash at 31 December 20X4	400	

Workings

Non-current assets

NON-CURRENT ASSETS AT COST

	$		$
Opening balance	8,000	Disposal	800
Revaluation	500	Closing balance	11,000
Additions (balance figure)	3,300		
	11,800		11,800

NON-CURRENT ASSETS – ACCUMULATED DEPRECIATION

	$		$
Disposal (800 – 350)	450	Opening balance	4,800
Closing balance	5,600	Charge for year (balance figure)	1,250
	6,050		6,050

19.6 **Snowdrop**

SNOWDROP LIMITED
STATEMENT OF CASH FLOWS FOR THE YEAR ENDED 31 MAY 20X5

	$'000	
Cash flows from operating activities		
Net profit before tax	1,032	Before
Adjustments for		
Depreciation	700	Add
Loss on disposal of non-current assts	20	Add
Increase in inventory	(80)	Subtract
Increase in receivables	(130)	Subtract
Increase in payables	85	Add
Income taxes paid (W1)	(145)	Subtract
Dividends paid	(270)	Subtract
Cash flow from investing activities		
Purchase of non-current assets (W2)	(2,800)	
Receipts from sales of tangible non-current assets	180	
Cash flows from financing activities		
Proceeds from issue of share capital	1,280	Add
Repayment of long term borrowing	(100)	Subtract
Net increase/(decrease) in cash and cash equivalents	(228)	
Cash and cash equivalents at the beginning of period	170	
Cash and cash equivalents at end of period	(58)	

Note. Dividends paid and interest paid may be shown in either operating activities or financing activities.

Workings

1   *Tax paid*

TAXATION

	$'000		$'000
Tax paid (bal fig)	145	Balance b/fwd	145
Balance c/fwd	180	Statement of profit or loss	180
	325		325

2   *Payments for tangible non-current assets*

TANGIBLE NON-CURRENT ASSETS

	$'000		$'000
Balance b/fwd	2,700	Depreciation	700
Additions (bal fig)	2,800	Disposals (carrying amount)	200
		Balance c/fwd	4,600
	5,500		5,500

19.7 Geofrost

GEOFROST
STATEMENT OF CASH FLOWS FOR THE YEAR ENDED 31 OCTOBER 20X7

	$	
Cash flows from operating activities		
Net profit before tax	15,000	Before tax
Adjustments for		
Depreciation	4,658	Add
Profit on disposal of non-current assets (W1)	(720)	Subtract
Decrease in inventory	6,075	Add
Increase in receivables	(1,863)	Subtract
Increase in payables	3,198	Add
Tax paid (W2)	(4,090)	Subtract
Cash flows from investing activities		
Payments to acquire tangible non-current assets	(24,340)	Subtract
Proceeds from sale of non-current assets	2,694	Add
Cash flows from financing activities		
Proceeds from issue of share capital	1,869	Add
Repayment of long term borrowing	(2,300)	Subtract
Net increase in cash and cash equivalents	181	Increase
Cash and cash equivalents at the beginning of period	634	
Cash and cash equivalents at end of period	815	

Workings

1   *Profit on sale of tangible non-current asset*

	$'000
Sale proceeds	2,694
Net book value	1,974
Profit	720

2   *Tax paid*

TAXATION

	$'000		$'000
Tax paid (bal fig)	4,090	Balance b/f	2,760
Balance c/f	3,020	Statement of profit or loss	4,350
	7,110		7,110

20 Incomplete records

20.1 C

	$
Opening inventory	386,200
Purchases	989,000
Closing inventory	(422,700)
Cost of sales	952,500

952,500 × 100/60 = 1,587,500

20.2 A   Closing net assets plus drawings minus capital introduced minus opening net assets.

20.3 B   Cost of sales = $114,000

Therefore sales should be = $114,000 × 100/60 = $190,000

Theft = $190,000 – 181 600 = $8,400

20.4 $744,960

TOTAL RECEIVABLES ACCOUNT

	$		$
Opening balance	130,000	Cash received	687,800
Sales (balancing figure)	744,960	Irrecoverable debts	4,160
		Contra	2,000
		Closing balance	181,000
	874,960		874,960

20.5 D

TOTAL PAYABLES ACCOUNT

	$		$
Cash paid	302,800	Opening balance	60,000
Discounts received	2,960	Purchases (balancing figure)	331,760
Contra	2,000		
Closing balance	84,000		
	391,760		391,760

20.6 C   Cost of sales = $281,250 × 2/3 = $187,500
Loss of inventory = $228,200 – 187,500 = $40,700

20.7 D

	$
Opening inventory	318,000
Purchases	412,000
Closing inventory	(214,000)
	516,000
Notional cost of sales (612,000 × 75%)	(459,000)
Inventory lost	57,000

20.8 A

	$'000
Profit for the year	1,175
Add back depreciation	100
	1,275
Add: issue of shares	1,000
Less: repayment of loan notes	(750)
Less: purchase of non current assets	(200)
	1,325
Less: increase in working capital	(575)
Increase in bank balance	750

20.9 C

	$
Capital at 1 April 20X7	6,500
Add: profit (after drawings)	32,500
Less: sales tax element	(70)
Capital at 31 March 20X8	38,930

20.10 $937,050

PURCHASES CONTROL ACCOUNT

	$		$
Payments to suppliers	888,400	Opening balance	130,400
Discounts received	11,200	Goods taken	1,000
Closing balance	171,250	Refunds received	2,400
		Purchases (bal fig)	937,050
	1,070,850		1,070,850

20.11 A $669,375

Cost of sales

	$
Opening inventory	243,000
Purchases	595,400
Less: purchases returns	(41,200)
	797,200
Less: closing inventory	(261,700)
	535,500

Sales = 535,500 × 100/80 = $669,375

20.12 A

Sales = 381,600 + 6,800 + 112,900 + 7,200 = $508,500

20.13 D   Cost of sales: $17,000 + $91,000 − $24,000 = $84,000

Sales	100%
Cost of sales	60%
Gross profit	40%

Sales: $\dfrac{\$84,000}{60\%}$ = $140,000

20.14 B

	$
Sales (100%)	64,800
Cost of sales (70%)	45,360
Gross profit (30%)	19,440

	$
Opening inventory	28,400
Purchases	49,600
	78,000
Calculated closing inventory (bal fig)	(32,640)
Cost of sales	45,360
Calculated closing inventory	32,640
Actual closing inventory	−
Destroyed by fire	32,640

20.15 A

	$
Cost of sales	
Opening inventory	38,000
Purchases	637,000
Less: closing inventory	(45,000)
	630,000

Sales 630,000 × 100/70 = $900,000

20.16 C   Opening net assets + Profit + Capital introduced − Drawings = Closing net assets
             210,000 + Profit + 100,000 − 48,000 = 400,000

Profit = $138,000

21 Company financial statements

21.1 D The revaluation surplus is part of equity. Dividends paid on redeemable preference shares are treated like interest paid on loans, and are therefore accrued for as finance costs in the financial statements.

21.2 B, D Profit on disposal of properties will be included in profit in the statement of profit or loss and other comprehensive income. Equity dividends proposed after the reporting period are disclosed by note.

21.3 B

	$
Receivables and prepayments	
Insurance 9,000 × 8/12 prepayment	6,000
Loan (receivable)	12,000
Interest due 12,000 × 2% (receivable)	240
Rent due (receivable)	4,000
	22,240

21.4 D All of these items must be disclosed, either on the face of the main financial statements or in the notes. Although dividends proposed are not included in the statement of changes in equity, they must still be disclosed in the notes.

21.5 The correct answers are:

In preparing a statement of cash flows, either the direct or the indirect method may be used. Both lead to the same figure for net cash from operating activities.	**True**	
Loan notes can be classified as current or non-current liabilities.	**True**	
Financial statements must disclose a company's total expense for depreciation, if material.	**True**	
A company must disclose, by note, details of all adjusting events allowed for in the financial statements.		**False**

Adjusting events after the reporting period should be adjusted for, not just disclosed.

21.6 A, C The loss on sale of investments will have been recognised in the statement of profit or loss and other comprehensive income. Dividends proposed after the year end are disclosed in the notes, they are not recognised in the financial statements.

21.7 D Loan stock is a non-current liability.
Share premium account is a statutory reserve.
Retained earnings is otherwise known as the revenue reserve.
Revaluation surplus is an unrealised reserve.

21.8 B The total will be $260,000, of which $60,000 will be credited to share premium.

21.9 C A revaluation surplus arises when a non-current asset is **revalued**. Loan notes are not part of share capital.

21.10 $22,500

The under provision for the previous year of $2,500 plus the provision for the current year of $20,000 gives a charge to the statement of profit or loss of $22,500.

22 Disclosure notes

22.1   A   Disclosure notes provide more detail about the information in the main financial statements.

22.2   B   A reconciliation of the opening and closing carrying amounts is required by IAS 16 for tangible non-current assets and by IAS 38 for intangible assets.

22.3   B   IAS 2 requires disclosure of the accounting policies adopted in measuring inventories, including the cost formula used, the total carrying amount of inventories and the carrying amount in classifications appropriate to the entity and the carrying amount of inventories carried at net realisable value.

22.4   A   IAS 38 does not require the net realisable value of deferred development costs to be disclosed.

22.5   C   Both statements are correct.

22.6   B   These are the disclosure requirements given in IAS 37 for contingent liabilities.

22.7   C   IAS 16 does not require disclosure of the market value of all tangible non-current assets.

22.8   B   Inventories must be valued at the lower of cost and net realisable value. The amount of any write-down in the period must be disclosed, and so too must the carrying amount of inventories classified by type and the cost of inventories recognised as an expense in the period. There is no requirement to disclose the original cost of inventories that have been written down in value.

22.9   D   IAS 10 requires disclosure of the nature of material non-adjusting events after the reporting period and either an estimate of the financial effect of the event or a statement that a reasonable estimate cannot be made.

23 Events after the reporting period

23.1   A   All of these events are indicative of conditions that existed at the reporting period.

23.2   A, D   B and C do not affect the company's position at the end of the reporting period.

23.3   B   These affect valuation of receivables and inventory at the end of the reporting period.

23.4   B   These events are adjusting if discovered between the reporting date and the date the financial statements are authorised for issue as they provide evidence about conditions that existed at the reporting date: insolvency of an account receivable which was outstanding at the end of the reporting period, discovery of fraud or error which shows that the financial statements were incorrect, sale of inventory which gives evidence about its value at the end of the reporting period.

23.5   B   (2) and (4) both affect the valuation of assets at the end of the reporting period.

23.6   C   IAS 10 requires the financial statements to be adjusted for events that reflect conditions that existed at the reporting date. Only Event (3) is indicative of conditions at the reporting date – ie the recoverability of the receivable balance. Events (1) and (2) are non-adjusting events, however, they are material so they should be disclosed.

23.7   D   None of these events require adjustment in the financial statements.

23.8   A   An adjusting event after the reporting date is event that occurs between the reporting date and the date on which the financial statements are authorised for issue that provides further evidence of conditions that existed at the reporting date. The event must occur **after** the reporting period but **before** the date the financial statements are authorised for issue.

23.9   A   The nature of the event and an estimate of the financial effect (or a statement that such an estimate cannot be made) should be disclosed.

24 Statements of cash flows

24.1 C   Only the proceeds of a share issue and dividends received involve the movement of cash.

24.2 D   Loss on sale of non-current assets should be added back to net profit before tax.

24.3 D

	$
Add: depreciation charge	980,000
Less: profit on sale of assets	(40,000)
Less: increase in inventories	(130,000)
Add: decrease in receivables	100,000
Add: increase in payables	80,000
Addition to operating profit	990,000

24.4 B   Depreciation should be added back as it not a cash flow and proceeds of sale of non-current assets appears under 'investing' cash flows.

24.5 D   None of them

(1)   Proceeds from sale of premises appears under investing activities.
(2)   Dividends received appears under operating or investing activities.
(3)   A bonus issue of shares is not a cash flow.

24.6 C   (3) only

(1)   The direct and indirect methods will give the correct figure.

(2)   A rights issue of shares is a cash flow.

(4)   The profit on sale of a non-current asset appears as an adjustment to profit in order to reach net cash flow from operations.

24.7 A, D   The depreciation charge and the increase in payables should both have been added.

24.8 B   Neither a proposed dividend nor a bonus issue of shares involve the movement of cash.

24.9 B   Proceeds from sale of equipment are included in investing activities.

24.10 B

		$'000
Cash flows from financing:		
Issue of share capital	(120 + 60) – (80 + 40)	60
Repayment of bank loan	(100 – 150)	(50)
		10

24.11 D   (2) and (4). Decrease in inventories should be added, decrease in payables should be deducted.

24.12 B   The corrected extract is as follows:

	$'000
Net cash flow from operating activities	
Profit before tax	484
Depreciation charges	327
Profit on sale of property, plant and equipment	(35)
Increase in inventories	(74)
Decrease in trade and other receivables	41
Increase in trade payables	29
Cash generated from operations	772

24.13 D   Interest received and proceeds from the sale of property are cash flows from investing activities; taxation paid is a cash flow from operating activities.

24.14 A   The net cash flows from operating activities will be the same using the two methods.

24.15 $204,000

	$'000
Carrying amount of assets at beginning of the year	462
Increase in revaluation surplus during the year	50
Book value of assets disposed of (110 – 65)	(45)
Depreciation charge for the year	(38)
	429
Carrying amount of assets at end of the year	633
Purchases of property, plant and equipment during the year	204

24.16 C   A loss on disposal of a non-current asset is added back as an adjustment in the calculation of cash flows from operating activities (using the indirect method), and the cash received from the disposal is included within cash flows from investing activities

24.17 B
Cash flows from operating activities	$
Cash received from customers ($400 + $33,400 – $900)	32,900
Cash paid to suppliers ($1,000 + $18,500 – $2,550)	(16,950)
Cash paid to employees ($1,500 + $9,500 – $750)	(10,250)
Interest paid	(2,100)
Interest received	175
Net cash flow from operating activities	3,775

24.18 C   A business may make a profit but have negative cash flow.

24.19 D   Jo is correct. A business that does not have cash available to fund operations is likely to fail.

24.20 B   There is an opportunity to reclassify some cash outflows that might have been reported in the operating section as investing cash outflows. For example, questionable capitalisation of expenses.

24.21 D   This question is focused around the cash actually received during the financial year ended 31 March 2017. Therefore, we need to consider (i) the amount owed to the company at the beginning of the year that will be paid during the financial year ie the receivables at 1 April 2016, (ii) the sales during the year, and (iii) the amounts owed to the company at the end of the year ie receivables at 31 March 2017.

The calculation can be summarised as follows:

	$
Receivables at 1 April 2016	163,000
Sales during the year	750,000
Total	913,000
Less receivables at 31 March 2017	184,000
	729,000

25 15 mark questions: preparing simple consolidated financial statements

25.1   **Swing and Cat**

Task 1

	$	$'000
Fair value of consideration transferred		120
Plus fair value of non-controlling interest at acquisition		40
Less fair value of net assets acquired as represented by		
Ordinary share capital	100	
Retained earnings	50	
		(150)
Goodwill		10

Task 2

$ 10,000

	$
Profit on intra-group sale (100,000 – 80,000)	20,000
Unrealised profit (50% × 20,000)*	10,000

- 50% of the inventories from the intra-group sales remain in inventories at the year end, therefore the unrealised profit is 50% of the overall profit made on the intra-group sales. The rest of the profit from the intra-group sales is now realised as the inventories have been sold outside the group.

Task 3

Consolidated cost of sales is $3,410,000

	$'000
Swing	2,900
Cat	600
Intragroup purchases	(100)
Unrealised profit	10
	3,410

Task 4

The correct statements are:

Non-controlling interest describes shares in the subsidiary not held by the parent

20% of Cat's profit after tax will be allocated to the non-controlling interest

Task 5

	Swing $'000	Cat $'000
Per question	400	200
Adjustment (unrealised profit (W2))	(10)	
Pre-acquisition retained earnings		(50)
		150
Group share of Cat (80% × 150)	120	
Group retained earnings	510	

25.2 **Black and Bury**

Task 1

$21,000,000

	$'000
Fair value of net assets acquired:	
Share capital	30,000
Retained earnings	2,000
Goodwill acquired	800
Less fair value of NCI	(11,800)
Consideration transferred	21,000

Task 2

The dividend due to Black from Bury will be eliminated on consolidation.

This is an intragroup item.

The dividend due to be paid by Black will be shown in current liabilities.

This is not intragroup, it is owed to third parties. It is not deducted from profit as it is a distribution, not an expense.

Task 3

The unrealised profit is $1,440,000 (12m × 40% × 30%)

This is posted: DR Retained earnings / CR Inventory

Task 4

Dr Payables / Cr Receivables

This removes the intragroup amount from payables and receivables

Task 5

Non-controlling interest in the consolidated SPL is $4,500,000 (15,000,000 × 30%)

Non-controlling interest in the consolidated SFP:

	$'000
Fair value at acquisition	11,800
Share of post-acquisition retained earnings ((10,280 − 2,000) × 30%)	2,484
Total	14,284

25.3 **Prestend**

Task 1

	$'000
Fair value of consideration transferred	3,345
Plus fair value of NCI at acquisition	1,415
Total A	1,930
Fair value of net assets acquired:	
Ordinary share capital	4,000
Retained earnings at acquisition	60
Total B	4,060

Formula for goodwill = A − 100%B

Task 2

Unrealised profit on intragroup sales = $20,000 (240,000 × 20/120 × 50%)

Task 3

The correct answers are:

Ownership of more than 50% of equity shares

Power to appoint or remove the majority of board members

Ownership of preference shares does not give control as they are usually non-voting. Significant influence is not the same as control.

Task 4

	Prestend	Northon	
	$'000	$'000	
Per question	525	200	
Adjustment for unrealised profit	(20)		Subtract
Pre-acquisition retained earnings		(60)	Subtract
Total Northon		140	
Group share of Northon (70% × 140)	98		
Group retained earnings	603		

25.4 **Liverton and Everpool**

Task 1

	$'000
Fair value of consideration transferred	3,500
Fair value of NCI at acquisition	1,000
Total	4,500
Fair value of net assets acquired	
Share capital	4,000
Retained earnings at acquisition	200
Total	4,200
Goodwill	300

Task 2

Unrealised profit: ((200,000 – 120,000) × 60%) = $48,000

Task 3

CONSOLIDATED STATEMENT OF PROFIT OR LOSS FOR THE YEAR ENDED 31 MAY 20X6

	$'000
Sales revenue (6,400 + 2,600 – 200)	8,800
Cost of sales (3,700 + 1,450 – 200 + 48)	(4,998)
Gross profit	3,802
Distribution costs (1,110 + 490)	(1,590)
Administration expenses (700 + 320)	(1,020)
Profit before tax	1,192
Tax (400 + 80)	(480)
Profit for the year	712
Profit attributable to	
Owners of the parent	647
Non-controlling interest (25% × 260)	65
	712

26 Consolidated financial statements

26.1 C

	$	$
Fair value of consideration		270,000
Plus fair value of NCI at acquisition		42,000
Less net acquisition-date fair value of identifiable assets acquired and liabilities assumed:		
Share capital	100,000	
Retained earnings at acquisition	90,000	
		190,000
Goodwill in statement of financial position		122,000

26.2 A

	$
Non-controlling interest	
Fair value of NCI at acquisition	42,000
Plus NCI's share of post-acq'n retained earnings (10% × (160 – 90))	7,000
NCI at reporting date	49,000

26.3

$273,000	$
Alpha retained earnings	210,000
Group share post-acq'n ret'd earnings:	
Beta ((160,000 – 90,000) × 90%)	63,000
	273,000

26.4 C   Iota is a subsidiary as Gamma has power to cast a majority of votes at meetings of the board of directors. Kappa is a subsidiary as Gamma owns >50% of the ordinary shares of Kappa, it doesn't make any difference that Kappa is based overseas or pays tax in that country. Zeta is not a subsidiary of Gamma because Gamma's investment in the non-voting preference shares will not give it the ability to control Zeta.

26.5 C

	$	$
Fair value of consideration		280,000
Plus fair value of NCI at acquisition		65,000
Less net acquisition-date fair value of identifiable assets acquired and liabilities assumed:		
Share capital	140,000	
Share premium	50,000	
Retained earnings at acquisition	60,000	
		250,000
Goodwill		95,000

26.6 C

Non-controlling interest	$
Fair value of NCI at acquisition	65,000
Plus NCI's share of post-acq'n retained earnings (20% × (100 – 60))	8,000
NCI at reporting date	73,000

26.7 D

	$'000
Fair value of net assets acquired:	
Ordinary shares	400
Retained earnings at 1 January 20X7	100
Retained earnings for 9 months to acquisition date (80 × 9/12)	60
	560
Add goodwill	30
	590

26.8 B Deciduous is an associate of Evergreen. Under equity accounting, the Evergreen group's share of the profit after tax of Deciduous is added to the group profit before tax.

26.9 A

	$
Mercedes Co retained earnings	450,000
Benz Co retained earnings	
Unrealised profit in closing inventory (50,000 × 25/125)	(10,000)
Consolidated retained earnings at 31 March 20X9	560,000

26.10 B

	$	$
Fair value of consideration		300,000
Plus fair value of NCI at acquisition		75,000
Less net acquisition-date fair value of identifiable assets acquired and liabilities assumed:		
Share capital	100,000	
Retained earnings at acquisition	156,000	
Fair value adjustment at acquisition	20,000	
		276,000
Goodwill		99,000

26.11 D

	$'000
Unrealised profit (30,000 × 25% × 40%)	3
Gross profit (330 + 300 – 3)	627

26.12 A, B An investor must have significant influence over the investee in order for the investee to be classified as an associate. If the investor holds 20% or more of the voting power of the entity, significant influence can be assumed (unless it can clearly be shown that this is not the case). Therefore (A) is true. For an investee to be classified as a subsidiary, the investor (the parent) must have control over the investee (the subsidiary). Control can be demonstrated if the investor has the power to appoint the majority of board members of the investee, so (B) is true. (C) is incorrect because the power to govern the financial and operating policies of Fef make Fef a subsidiary of Ear. Likewise, (D) is incorrect as the power to govern the financial and operating policies of Hay makes Hay a subsidiary of Gee.

26.13 C Tangerine is an associate of Clementine, however because Clementine has no other investments in other companies, it will not produce consolidated financial statements. Under IAS 27, Tangerine can choose to account for the investment at cost, or the equity method. In this scenario, it has chosen to account for the investment at cost, therefore the investment will appear in the single company financial statements of Clementine as a simple investment. The statement of financial position will show an investment at cost and the statement of profit or loss will show dividends received from Tangerine. If Clementine instead did produce consolidated financial statements, Tangerine would have to be accounted for in the consolidated financial statements using the equity method.

26.14 B A parent may hold less than 50% of the share capital but more than 50% of the voting rights. Goodwill only appears in the **consolidated** statement of financial position. Consolidated financial statements present the substance of the relationship between parent and subsidiaries, rather than the legal form.

26.15 D S is not a subsidiary as P's shareholdings in S do not give it the power to control S. R is a subsidiary as P has the right to appoint or remove the directors of R, and so control it.

26.16 C Investments in associates are accounted for using equity accounting. An investment is an associate if the investor has significant influence over the investee. Significant influence is presumed if the investor owns at least 20% of the voting equity of the investee. Therefore (2) is not an associate. (1) and (4) are subsidiaries as Company A investor has control over them.

26.17 C

	$'000	$'000
Fair value of consideration (bal fig)		620
Plus fair value of NCI at acquisition		150
Less net acquisition-date fair value of identifiable assets acquired and liabilities assumed:		
Share capital	500	
Retained earnings at acquisition	150	
Revaluation surplus at acquisition	50	
		(700)
Goodwill		70

26.18 A $950 + $1,250 + $50 = $2,250,000

26.19 A The $30,000 owed by Seven Co to Six Co is included within the receivables of Six Co and the payables of Seven Co. These intra-group balances should be eliminated for the purpose of consolidation.

Trade receivables = $(64,000 + 39,000 – 30,000) = $73,000

Trade payables = $(37,000 + 48,000 – 30,000) = $55,000

The unrealised profit on closing inventory will be an adjustment to inventory on consolidation, and does not affect consolidated receivables and payables.

26.20 $27,800

	$
Fair value of NCI at date of acquisition	25,000
NCI share of retained post-acquisition earnings: 20% × $(60,000 – 40,000)	4,000
	29,000
NCI share in unrealised profit: 20% × 50% × $12,000	(1,200)
Non-controlling interest at 31 December 20X4	27,800

26.21 A   Retained post-acquisition earnings of Lava Co = 4/12 × $(336,000 – 264,000) = $24,000.

	$000
Volcano retained earnings	650
Parent company share of post-acquisition earnings: 75% × $24,000	18
Parent company's share of consolidated retained earnings at 31 Dec 20X3	668

26.22 B   Post-acquisition earnings of Drum Co = 9/12 × $60,000 = $45,000.

	$
Tin Co profit for the year	70,000
Parent company share of post-acquisition profit of Drum Co: 90% × $45,000	40,500
Parent company's share of consolidated retained earnings at 31 Dec 20X3	110,500

26.23 C   The unrealised profit in the closing inventory of Sand Co = 25% × 40% × $40,000 = $4,000.
The NCI share of this is 20% × $4,000 = $800.

	$	$
NCI share of profit of Sun Co: 20% × $35,000		7,000
Less: NCI share of unrealised profit		(800)
		6,200
Combined profits of Sand Co and Sun Co: (120,000 + 35,000)	155,000	
Less: Unrealised profit in closing inventory	(4,000)	
Total consolidated profit for the year		151,000
Attributable to the parent company		144,800

26.24 B

	$'000
Shares (18m × 2/3 × $5.75)	69,000

26.25 B

	X Co $'000	Y Co × 2/12 $'000	Adj $'000	Group $'000
Revenue	3,400	400	(10)	3,790
Cost of sales	1,500	300	(10 –1*)	1,791
				1,999

* Unrealised profit

		$
Sale price	125%	10,000
Cost price	100%	(8,000)
Gross profit	25%	2,000
Unrealised profit	(2,000 × 50%)	1,000

26.26 D

Eliminate unrealised profit on goods in inventory of WX:

		$
Sale price	120%	60,000
Cost price	100%	(50,000)
Gross profit	20%	10,000

Unrealised profit attributable to NCI = $10,000 × 25% = $2,500

Unrealised profit attributable to WX = $10,000 × 75% = $7,500

26.27 D

	$'000
Net profit of S	60 000
NCI share of profit of S (20%)	(12,000)

Because the sale was made from the parent, P to the subsidiary, S, there is no unrealised profit attributable to the non-controlling interest.

27 15 mark question: interpretation of financial statements

Binky and Smokey

Task 1

		Binky		Smokey	

Gross profit % $\dfrac{\text{Gross profit}}{\text{Sales}} \times 100$ $\dfrac{129}{284} \times 100$ = 45.4% $\dfrac{154}{305} \times 100 = 50.5\%$

Net profit % $\dfrac{\text{Net profit}}{\text{Sales}} \times 100$ $\dfrac{61}{284} \times 100$ = 21.5% $\dfrac{47}{305} \times 100 = 15.4\%$

Asset turnover $\dfrac{\text{Sales}}{\text{Capital employed}} \times 100$ $\dfrac{284}{258} \times 100$ = 110.1% $\dfrac{305}{477} \times 100 = 63.9\%$

Current ratio $\dfrac{\text{Current assets}}{\text{Current liabilities}}$ $\dfrac{201}{188}$ = 1.1:1 $\dfrac{383}{325} = 1.2:1$

Quick ratio $\dfrac{\text{Current assets} - \text{inventory}}{\text{Current liabilities}}$ $\dfrac{110}{188}$ = 0.6:1 $\dfrac{90}{325} = 0.3:1$

Receivables collection period $\dfrac{\text{Receivables}}{\text{Sales}} \times 365$ $\dfrac{46}{284} \times 365$ = 59.1 days $\dfrac{75}{305} \times 365 = 89.8$ days

Task 2

Of the two companies **Binky** has the higher net profit percentage. This is due to **lower expenses**.

Both companies have low quick ratios. In Smokey's case this is because much of its working capital is tied up in **inventory**. This has given rise to **liquidity** problems.

Smokey needs to improve credit control.

The **asset turnover** ratio shows that Binky is making better use of its working capital than Smokey.

28 Interpretation of financial statements

28.1 A   Issuing further loan notes and paying dividends will **increase** gearing. A bonus issue simply capitalises reserves, so has no effect.

28.2 D   Understatement of the December 20X1 closing inventory will lead to understatement of December 20X2 opening inventory and therefore understatement of cost of sales.

28.3 A   Profit will be an addition to owner's capital.

28.4 D   Purchases = \$(32,500 – 6,000 + 3,800)
= \$30,300

∴ Accounts payable payment period = $\dfrac{4,750}{30,300} \times 365 = 57$ days

TOKEN		Question 28.5	Question 28.6	Question 28.7
		Gearing	Quick ratio	Current ratio
		13%	1.75	2.56
16%				
20%				
24%				
2.88				
3.20				

28.5 $$\text{Gearing} = \frac{\text{Total long term debt}}{\text{Total long term debt} + \text{share holders equity}} = \frac{75}{75+500} = 13\%$$

28.6 $$\text{Quick ratio} = \frac{\text{Current assets} - \text{Inventory}}{\text{Current liabilities}} = \frac{205-65}{80} = 1.75$$

28.7 $$\text{Current ratio} = \frac{\text{Current assets}}{\text{Current liabilities}} = \frac{205}{80} = 2.56$$

28.8 C The gearing ratio is used to assess how much the company owes in relation to its size.

28.9 B

	%	$
Sales	100	2,400
Cost of sales	66 2/3	1,600
Gross profit	33 1/3	800
Expenses	28 1/3	680
Net profit	5	120

28.10 C Current ratio is 2,900 : 1,100 = 2.6: 1 ie high compared to the industry norm.

28.11 B Analysis of financial statements is carried out so that the significance of the financial statements can be better understood. Comparisons through time and with other companies help to show how well the company is doing.

29 Mixed bank 1

29.1 $126,000

	$
Increase in net assets	88,000
Capital introduced	(50,000)
Drawings (68,000 + 20,000)	88,000
Profit for the year	126,000

29.2 A

	$
Debit cash	1,100,000
Credit share capital	250,000
Credit share premium	850,000

29.3 C Closing inventory should be valued at the lower of cost and NRV as per IAS 2.

29.4 D

	Share capital $	Share premium $
1 July 20X4	500,000	400,000
1 January 20X5 – bonus issue (250,000 × 50c)	125,000	(125,000)
1 April 20X5 – rights issue	62,500	125,000
	687,500	400,000

29.5 B

RECEIVABLES LEDGER CONTROL ACCOUNT

	$		$
Opening balance	138,400	Cash received	78,420
Credit sales	80,660	Payables contra	1,000
Dishonoured cheques	850	Irrecoverable debts written off	4,950
		Closing balance	135,540
	219,910		219,910

29.6 A

SUSPENSE ACCOUNT

	$		$
Opening balance	14,550	To cash account	10,000
		To rent account	4,550

29.7 B, D A revaluation of a non-current asset and a bonus issue of shares are both non-cash transactions.

29.8 D

	$
Opening inventory	138,600
Purchases	716,100
Closing inventory	(149,100)
Cost of sales	705,600

Sales = 705,600 × 100/70 = 1,008,000

29.9 C

	SPL	SOFP
	$	$
Prepaid insurance	8,200	
Payment January 20X5	38,000	
Prepayment July-Sept 20X5	(9,500)	9,500
	36,700	9,500

29.10 D All three statements are correct.

29.11 D Beta has issued a credit note for $500 to Alpha which Alpha has not yet received.

29.12 A Research expenditure is never capitalised.

29.13 D (i) and (iv) provide information about conditions which existed at the reporting date and are therefore adjusting.

29.14 $84,000

RENT RECEIVED

	$		$
Arrears b/f	3,800	In advance b/f	2,400
Rent in advance	3,000	Cash received	83,700
Rental income	84,000	In arrears	4,700
	90,800		90,800

29.15 B

	$
Allowance for receivables ((517,000 – 37,000) × 5%)	24,000
Previous allowance	(39,000)
Reduction	(15,000)
Debts written off	37,000
Charge to statement of profit or loss	22,000

29.16 D 2 and 3 only. Attributable overheads should be included in finished goods inventories.

29.17 B The proceeds will appear under **investing activities** and any profit will be deducted under **operating activities**.

29.18 C All four items will appear in the statement of changes in equity.

29.19 A

	$
Balance per bank statement	(38,600)
Bank charges	200
Lodgements	14,700
Cheque payments	(27,800)
Cheque payment misposted	8,400
Balance per cash book	(43,100)

30 Mixed bank 2

30.1 C

	$
Balance b/f ((280,000 − 14,000) × 20%)	53,200
Addition 1 April (48,000 × 20% × $\frac{9}{12}$)	7,200
Addition 1 Sept (36,000 × 20% × $\frac{4}{12}$)	2,400
	62,800
Sale (14,000 × 20% × $\frac{1}{2}$)	1,400
	64,200

30.2 D   Item 1 is wrong, as inventory should be valued at the **lower** of cost and net realisable value. Items 2, 3 and 4 are all correct.

30.3 D

RENT RECEIVABLE

	$			$
31.1.X6 Statement of profit or loss	27,500	1.2.X5 Balance b/f ($\frac{2}{3}$ × $6,000)		4,000
		1.4.X5 Received		6,000
		1.7.X5 Received		7,500
		1.10.X5 Received		7,500
31.1. X6 Balance c/f ($\frac{2}{3}$ × $7,500)	5,000	1.1.X6 Received		7,500
	32,500			32,500

30.4 D   20%. ROCE is defined as the profit on ordinary activities before interest and tax divided by capital employed = $300,000/$1.5m = 20%

30.5 D   Items (1) and (4) are adjusting events. Item (2) is a non-adjusting event but might be disclosed by way of note if material. Item (3) is a non-adjusting event that is disclosed by way of note.

30.6 $100

	$
Balance per Alta	3,980
Cheque not yet received	(270)
Goods returned	(180)
Contra entry	(3,200)
Revised balance per Alta	330
Balance per Ordan	(230)
Remaining difference	100

30.7 B, D   For returns, we need to debit the purchases returns account $130 to reverse the entry and debit the sales returns account $130 to record the entry correctly. The credit of $260 will be to suspense. So journal B is correct.

For machinery, we need to debit plant and machinery $18,000 and credit suspense $18,000. So journal D is correct.

30.8 B   Item (1), as the plant register is not part of the double entry system, the adjustment does not go through the suspense account.

Item (2), the transaction has been completely omitted from the records.

Therefore only items (3) and (4) affect the suspense account.

30.9 D

	$
Initial profit	630,000
Item (1) – increase in depreciation (4,800 – 480)	(4,320)
Item (2) – bank charges	(440)
Item (3) – no effect on P/L	–
Item (4) – no effect on P/L	–
Revised profit	625,240

30.10 A Statements (1) and (2) are correct.

30.11 C Only Statements (2) and (3) are correct.

30.12 B

	$
Closing receivables	458,000
Irrecoverable debts w/off	(28,000)
	430,000
Allowance required (5% × 430,000)	21,500
Existing allowance	(18,000)
Increase required	3,500
Charge to statement of profit or loss (28,000 + 3,500)	31,500

30.13 A

PLCA

	$		$
Cash paid to suppliers	988,400	Opening balance	384,600
Discounts received	12,600	Purchases	963,200
Purchases returns	17,400		
Contras	4,200		
Closing balance	325,200		
	1,347,800		1,347,800

30.14 A We need to increase drawings (debit) and reduce purchases (credit). Therefore journal A is the correct answer. Remember that we only adjust inventory at the year end.

30.15 D

	$	$
Sales (balancing figure)		1,080,000
Opening inventory	77,000	
Purchases	763,000	
	840,000	
Closing inventory	84,000	
Cost of sales (70%)		756,000
Gross profit ($\frac{30}{70}$ × 756,000)		324,000

30.16 C Statements (3) and (4) are correct. Statement (1) is incorrect because land is not usually depreciated. Statement (2) is incorrect as the gain on revaluation for property accounted for in accordance with IAS 16 is shown in the statement of profit or loss and other comprehensive income, under 'other comprehensive income' or in the separate statement of other comprehensive income. (NB gains on property classified as investment property per IAS 40 are recognised in profit or loss, but this is beyond the scope of this syllabus).

30.17 B

	$
Balance per bank (overdrawn)	(38,640)
Add outstanding lodgements	19,270
	(19,370)
Less unpresented cheques	(14,260)
Balance per cash book (overdrawn)	(33,630)

30.18 C 48,000 + 400 + 2,200 = 50,600

30.19 B   Opening inventory: debit statement of profit or loss, credit inventory account

Closing inventory: debit inventory account, credit statement of profit or loss

Remember that inventory is part of cost of sales, which is included in the statement of profit or loss.

30.20 D

	$'000
Fair value of consideration	4,000
Plus fair value of NCI at acquisition	2,200
Less net acquisition-date fair value of identifiable assets acquired and liabilities assumed	(4,750)
Goodwill	1,450

31 Mixed bank 3

31.1 A

	$
Sales (100%)	650,000
Cost of sales (70%)	455,000
Gross profit (30%)	195,000
Opening inventory	380,000
Purchases	480,000
	860,000
Closing inventory (bal. fig.)	(405,000)
Cost of sales	455,000
Calculated inventory	405,000
Actual inventory	220,000
Lost in fire	185,000

31.2 B   Income from investments and dividends paid on redeemable preference shares are recognised in the statement of profit or loss.

31.3 D   Dividends paid go through the SOCIE, not the statement of profit or loss and other comprehensive income. Also dividends declared after the end of the reporting period, are disclosed by way of note to the financial statements.

31.4 D   Goose Co has control over all three of these investments, and hence they are all subsidiaries.

31.5 B   Trade receivables = 838,000 – 72,000

= 766,000

Allowance for receivables = 60,000

Net balance = 766,000 – 60,000

= 706,000

31.6 A, D   Overheads must be included in the value of finished goods. Inventories should be valued at the lower of cost and net realisable value, not replacement cost.

31.7 C   Inventory is correctly recorded, so (2) and (4) are incorrect. Purchases are understated, so cost of sales are understated and so profit for 20X6 is overstated. Therefore (1) only is the correct answer.

31.8 D   1.26:1. (Receivables 176,000)/(trade payables 61,000 + overdraft 79,000).

31.9 A   All four items are correct.

31.10 A

INSURANCE

	$		$
Prepayment b/f	8,100	SPL	11,100
(3/4 × 10,800)		Prepayments c/f	9,000
Paid	12,000	(3/4 × 12,000)	
	20,100		20,100

31.11 C Statements (2) and (3) are incorrect. A bounced cheque is credited to the cash book and bank errors do not go through the cash book at all.

31.12 B

SHARE CAPITAL

	$m		$m
		Bal b/f	100
		Bonus (1/2 × 100m)	50
Bal c/f	210	Rights (2/5 × 150m)	60
	210		210

SHARE PREMIUM

	$m		$m
Bonus	50	Bal b/f	80
Bal c/f	60	Rights	30
	110		110

31.13 A All three statements are correct

31.14 A Items (2), (3) and (4) preserve double entry and so would not show up in a trial balance.

31.15 $2,850,000

	$'000
Fair value of consideration transferred	8,000
Plus fair value of NCI at acquisition ($1.20 × 3,000,000)	3,600
Less net acquisition-date fair value of identifiable assets acquired	
and liabilities assumed	(8,750)
Goodwill	2,850

31.16 B

	$
Opening inventory	40,000
Purchases	60,000
	100,000
Closing inventory	(50,000)
Cost of sales	50,000
This implies sales of	100,000 (50,000 × 2)

So either (1) is correct or (3) is correct.

31.17 D

RENT RECEIVED

	$		$
Arrears b/f	4,800	Prepayments b/f	134,600
		Cash received	834,600
Profit or Loss	828,700		
Prepayments c/f	144,400	Arrears c/f	8,700
	977,900		977,900

31.18 C

RECEIVABLES LEDGER CONTROL ACCOUNT

	$		$
Opening balance	284,680	Cash received	179,790
Credit sales	189,120	Irrecoverable debts written off	5,460
		Sales returns	4,920
		Contras	800
		Closing balance	282,830
	473,800		473,800

31.19 A $150,000

	$
Carrying amount at 01 August 20X0	200,000
Less depreciation	(20,000)
	180,000
Proceeds	25,000
Loss	5,000
Carrying amount of asset sold	(30,000)
Therefore carrying amount	150,000

32 Mixed bank 4

32.1 A   Share capital (1m × $1)   =   1,000,000

Share premium (1m × 50c) =   500,000

32.2 C   The correct answer is decrease current ratio and decrease quick ratio. Proposed dividends are not accrued for, so the only impact on the financial statements is to decrease cash.

32.3 D

RENTAL INCOME

	$		$
Arrears b/f	42,300	Prepayments b/f	102,600
Profit or Loss	858,600	Received	838,600
Prepayments c/f	88,700	Arrears c/f	48,400
	989,600		989,600

32.4 C   Journals A and B have their entries reversed and Journal D should not include the suspense account at all.

32.5 A   Per IAS 37 **provide** for probable losses of known amount and for which there is a constructive obligation, disclose possible losses, ignore remote ones.

32.6 A

RENT PAID

	$		$
Prepayment b/f	10,000		
(1/12 × 120,000)			
Paid – 1/1	30,000	SPL	136,000
– ¼	36,000		
– 1/7	36,000		
– 1/10	36,000	Prepayments c/f	12,000
		(1/3 × 36,000)	
	148,000		148,000

32.7 A

	$	$
Trade receivables	863,000	
Irrecoverable debts w/off	(23,000)	
	840,000	
Closing allowance for receivables (5% × 840,000)		42,000
Opening allowance		49,000
Reduction		(7,000)

Charge = 23,000 – 7,000
       = 16,000

32.8 C

SHARE CAPITAL

	$m		$m
		Bal b/f	1.0
		Share issue (note 1)	0.5
Bal c/f	2.0	Bonus (note 2)	0.5
	2.0		2.0

SHARE PREMIUM

	$m		$m
Bonus (note 2)	0.5	Bal b/f	1.4
Bal c/f	1.8	Share issue (note 1)	0.9
	2.3		2.3

Notes

1   Share issues of 1,000,000 shares raises $1,400,000. Shares are 50c each, so share capital is $500,000 and share premium $900,000.

2   Share capital is $1.5m or 3m shares. Therefore the bonus issue is 1m shares.

32.9 C   Inventory should be valued at the lower of cost and net realisable value, so Statement (1) is incorrect.

32.10 $192,600

	$
Held all year ((960,000 – 84,000) × 20%)	175,200
Addition (48,000 × 20% × ½)	4,800
Disposal (84,000 × 20% × ¾)	12,600
	192,600

32.11 B, C   Items A and D involve completed double entry and so do not go through the suspense account.

32.12 D   Debit drawings and credit the cost to purchases.

32.13 D

Cost	+	Profit	=	Selling price
100		25		125

PUP = (25/125 × 15,000) × 2/3   = $2,000

Inventories = $40,000 + $20,000 – $2,000   = $58,000

32.14 D   Tax is separately disclosed in the statement of profit or loss and other comprehensive income only, while profit for the period is shown in the statement of profit or loss and other comprehensive income and in the statement of changes in equity.

32.15 D   The reducing balance method charges more depreciation in earlier years.

32.16 D   A decrease in receivables should be added and so should an increase in payables. Therefore (3) and (4) are correct.

32.17 C $47,429

		$	$
Balance per P Johnson			46,747
Add:	Whitchurch Co invoice, previously omitted from ledger	267	
	Rectofon Co balance, previously omitted from list	2,435	
			3,102
			49,449
Less:	Error on posting of Bury Inc's credit note to ledger	20	
	P Fox & Son (Swindon) Co's balance included twice	2,000	
			2,020
Revised balance per receivables ledger			47,429

33   Mixed bank 5

33.1 B   Closing inventory $1,700

Purchases Units	Sales Units	Balance Units	Inventory value $	Unit cost $
10		10	3,000	300
12			3,000	250
		22	6,000	
	8		(2,400)	
		14	3,600	
6			1,200	200
		20	4,800	
	12		(3,100)*	
		8	1,700	

* 2 @ $300 + 10 @ $250 = $3,100

33.2 A   The IFRS Advisory Council

33.3 D

SUSPENSE ACCOUNT

	$		$
Cash	1,512	Bal b/f	759
		Receivables	131
		Bal c/f	622
	1,512		1,512

33.4 D   The sales daybook has been totalled incorrectly so the incorrect total has been posted to the control account. Each individual transaction has been posted to the individual accounts so when the two are compared there will be a difference of $200.

33.5 C

	$
Receivables allowance at 30.11.X8 (598,600 × 2%)	11,972
Opening allowance at 1.12.X7	(12,460)
Reduction in allowance (credit to statement of profit or loss)	(488)

Total credit to statement of profit or loss = 488 + 635 = $1,123

33.6 C

	$
Rent accrual (4/12 × $12,000)	(4,000)
Insurance prepayment (10/12 × $6,000)	5,000
Net increase in profit	1,000

33.7 D

	$
Non-current assets at 1 December 20X7	2,500,000
Depreciation charge for the year	(75,000)
Non-current asset disposed of (carrying amount)	(120,000)
Revaluation of non-current assets	500,000
	2,805,000
Non-current assets at 30 November 20X8	4,200,000
Therefore non-current assets acquired during the year	(1,395,000)
Sales proceeds from disposal of non-current asset	150,000
To be included in 'net cash flows from investing activities'	(1,245,000)

NON-CURRENT ASSETS

	$'000		$'000
Bal b/f	2,500	Depreciation	75
Revaluation	500	Disposal	120
Additions (bal fig)	1,395	Bal c/f	4,200
	4,395		4,395

33.8 A A transposition error in the sales day book will not cause a difference between the SLCA and the receivables ledger as the total of the SDB is posted to the SLCA and the individual balances in the SDB to the receivables ledger, therefore the same error will be posted to both the SLCA and the receivables ledger.

33.9 A Make sure you read the **dates carefully** as some of the goods are returned after 31 May and we are only concerned with sales returns at that date, which is the goods with a list price of $3,000. The value of the original sale is after the trade discount of 10%, so the actual amount invoiced for those goods is $2,700 ($3,000 × 90%).

33.10 C Only Statement (2) is correct. Development expenditure should be capitalised in accordance with IAS 38, however, research expenditure should be written off to the statement of profit or loss as incurred. Goodwill arising in a business combination should be capitalised as a non-current asset in the statement of financial position.

33.11 D All of the suggestions are flawed. LIFO is not permitted under IAS 2. Provisions cannot be created unless a constructive obligation exists, the amount can be reliably estimated and the likelihood of having to pay out cash is probable – none of these conditions are met, therefore a provision cannot be made. Development expenditure must be amortised over its useful life.

33.12 C Journal entries (1) and (2) should both be reversed.

33.13 C Carriage outwards is a distribution expense.

33.14 C

	Frog $'000	Toad $'000
Per question	650	160
Pre-acquisition retained earnings		(145)*
		15
Post-acquisition retained earnings of Toad	15	
Group retained earnings	665	

* 100 + (60/12 × 9)

33.15 D

	$
Profit before tax	36,000
Dividend	(21,000)
Added to retained earnings	15,000

33.16 D It reduces receivables.

33.17 A $2,185. Prepayment b/f $60 (2/3 × 90) + $2,145 – prepayment c/f $60 – accrual b/f $80 + accrual c/f $120 = $2,185.

33.18 B In Option (2), receivables and drawings are debits but discount received is a credit. In Option (4), capital and trade payables are credits but operating expenses are debits.

33.19 $205,000

Profit = Drawings + Increase in net assets – Capital introduced
= $77,000 + $173,000 – $45,000
= $205,000

33.20 B $130 loss

Capital = Assets – Liabilities

$50 + $100 + profit for the year = $90 – $70

$150 + profit for the year = $20

Therefore, the profit for the year is in fact a *loss* of $130.

34 Mixed bank 6

34.1 A X is a receivable of Y.

34.2 A $47,429

RECEIVABLES LEDGER CONTROL

	$		$
Balance b/d	50,241	Returns inwards	41,226
Sales	472,185	Irrecoverable debts written off	4,586
Cheques dishonoured	626	Cheques received	429,811
		Balance c/d	47,429
	523,052		523,052

34.3 A $2,098

CASH BOOK

	$		$
20X3		*20X3*	
31 May Balance b/d	873	31 May Bank charges	630
Error $(936 – 693)	243	Trade journals	52
Balance c/d	2,098	Insurance	360
		Business rates	2,172
	3,214		3,214
		1 May Balance b/d	2,098

34.4 B $87 loss

	$
Carrying amount: 9,000 × 0.7 × 0.7 × 0.7	3,087
Proceeds of sale	(3,000)
Loss on disposal	87

34.5 A Depreciation is an application of the accruals principle.

34.6 C Original annual depreciation = $(160,000 – 40,000)/8 years = $15,000 per year.

The change in the estimated life of the asset is made on 31 December 20X3, and this means that the change should be applied for the year ending 31 December 20X3.

		$
Cost		160,000
Accumulated depreciation to 31 December 20X2	(2 years × $15,000)	30,000
Carrying amount at 1 January 20X3		130,000
Residual value		40,000
Remaining depreciable amount as at 1 January 20X3		90,000

Remaining life from 1 January 20X3 = 4 years

Annual depreciation = $90,000/4 years = $22,500.

Net book value (carrying amount at 31 December 20X3 =

$130,000 – $22,500 = $107,500.

34.7 B $200 debit which should have been credited – correction will bring trial balance into agreement

34.8 C IAS 1 requires revenue to be disclosed on the face of the statement of profit or loss and other comprehensive income. It does not specify that a company must disclose profit before tax or gross profit on the face of the statement of profit or loss and other comprehensive income, however, most companies choose to do this. Dividends are disclosed in the statement of changes in equity if they are paid or are declared before the period end.

34.9 D ($73,680) + 102,480 – 87,240 = (58,440) $58,440 overdrawn

34.10 C (1), (2) and (3) are all incorrect.

34.11 A Cash received from customers, irrecoverable debts written off, and credits for goods returned by customers are credits to the sales ledger control account.

34.12 B $952,500 × 100/60 = $1,587,500

34.13 C

	$
Theoretical gross profit ($130,000 × 30%)	39,000
Actual gross profit ($130,000 – $49,800 – $88,600 + $32,000)	23,600
Shortfall – missing inventory	15,400

34.14 A

	$	$
Sales		240,000
Purchases	134,025	
∴ Drawings	(2,640)	
Inventory adjustment	(11,385)	
Cost of sales (50% × 240,000)		120,000
		120,000

34.15 D Incorrect answers: Goods purchased for cash – current assets remain the same, Payables paid out of an overdraft – current liabilities remain the same

34.16 D

PUP = 50,000 × 25/125 × 40% = $4,000

	Lexus group $'000
Revenue (350 + 150 – 50*)	450
Cost of sales (200 + 60 – 50* + 4)	214

* to remove intragroup sales

34.17 D

Share capital 75,000 + 15,000 + 30,000 =	120,000
Share premium 200,000 + 57,000 – 30,000 =	227,000
(Remember shares are 25c)	

34.18 D

35 Mixed bank 7

35.1 A

PLANT AND EQUIPMENT (CARRYING AMOUNT)

	$'000		$'000
b/d	155	Depreciation charge in year	25
Purchases of P+E	10	∴ Carrying amount of sale	15
		c/d	125
	165		165

	$'000
So, Carrying amount	15
Proceeds	(7)
Loss	8

35.2 D (2c + 3c) × 10,000,000. The final ordinary dividend is declared before the year end and so is accrued for. The preference dividend is classified as a finance cost.

35.3 A Working capital is increased as the company will receive cash for the share issue. Share premium is not reduced as it is not a bonus issue of shares, it will probably increase as the shares will probably be issued at a premium.

35.4 D A revaluation surplus will be presented as part of equity, not current liabilities.

35.5 C In Statement (i) both sides of the double entry posting from the cash book would be incorrect but equal in value, so this would not cause a trial balance imbalance. In Statement (ii), both expenses and non-current assets are debit balances in the trial balance, so posting to the wrong account in this case would not cause a trial balance imbalance.

35.6 D The dividends actually paid will go through the statement of changes in equity. The final proposed dividend of $120,000 is disclosed in the notes to the statement of financial position.

35.7 D Deferred development expenditure should be amortised over its useful life. If the conditions in IAS 38 are met, development expenditure **must** be capitalised. Trade investments are not intangible assets, they should be reported under non-current assets: investments in the SOFP.

35.8

RENT

	$		$
Bal b/f (rent in arrears)	4,800	Bal b/f (rent in advance)	134,600
SPL	828,700	Bank (bal. fig.)	834,600
Bal c/f (rent in advance)	144,400	Bal c/f (rent in arrears)	8,700
	977,900		977,900

35.9 D A, B and C are all income items reflected in the statement of profit or loss and other comprehensive income. In contrast D is reflected in the statement of financial position.

35.10 B Items A, C and D are all capital items, reflected in the statement of financial position.

35.11 A

PAYABLES LEDGER CONTROL ACCOUNT

	$		$
Cash paid to suppliers	1,364,300	Opening balance	318,600
Discounts received	8,200	Purchases	1,268,600
Purchases returns	41,200	Refunds received from suppliers	2,700
Contras	48,000		
Closing balance	128,200		
	1,589,900		1,589,900

35.12 C We need to increase the rent expenses (debit) and set up a liability to pay this amount (credit accruals).

35.13 C Wastage of inventory means that cost of sales is high relative to revenue.

35.14 A   Sales: current assets = 5:1

Therefore current assets ($30m/5) = $6m

Current ratio = 2:1

Therefore current liabilities ($6m/2) = $3m

Acid test ratio = 1.5:1

Therefore current assets – inventory ($3m × 1.5) = $4.5m

Hence, Inventory ($6m – $4.5m) = $1.5m

35.15 C   All three statements are correct.

35.16 A   485,000 + 48,600 + 18,100 – 368,400

35.17 B   = 60,000 + ((1,232,000 – 60,000) × 5%) – 90,000

35.18 A   Although we may use a trial balance as a step in preparing management or financial statements, the main reason is A.

Mock Exam 1

Foundations in Accountancy Financial Accounting (FFA)

Mock Exam 1 (Specimen Exam)

Questions	
Time allowed	2 hours
This exam is divided into two sections:	
Section A – ALL 35 questions are compulsory and MUST be attempted	
Section B – BOTH questions are compulsory and MUST be attempted	

DO NOT OPEN THIS EXAM UNTIL YOU ARE READY TO START UNDER EXAMINATION CONDITIONS

SECTION A – ALL 35 questions are compulsory and MUST be attempted

1   Which of the following calculates a sole trader's net profit for a period?

    A   Closing net assets + drawings – capital introduced – opening net assets
    B   Closing net assets – drawings + capital introduced – opening net assets
    C   Closing net assets – drawings – capital introduced – opening net assets
    D   Closing net assets + drawings + capital introduced – opening net assets   **(2 marks)**

2   Which of the following explains the imprest system of operating petty cash?

    A   Weekly expenditure cannot exceed a set amount.
    B   The exact amount of expenditure is reimbursed at intervals to maintain a fixed float.
    C   All expenditure out of the petty cash must be properly authorised.
    D   Regular equal amounts of cash are transferred into petty cash at intervals.   **(2 marks)**

3   Which of the following statements are **TRUE** of limited liability companies?

    1   The company's exposure to debts and liability is limited.
    2   Financial statements must be produced.
    3   A company continues to exist regardless of the identity of its owners.

    A   1 and 2 only
    B   1 and 3 only
    C   2 and 3 only
    D   1, 2 and 3   **(2 marks)**

4   Annie is a sole trader who does not keep full accounting records. The following details relate to her transactions with credit customers and suppliers for the year ended 30 June 20X6:

	$
Trade receivables, 1 July 20X5	130,000
Trade payables, 1 July 20X5	60,000
Cash received from customers	686,400
Cash paid to suppliers	302,800
Discounts received	2,960
Contra between payables and receivables ledgers	2,000
Trade receivables, 30 June 20X6	181,000
Trade payables, 30 June 20X6	84,000

What figure should appear for purchases in Annie's statement of profit or loss for the year ended 30 June 20X6?

$_____   **(2 marks)**

5   Which **TWO** of the following errors would cause the total of the debit column and the total of the credit column of a trial balance not to agree?

    1   A transposition error was made when entering a sales invoice into the sales day book.
    2   A cheque received from a customer was credited to cash and correctly recognised in receivables.
    3   A purchase of non-current assets was omitted from the accounting records.
    4   Rent received was included in the trial balance as a debit balance.   **(2 marks)**

6   At 31 December 20X5 the following require inclusion in a company's financial statements:

1   On 1 January 20X5 the company made a loan of $12,000 to an employee, repayable on 1 January 20X6, charging interest at 2% per year. On the due date she repaid the loan and paid the whole of the interest due on the loan to that date.

2   The company paid an annual insurance premium of $9,000 in 20X5, covering the year ending 31 August 20X6.

3   In January 20X6 the company received rent from a tenant of $4,000 covering the six months to 31 December 20X5.

For these items, what total figures should be included in the company's statement of financial position as at 31 December 20X5?

A   Current assets $10,000   Current liabilities $12,240
B   Current assets $22,240   Current liabilities $nil
C   Current assets $10,240   Current liabilities $nil
D   Current assets $16,240   Current liabilities $6,000   **(2 marks)**

7   A company's statement of profit or loss for the year ended 31 December 20X5 showed a net profit of $83,600. It was later found that $18,000 paid for the purchase of a motor van had been debited to the motor expenses account. It is the company's policy to depreciate motor vans at 25% per year on the straight line basis, with a full year's charge in the year of acquisition.

What would the net profit be after adjusting for this error?

$_____   **(2 marks)**

8   Xena has the following working capital ratios:

	20X9	20X8
Current ratio	1.2:1	1.5:1
Receivables days	75 days	50 days
Payables days	30 days	45 days
Inventory turnover	42 days	35 days

Which of the following statements is **CORRECT**?

A   Xena's liquidity and working capital has improved in 20X9.
B   Xena is receiving cash from customers more quickly in 20X9 than in 20X8.
C   Xena is suffering from a worsening liquidity position in 20X9.
D   Xena is taking longer to pay suppliers in 20X9.   **(2 marks)**

9   Are the following statements true or false?

	True	False
A statement of cash flows prepared using the direct method produces a different figure to net cash from operating activities from that produced if the indirect method is used	True	False
Rights issues of shares do not feature in a statement of cash flows.	True	False
A surplus on revaluation of a non-current asset will not appear as an item in a statement of cash flows.	True	False
A profit on the sale of a non-current asset will appear as an item under cash flows from investing activities in the statement of cash flows.	True	False

(2 marks)

10   A company receives rent from a large number of properties. The total received in the year ended 30 April 20X6 was $481,200.

The following were the amounts of rent in advance and in arrears at 30 April 20X5 and 20X6:

	30 April 20X5	30 April 20X6
	$	$
Rent received in advance	28,700	31,200
Rent in arrears (all subsequently received)	21,200	18,400

What amount of rental income should appear in the company's statement of profit or loss for the year ended 30 April 20X6?

A $486,500
B $460,900
C $501,500
D $475,900   **(2 marks)**

11   Which **TWO** of the following are differences between sole traders and limited liability companies?

1   A sole trader's financial statements are private; a company's financial statements are sent to shareholders and may be publicly filed.

2   Only companies that have capital invested into the business.

3   A sole trader is fully and personally liable for any losses that the business might make.

4   Revaluations can be carried out in the financial statements of a company, but not in the financial statements of a sole trader.

(2 marks)

12   Which of the following statements is **TRUE**?

A   The interpretation of an entity's financial statements using ratios is only useful for potential investors.

B   Ratios based on historical data can predict the future performance of an entity.

C   The analysis of financial statements using ratios provides useful information when compared with previous performance or industry averages.

D   An entity's management will not assess an entity's performance using financial ratios. **(2 marks)**

13   A company's motor vehicles (at cost) account at 30 June 20X6 is as follows:

MOTOR VEHICLES (AT COST)

	$		$
Balance b/f	35,800	Disposal	12,000
Additions	12,950	Balance c/f	36,750
	48,750		48,750

What opening balance should be included in the following period's trial balance for Motor vehicles (at cost) at 1 July 20X6?

A $36,750 Dr
B $48,750 Dr
C $36,750 Cr
D $48,750 Cr   **(2 marks)**

14 Which **TWO** of the following items must be disclosed in the note to the financial statements for intangible assets?

1   The useful lives of intangible assets capitalised in the financial statements
2   A description of the development projects that have been undertaken during the period
3   A list of all intangible assets purchased or developed in the period
4   Impairment losses written off intangible assets during the period

(2 marks)

15 Which of the following statements are **CORRECT**?

1   Capitalised development expenditure must be amortised over a period not exceeding five years.

2   Capitalised development costs are shown in the statement of financial position under the heading of non-current assets.

3   If certain criteria are met, research expenditure must be recognised as an intangible asset.

A   2 only
B   2 and 3
C   1 only
D   1 and 3   (2 marks)

16 The following transactions relate to Rashid's electricity expense ledger account for the year ended 30 June 20X9:

	$
Prepayment brought forward	550
Cash paid	5,400
Accrual carried forward	650

What amount should be charged to the statement of profit or loss in the year ended 30 June 20X9 for electricity?

A $6,600
B $5,400
C $5,500
D $5,300   (2 marks)

17 At 30 June 20X5 a company's allowance for receivables was $39,000. At 30 June 20X6 trade receivables totalled $517,000. It was decided to write off debts totalling $37,000. The receivables allowance was to be adjusted to an amount equivalent to 5% of the trade receivables based on past events.

What figure should appear in the statement of profit or loss for the year ended 30 June 20X6 for these items?

$_____   (2 marks)

18 The total of the list of balances in Valley's payables ledger was $438,900 at 30 June 20X6. This balance did not agree with Valley's payables ledger control account balance. The following errors were discovered:

1   A contra entry of $980 was recorded in the payables ledger control account, but not in the payables ledger.

2   The total of the purchase returns daybook was undercast by $1,000.

3   An invoice for $4,344 was posted to the supplier's account as $4,434.

What amount should Valley report in its statement of financial position as accounts payable at 30 June 20X6?

A $436,830
B $438,010
C $439,790
D $437,830   (2 marks)

19 According to IAS 2 *Inventories*, which **TWO** of the following costs should be included in valuing the inventories of a manufacturing company?

    1   Carriage inwards
    2   Carriage outwards
    3   Depreciation of factory plant
    4   General administrative overheads   **(2 marks)**

20 Prisha has not kept accurate accounting records during the financial year. She had opening inventory of $6,700 and purchased goods costing $84,000 during the year. At the year end she had $5,400 left in inventory. All sales are made at a mark up on cost of 20%.

What is Prisha's gross profit for the year?

$_____   **(2 marks)**

21 At 31 December 20X4 a company's capital structure was as follows:

	$
Ordinary share capital (500,000 shares of 25c each)	125,000
Share premium account	100,000

In the year ended 31 December 20X5 the company made a rights issue of one share for every two held at $1 per share and this was taken up in full. Later in the year the company made a bonus issue of one share for every five held, using the share premium account for the purpose.

What was the company's capital structure at 31 December 20X5?

	Ordinary share capital	*Share premium account*
A	$450,000	$25,000
B	$225,000	$250,000
C	$225,000	$325,000
D	$212,500	$262,500

(2 marks)

22 Which of the following should appear in a company's statement of changes in equity?

    1   Total comprehensive income for the year
    2   Amortisation of capitalised development costs
    3   Surplus on revaluation of non-current assets

    A   1, 2 and 3
    B   2 and 3 only
    C   1 and 3 only
    D   1 and 2 only   **(2 marks)**

23 The plant and machinery account (at cost) of a business for the year ended 31 December 20X5 was as follows:

PLANT AND MACHINERY (AT COST)

20X5	$	20X5	$
1 Jan Balance b/f	240,000	31 Mar Transfer to disposal account	60,000
30 Jun Cash purchase of plant	160,000	31 Dec Balance c/f	340,000
	400,000		400,000

The company's policy is to charge depreciation at 20% per year on the straight-line basis, with proportionate depreciation in the years of purchase and disposal.

What should be the depreciation charge for the year ended 31 December 20X5?

    A $68,000
    B $64,000
    C $61,000
    D $55,000   **(2 marks)**

24   The following extracts are from Hassan's financial statements:

	$
Profit before interest and tax	10,200
Interest	(1,600)
Tax	(3,300)
Profit after tax	5,300
Share capital	20,000
Reserves	15,600
	35,600
Loan liability	6,900
	42,500

What is Hassan's return on capital employed?

_____ %   (2 marks)

---

25   Is each of the following statements about sales tax true or false?

Sales tax is an expense to the ultimate consumer of the goods purchased.	True	False
Sales tax is recorded as income in the accounts of the entity selling the goods.	True	False

(2 marks)

---

26   Q's trial balance failed to agree and a suspense account was opened for the difference. Q does not keep receivables and payables control accounts. The following errors were found in Q's accounting records:

1   In recording an issue of shares at par, cash received of $333,000 was credited to the ordinary share capital account as $330,000.

2   Cash of $2,800 paid for plant repairs was correctly accounted for in the cash book but was credited to the plant asset account.

3   The petty cash book balance of $500 had been omitted from the trial balance.

4   A cheque for $78,400 paid for the purchase of a motor car was debited to the motor vehicles account as $87,400.

Which of the errors will require an entry to the suspense account to correct them?

A   1, 2 and 4 only
B   1, 2, 3 and 4
C   1 and 4 only
D   2 and 3 only   (2 marks)

---

27   Prior to the financial year end of 31 July 20X9, Cannon Co has received a claim of $100,000 from a customer for providing poor quality goods which have damaged the customer's plant and equipment. Cannon Co's lawyers have stated that there is a 20% chance that Cannon will successfully defend the claim.

Which of the following is the correct accounting treatment for the claim in the financial statements for the year ended 31 July 20X9?

A   Cannon should neither provide for nor disclose the claim.
B   Cannon should disclose a contingent liability of $100,000.
C   Cannon should provide for the expected cost of the claim of $100,000.
D   Cannon should provide for an expected cost of $20,000.   (2 marks)

28   Gareth, a sales tax registered trader purchased a computer for use in his business. The invoice for the computer showed the following costs related to the purchase:

	$
Computer	890
Additional memory	95
Delivery	10
Installation	20
Maintenance (one year)	25
	1,040
Sales tax (17.5%)	182
Total	1,222

How much should Gareth capitalise as a non-current asset in relation to the purchase?

$_____   **(2 marks)**

29   The following bank reconciliation statement has been prepared by a trainee accountant:

	$
Overdraft per bank statement	3,860
Less: Unpresented cheques	9,160
	5,300
Add: Outstanding lodgements	16,690
Cash at bank	21,990

What should be the correct balance per the cash book?

A $21,990 balance at bank as stated
B $3,670 balance at bank
C $11,390 balance at bank
D $3,670 overdrawn   **(2 marks)**

30   The IASB's *Conceptual Framework for Financial Reporting* identifies characteristics which make financial information faithfully represent what it purports to represent.

Which **TWO** of the following are examples of those qualitative characteristics?

1   Accruals
2   Completeness
3   Going concern
4   Neutrality   **(2 marks)**

31   The following control account has been prepared by a trainee accountant:

RECEIVABLES LEDGER CONTROL ACCOUNT

	$		$
Opening balance	308,600	Cash	148,600
Credit sales	154,200	Interest charged on overdue	
		accounts	2,400
Cash sales	88,100	Irrecoverable debts	4,900
Contras against credit balances	4,600	Allowance for receivables	2,800
in payables ledger			
		Closing balance	396,800
	555,500		555,500

What should the closing balance be when all the errors made in preparing the receivables ledger control account have been corrected?

A $395,200
B $304,300
C $309,500
D $307,100   **(2 marks)**

32   Are the following material events, which occured after the reporting date and before the financial statements are approved, adjusting events?

A valuation of property providing evidence of impairment in value at the reporting date	Yes	No
Sale of inventory held at the reporting date for less than cost	Yes	No
Discovery of fraud or error affecting the financial statements	Yes	No
The insolvency of a customer with a debt owing at the reporting date which is still outstanding	Yes	No

(2 marks)

33   A company values its inventory using the FIFO method. At 1 May 20X5 the company had 700 engines in inventory, valued at $190 each. During the year ended 30 April 20X6 the following transactions took place:

20X5
1 July   Purchased 500 engines at $220 each
1 November   Sold 400 engines for $160,000

20X6
1 February   Purchased 300 engines at $230 each
15 April   Sold 250 engines for $125,000

What is the value of the company's closing inventory of engines at 30 April 20X6?

A $188,500
B $195,500
C $166,000
D $106,000

(2 marks)

34   Amy is a sole trader and had assets of $569,400 and liabilities of $412,840 on 1 January 20X8. During the year ended 31 December 20X8 she paid $65,000 capital into the business and she paid herself wages of $800 per month.

At 31 December 20X8, Amy had assets of $614,130 and liabilities of $369,770.

What is Amy's profit for the year ended 31 December 20X8?

$_____

(2 marks)

35   Bumbly Co extracted the trial balance for the year ended 31 December 20X7. The total of the debits exceeded the credits by $300.

Which of the following could explain the imbalance?

A   Sales of $300 were omitted from the sales day book.
B   Returns inward of $150 were extracted to the debit column of the trial balance.
C   Discounts received of $150 were extracted to the debit column of the trial balance.
D   The bank ledger account did not agree with the bank statement by a debit of $300.   (2 marks)

SECTION B – BOTH questions are compulsory and MUST be attempted

Background

36   Keswick Co acquired 80% of the share capital of Derwent Co on 1 June 20X5. The summarised draft statements of profit or loss for Keswick Co and Derwent Co for the year ended 31 May 20X6 are shown below:

	Keswick Co	Derwent Co
	$'000	$'000
Revenue	8,400	3,200
Cost of sales	(4,600)	(1,700)
Gross profit	3,800	1,500
Distribution costs	(1,500)	(510)
Administrative costs	(700)	(450)
Profit before tax	1,600	540
Tax	(600)	(140)
Profit of the year	1,000	400

During the year Keswick Co sold goods costing $1,000,000 to Derwent Co for $1,500,000. At 31 May 20X6, 30% of these goods remained in Derwent Co's inventory.

Task 1

Use the information above to complete the following financial statement:

	$'000
Revenue	_____
Less: Cost of sales	_____
Gross profit	_____
Less:	
Distribution costs	_____
Administrative costs	_____
Profit before tax	_____
Less: Tax	_____
Profit for the year	_____
Attributable to:	
Equity owners of Keswick Co	_____
Non-controlling interest	_____

(11 marks)

Task 2

Does each of the following factors illustrate the existence of a parent – subsidiary relationship?

1.	50% of all shares and debt being held by an investor	Yes	No
2.	Greater than 50% of the preference shares being held by an investor	Yes	No
3.	Control	Yes	No
4.	Greater than 50% of the equity shares being held by an investor	Yes	No
5.	100% of the equity shares being held by an investor	Yes	No
6.	Significant influence	Yes	No
7.	Non-controlling interest	Yes	No
8.	Greater than 50% of preference shares and debt being held by an investor	Yes	No

(4 marks)

(Total = 15 marks)

37 Malright, a limited liability company, has an accounting year end of 31 October. The accountant is preparing the financial statements as at 31 October 20X7. A trial balance has been prepared.

Task 1

Do each of the following items belong on the statement of financial position (SOFP) as at 31 October 20X7?

	Dr $'000	Cr $'000	Belongs on SOFP as at 31 October 20X7
Buildings at cost	740		Yes/No
Buildings accumulated depreciation at 1 November 20X6		60	Yes/No
Plant at cost	220		Yes/No
Plant accumulated depreciation at 1 November 20X6		110	Yes/No
Bank balance		70	Yes/No
Revenue		1,800	Yes/No
Net purchases	1,140		Yes/No
Inventory at 1 November 20X6	160		Yes/No
Cash	20		Yes/No
Trade payables		250	Yes/No
Trade receivables	320		Yes/No
Administrative expenses	325		Yes/No
Allowance for receivables at 1 November 20X6		10	Yes/No
Retained earnings at 1 November 20X6		130	Yes/No
Equity shares, $1		415	Yes/No
Share premium account		80	Yes/No
	2,925	2,925	

(4 marks)

Task 2

The allowance for receivables is to be increased to 5% of trade receivables. The allowance for receivables is treated as an administrative expense.

The year end journal for allowance for receivables is given below. Prepare the double entry by selecting the correct option for each row.

Trade receivable	Debit / Credit / No debit or credit
Administrative expenses	Debit / Credit / No debit or credit
Allowance for receivables	Debit / Credit / No debit or credit
Revenue	Debit / Credit / No debit or credit

Complete the following:

The amount included in the statement of profit or loss after the allowance is increased to 5% of trade receivables is $_____'000. (3 marks)

Task 3

Plant is depreciated at 20% per annum using the reducing balance method and buildings are depreciated at 5% per annum on their original cost. Depreciation is treated as a cost of sales expense.

The year end journal for buildings and plant depreciation is given below. Using the information above, prepare the double entry by selecting the correct option for each row.

Administrative expenses	Debit / Credit / No debit or credit
Cost of sales	Debit / Credit / No debit or credit
Buildings cost	Debit / Credit / No debit or credit
Plant cost	Debit / Credit / No debit or credit
Buildings accumulated depreciation	Debit / Credit / No debit or credit
Plant accumulated depreciation	Debit / Credit / No debit or credit

Calculate the depreciation charge for the below for the year ended 31 October 20X7. Use the information above to help you.

Buildings $_____'000
Plant $_____'000   **(5 marks)**

Task 4

Closing inventory has been counted and is valued at $75,000.

Ignoring the depreciation charge calculated earlier, what is the cost of sales for the year?

$_____'000   **(1.5 marks)**

Task 5

An invoice of $15,000 for energy costs relating to the quarter ended 30 November 20X7 was received on 2 December 20X7. Energy costs are included in administrative expenses.

Complete the following statements:

The double entry to post the year end adjustment for energy costs is:

Dr _____

Cr _____

The amount to be posted within the year end adjustment double entry above is $_____'000.

(1.5 marks)

(Total = 15 marks)

Answers to
Mock Exam 1
(Specimen Exam)

Note. The ACCA examining team's answers follow these BPP Learning Media answers.

SECTION A

1   A   Remember that: closing net assets = opening net assets + capital introduced + profit – drawings.

2   B   Under the imprest system, a reimbursement which equals the total of expense vouchers paid out, is made at intervals to maintain the petty cash balance at a certain amount.

3   C   The shareholder's exposure to debts is limited, not the company's.

4

PAYABLES CONTROL ACCOUNT

	$		$
Cash paid to suppliers	302,800	Balance b/f	60,000
Discounts received	2,960	**Purchases (bal fig)**	**331,760**
Contra	2,000		
Balance c/f	84,000		
	391,760		391,760

5   2,4   Errors (1) and (3) will not cause a trial balance imbalance. In error (1), the incorrect amount will be posted to both sales and receivables (Dr receivables, Cr sales). In error (3), the complete omission of the transaction will have no effect on the trial balance.

6   B

Current assets	$
Loan asset	12,000
Interest (12,000 × 12%)	240
Prepayment (8/12 × 9,000)	6,000
Accrued rent	4,000
	22,240

7

	$
Profit	83,600
Purchase of van	18,000
Depreciation 18,000 × 25%	(4,500)
	97,100

8   C   The ratios given relate to working capital and liquidity. The ratios have all worsened from 20X8 to 20X9, suggesting a worsening liquidity position. Receivables days have gone up, meaning that customers are taking longer to pay. Payables days have gone down, meaning that Xena is paying suppliers more quickly. Inventory turnover days have gone up, meaning inventories are being held for longer.

9   Only the third statement is true. The direct and indirect method both produce the same figure for cash from operating activities. A rights issue of shares does feature in a statement of cash flows as cash is received for the issue, a bonus issue, however, would not feature as no cash is received. A profit on the sale of a non-current asset would not appear as an investing cash flow, rather the cash received from the sale would appear as an investing cash flow and the profit on the sale would be added back to profit before tax under the indirect method of calculating cash from operating activities.

10   D

	$
Balance b/f (advance)	28,700
Balance b/f (arrears)	(21,200)
Cash received	481,200
Balance c/f (advance)	(31,200)
Balance c/f (arrears)	18,400
	475,900

11   1,3   A sole trader's financial statements are not publicly available, but they might be made available to some third parties, for example, the tax authorities.

12   C   Ratio analysis is useful for different users of financial statements, including management, potential investors, the government, employees and so on. Historical performance can give an indication of what might occur in the future, especially if a trend is shown, but it cannot be used to accurately predict the future.

13   A   Motor vehicles – cost account is an asset and so the balance brought forward must be a debit. It is $36,750 as this is the figure that balances the account.

14   1,4   An entity is **not** required to disclose a description of the development projects undertaken in the period, or a list of all intangible assets purchased or developed in the period. It is however, required to: disclose a description, the carrying amount and remaining amortisation period of any individual intangible asset that is **material** to the entity's financial statements, and distinguish between internally generated intangible assets capitalised in the period and those acquired in the period.

15   A   Statement (2) is the only correct statement. Statement (1) is incorrect because capitalised development expenditure is amortised over its useful life. Statement (3) is incorrect because research expenditure is never capitalised.

16   A

	$
Balance b/f	550
Expense incurred (cash)	5,400
Accrual c/f	650
	6,600

17

	$	$
Debts written off		37,000
Movement in allowance:		
(517 – 37) × 5%	24,000	
Less opening allowance	39,000	
		(15,000)
Receivables expense		22,000

18   D

	$
Balance per ledger	438,900
Less contra	(980)
Posting error	(90)
Corrected balance	437,830

The individual returns from the purchase returns day book are posted to the individual accounts in the memorandum payables ledger, so the list of balances does not need to be adjusted for error (2).

19   1,3   Carriage outwards is a distribution expense. General administrative overheads should not be included per IAS 2.

20   (6,700 + 84,000 – 5,400) × 20% = $17,060

21   B   Share capital = 125,000 + 62,500 rights issue of 250,000 25c shares (500,000/2) + 37,500 bonus issue of 150,000 25c shares (750,000/5) = 225,000

Share premium = 100,000 + 187,500 rights issue (250,000 × 75c) – 37,500 bonus issue (150,000 × 25c) = 250,000

22   C   Amortisation of development costs will appear in the statement of profit or loss, not the statement of changes in equity.

23   D

	$
Depreciation:	
Jan–Mar 240,000 × 20% × 3/12	12,000
Apr–Jun (240,000 – 60,000) × 20% × 3/12	9,000
Jul–Dec (180,000 + 160,000) × 20% × 6/12	34,000
	55,000

24   10,200/42,500 = 24%

25   Only the first statement is true. Sales tax is merely collected by the business, the ultimate consumer bears the expense.

26   B   All of the errors would require an entry to the suspense account to correct them.

27   C   It is probable that Canon will have to pay $100,000 for the claim, therefore a provision is required.

28   $1,015   1,040 – 25 = $1,015. The maintenance costs should not be capitalised. The sales tax is recoverable as Gareth is registered for sales tax, therefore is should not be capitalised.

29   B

	$
Overdraft per bank statement	(3,860)
Less: Unpresented cheques	(9,160)
Add: Outstanding lodgements	16,690
Cash at bank	3,670

30   2,4   Completeness and neutrality are two characteristics given in the *Conceptual framework*. Going concern is the underlying assumption and accruals is not a stated characteristic.

31   D

RECEIVABLES LEDGER CONTROL ACCOUNT

	$		$
Opening balance	308,600	Cash	148,600
Credit sales	154,200	Contras	4,600
Interest charged on overdue accounts	2,400	Irrecoverable debts	4,900
		Closing balance	**307,100**
	465,200		465,200

32   The answer is Yes for all of the statements. All of the events are adjusting events.

33   A   Closing inventory:

	$
50 × $190	9,500
500 × $220	110,000
300 × $230	69,000
	188,500

34   $32,400   Closing net assets = opening net assets + capital introduced + profit – drawings

	$
Opening assets	569,400
Opening liabilities	(412,840)
Capital introduced	65,000
Drawings (800 × 12)	(9,600)
	211,960
Profit (bal fig)	**32,400**
Closing net assets (614,130 – 369,770)	244,360

35   C   Discounts received are recorded as a credit balance and appear as other income in the statement of profit or loss: Dr payables, Cr discounts received.

SECTION B

36 **Task 1**

KESWICK GROUP

CONSOLIDATED STATEMENT OF PROFIT OR LOSS FOR THE YEAR ENDED 31 MAY 20X6

	$'000
Revenue (8,400 + 3,200 – 1,500)	10,100
Less: Cost of sales (4,600 + 1,700 – 1,500 + 150)	(4,950)
Gross profit	5,150
Less:	
Distribution costs	(2,010)
Administration costs	(1,150)
Profit before tax	1,990
Less: Tax (600 + 140)	(740)
Profit of the year	1,250

Attributable to:

Equity owners of Keswick Co	1,170
Non-controlling interest ($400,000 × 20%)	80

Task 2

1	Significant influence	No
2	Control	Yes
3	Non-controlling interest	Yes
4	Greater than 50% of the equity shares being held by an investor	Yes
5	100% of the equity shares being held by an investor	Yes
6	Greater than 50% of the preference shares being held by an investor	No
7	50% of all shares and debt being held by an investor	No
8	Greater than 50% of preference shares and debt being held by an investor	No

37 MALRIGHT CO

Task 1

	Belongs on SOFP as at 31 October 20X7?
Buildings at cost	Yes
Buildings accumulated depreciation at 1 November 20X6	No
Plant at cost	Yes
Plant accumulated depreciation at 1 November 20X6	No
Bank balance	Yes
Revenue	No
Net purchases	No
Inventory at 1 November 20X6	No
Cash	Yes
Trade payables	Yes
Trade receivables	Yes
Administrative expenses	No
Allowance for receivables at 1 November 20X6	No
Retained earnings at 1 November 20X6	No
Equity shares, $1	Yes
Share premium account	Yes

Task 2

The year end journal for the receivables allowance is:

Trade receivable	No debit or credit
Administrative expenses	Debit
Allowance for receivables	Credit
Revenue	No debit or credit

The amount included in the statement of profit or loss after the allowance is increased to 5% of trade receivables is $6,000,000.

Workings (in $'000):

Required end allowance is 320,000 × 5% = $16,000

As the allowance for doubtful debts has an existing balance of $10,000, the allowance must be increased by $6,000.

Task 3

The year end journal for buildings and plant depreciation is:

Administrative expenses	No debit or credit
Cost of sales	Debit
Buildings cost	No debit or credit
Plant cost	No debit or credit
Buildings accumulated depreciation	Credit
Plant accumulated depreciation	Credit

The depreciation charge for the year ended 31 October 20X7 is:

Buildings $37,000 (*Working*: 740 × 5%)
Plant $22,000 (*Working*: (220 −110) × 20%)

Task 4

The cost of sales for the year is $1,225,000.

Working	$'000
Opening inventory	160
Purchases	1,140
Closing inventory	(75)
	1,225

Task 5

The year end adjustment for energy costs is:

Debit Administrative expenses
Credit Accrual

Energy cost accrual
15,000 × 2/3 = $10,000

ACCA's exam answers to
Specimen Exam

FA and FFA Full Specimen Exam Answers

Question	Correct answer	Marks
1	Closing net assets + drawings – capital introduced – opening net assets	2
2	The exact amount of expenditure is reimbursed at intervals to maintain a fixed float	2
3	2 and 3 only	2
4	331,760	2
5	A cheque received from a customer was credited to cash and correctly recognised in receivables Rent received was included in the trial balance as a debit balance	2
6	Current assets: $22,240 Current liabilities: $nil	2
7	97,100	2
8	Xena is suffering from a worsening liquidity position in 20X9	2
9	A statement of cash flows prepared using the direct method produces a different figure to net cash from operating activites from that produced if the indirect method is used – **False** Rights issues of shares do not feature in a statement of cash flows – **False** A surplus on revaluation of a non-current asset will not appear as an item in a statement of cash flows – **True** A profit on the sale of a non-current asset will appear as an item under cash flows from investing activities in a statement of cash flows – **False**	2
10	$475,900	2
11	A sole trader's financial statements are private; a company's financial statements are sent to shareholders and may be publicly filed A sole trader is fully and personally liable for any losses that the business might make	2
12	The analysis of financial statements using ratios provides useful information when compared with previous performance or industry averages	2
13	$36,750 Dr	2
14	The useful lives of intangible assets capitalised in the financial statements Impairment losses written off intangible assets during the period	2

Question	Correct answer	Marks
15	2 only	2
16	$6,600	2
17	22,000	2
18	$437,830	2
19	Carriage inwards Depreciation of factory plant	2
20	17,060	2
21	Ordinary share capital: $225,000 Share premium account: $250,000	2
22	1 and 3 only	2
23	$55,000	2
24	24%	2
25	Sales tax is an expense to the ultimate customer of the goods purchased – **True** Sales tax is recorded as income in the accounts of the entity selling the goods – **False**	2
26	1, 2, 3 and 4	2
27	Cannon should provide for the expected cost of the claim of $100,000	2
28	1,015	2
29	$3,670 balance at bank	2
30	Completeness Neutrality	2
31	$307,100	2
32	Yes Yes Yes Yes	2
33	$188,500	2
34	$32,400	2
35	Discounts received of $150 was extracted to the debit column of the trial balance	2

MTQ 36

Task 1 (11 marks)

Consolidated statement of profit or loss for the year ended 31 May 20X6	
	$000
Revenue	8,400 + 3,200 – 1,500
Less: Cost of sales	4,600 + 1,700 – 1,500 + (30% × 500)
Gross profit	5,150
Less: Distribution costs	2,010
Administrative costs	1,150
Profit before tax	1,990
Less: Tax	740
Profit for the year	1,250
Attributable to:	
Equity owners of Keswick Co	Group profit after tax - Non-controlling interest
Non-controlling interest	80

Task 2 (4 marks)

Significant influence	No
Control	Yes
Non-controlling interest	Yes
Greater than 50% of the equity shares being held by an investor	Yes
100% of the equity shares being held by an investor	Yes
Greater than 50% of the preference shares being held by an investor	No
50% of all shares and debt being held by an investor	No
Greater than 50% of preference shares and debt being held by an investor	No

MTQ 37

Task 1 (4 marks)

Buildings at cost	Yes
Buildings accumulated depreciation at 1 November 20X6	No
Plant at cost	Yes
Plant accumulated depreciation at 1 November 20X6	No
Bank balance	Yes
Revenue	No
Net purchases	No

BPP
LEARNING MEDIA

Inventory at 1 November 20X6	No
Cash	Yes
Trade payables	Yes
Trade receivables	Yes
Administrative expenses	No
Allowance for receivables at 1 November 20X6	No
Retained earnings at 1 November 20X6	No
Equity shares, $1	Yes
Share premium account	Yes

Task 2 (3 marks)

Trade receivable	No debit or credit
Administrative expenses	Debit
Allowance for receivables	Credit
Revenue	No debit or credit
Profit or loss	6 thousand

Task 3 (5 marks)

Administrative expenses	No debit or credit
Cost of sales	Debit
Buildings cost	No debit or credit
Plant cost	No debit or credit
Buildings accumulated depreciation	Credit
Plant accumulated depreciation	Credit
Buildings depreciation charge	37 thousand
Plant depreciation charge	22 thousand

Task 4 (1.5 marks)

| Cost of sales | 1225 thousand |

Task 5 (1.5 marks)

Debit	Administrative expenses
Credit	Accrual
Adjustment value	10 thousand

Mock Exam 2

Foundations in Accountancy
Financial Accounting (FA)

Mock Exam 2

Questions	
Time allowed	2 hours
This exam is divided into two sections:	
Section A – ALL 35 questions are compulsory and MUST be attempted	
Section B – BOTH questions are compulsory and MUST be attempted	

DO NOT OPEN THIS EXAM UNTIL YOU ARE READY TO START UNDER EXAMINATION CONDITIONS

SECTION A

1   In accordance with IAS 37 *Provisions, Contingent Liabilities and Contingent Assets*, which of the following criteria must be present in order for a company to recognise a provision?

      1   There is a present obligation as a result of past events.
      2   It is probable that a transfer of economic benefits will be required to settle the obligation.
      3   A reliable estimate of the obligation can be made.

      A   All three criteria must be present
      B   1 and 2 only
      C   1 and 3 only
      D   2 and 3 only   **(2 marks)**

2   Which of the following types of book-keeping error is never indicated when a trial balance of nominal ledger account balances is extracted?

      A   Errors of commission
      B   Errors of omission
      C   Errors of principle
      D   Transposition errors   **(2 marks)**

3   Nooma Co owns 55% of the ordinary shares of Matic Co. What is the correct accounting treatment of the revenues and costs of Matic Co in the consolidated statement of profit or loss of the Nooma Group?

      A   The revenues and costs of Matic Co are added to the revenues and costs of Nooma Co on a line by line basis.

      B   55% of the profit after tax of Matic Co should be added to Nooma Co's consolidated profit after tax.

      C   55% of the revenues and costs of Matic Co are added to the revenues and costs of Nooma Co on a line by line basis.

      D   Only dividends received from Matic Co are shown in the consolidated statement of profit or loss of Nooma Co.   **(2 marks)**

4   Your firm's cash book at 30 April 20X8 shows a balance at the bank of $2,490. Comparison with the bank statement at the same date reveals the following differences:

	$
Unpresented cheques	840
Bank charges not in cash book	50
Receipts not yet credited by the bank	470
Dishonoured cheque not in cash book	140

      What is the adjusted bank balance per the cash book at 30 April 20X8?

      $_____ .   **(2 marks)**

5   W Co, a sales tax registered trader, bought a new printing machine. The cost of the machine was $80,000, excluding sales tax at 17.5%. The delivery costs were $2,000 and installation costs were $5,000. Before using the machine to print customers' orders, a test was undertaken and the paper and ink cost $1,000.

      What should be the cost of the machine in the company's statement of financial position?

      $_____   **(2 marks)**

6   Which of the following correctly defines 'equity' according to the IASB's *Conceptual Framework for Financial Reporting*?

A   Equity is a present obligation of the entity arising from past events, the settlement of which is expected to result in an outflow from the entity of resources embodying economic benefit.

B   Equity is a resource controlled by an entity as a result of past events and from which future economic benefits are expected to flow to the entity.

C   Equity is the residual interest in the assets of the entity after deducting all its liabilities.

D   Equity is increases in economic benefits during the accounting period in the form of inflows or enhancements of assets or decreases of liabilities.   **(2 marks)**

7   Which of the following is a qualitative characteristic of financial information included in the IASB's *Conceptual framework for financial reporting*?

A   Relevance
B   Fair presentation
C   Consistency
D   Accruals   **(2 marks)**

8   S & Co sell three products – A, B and C. The following information was available at the year end.

	Basic $ per unit	Super $ per unit	Luxury $ per unit
Original cost	10	9	20
Estimated selling price	9	12	26
Selling and distribution costs	1	4	5
	units	units	units
Units of inventory	500	1,250	850

In accordance with IAS2 *Inventories*, what is the value of inventory at the year end?

$_____   **(2 marks)**

9   A car was purchased by a business in May 20X1 for:

	$
Cost	10,000
Road fund licence	150
Total	10,150

The business adopts a date of 31 December as its year end.

The car was traded in for a replacement vehicle in August 20X4 at an agreed value of $5,000.

It has been depreciated at 25% per annum on the reducing-balance method, charging a full year's depreciation in the year of purchase and none in the year of sale.

What was the profit or loss on disposal of the vehicle during the year ended December 20X4?

A   Loss of $2,890
B   Profit of $781
C   Profit of $2,500
D   Profit of $3,750   **(2 marks)**

10   At 1 January 20X3, Attila Co had an allowance for receivables of $35,000. At 31 December 20X3, the trade receivables of the company were $620,000. It was decided to:

1   Write off (as uncollectable) receivables totalling $30,000; and
2   Adjust the allowance for receivables to an amount equivalent to 5% of receivables.

What is the combined expense that should appear in the company's statement of profit or loss for the year, for irrecoverable debts and the allowance for receivables?

A $24,500
B $26,000
C $34,000
D $35,500   **(2 marks)**

11   The annual sales of a company are $235,000 including sales tax at 17.5%. Half of the sales are on credit terms, half are cash sales. The receivables in the statement of financial position are $23,500.

What is the output tax?

$_____   **(2 marks)**

12   Beta purchased some plant and equipment on 1 July 20X1 for $40,000. The scrap value of the plant in ten years' time is estimated to be $4,000. Beta's policy is to charge depreciation on the straight line basis, with a proportionate charge in the period of acquisition.

What is the depreciation charge on the plant in Beta's financial statements for the year ended 30 September 20X1?

A $900
B $1,000
C $3,600
D $4,000   **(2 marks)**

13   The following figures are taken from the statement of financial position of GEN Co.

	$m
Inventory	2
Receivables	3
Cash	1
Payables	3
Bank loan repayable in 5 years time	3

What is GEN Co's current ratio?

A   1.33
B   2.00
C   1.00
D   0.33   **(2 marks)**

14   A particular source of finance has the following characteristics: fixed payments, a fixed repayment date, it is secured on the assets of the company and the payments are classified as an expense.

Which of the following best describes this source of finance?

A   A redeemable preference share
B   An irredeemable preference share
C   A loan note
D   An overdraft   **(2 marks)**

15   Tong Co acquired 100% of the $100,000 ordinary share capital of Cheek Co for $1,200,000 on 1 January 20X5 when the retained earnings of Cheek Co were $550,000 and the balance on the revaluation surplus was $150,000. At the date of acquisition the fair value of plant held by Cheek Co was $80,000 higher than its carrying value.

What is the goodwill arising on the acquisition of Cheek Co?

A $320,000
B $400,000
C $470,000
D $550,000   (2 marks)

16   During the year ended 31 December 20X1, Alpha Rescue had the following transactions on the receivables ledger.

	$
Receivables at 1 January 20X1	100,000
Receivables at 31 December 20X1	107,250
Goods returned	12,750
Amounts paid into the bank from receivables	230,000
Discount received	75,000

What were the sales for the year?

A $107,250
B $240,000
C $250,000
D $320,000   (2 marks)

17   Financial analysts calculate ratios from the published financial statements of large companies. Which one of the following reasons is **UNLIKELY** to be a reason why they calculate and analyse financial ratios?

A   Ratios can reduce lengthy or complex financial statements into a fairly small number of more easily-understood indicators.

B   Ratios can predict a company's future performance.

C   Ratios can help with comparisons between businesses in the same industry.

D   Ratios can indicate changes in the financial performance and financial position of a business over time.   (2 marks)

18   Cat Co has held 85% of the share capital of Dog Co for many years. During the current year Cat Co sold goods to Dog Co for $15,000, including a mark up of 25% on cost. 60% of these goods were still in inventory at the year end.

The following extract was taken from the accounting records of Cat Co and Dog Co at 31 March 20X8.

	Cat Co $'000	Dog Co $'000
Opening inventory	650	275
Closing Inventory	750	400

What is the figure for inventory to be included in the statement of financial position of the Cat Group at 31 March 20X8?

A $1,151,800
B $1,152,250
C $1,197,750
D $1,148,200   (2 marks)

19 A company's quick ratio has increased from 0.9:1 at 31 December 20X1 to 1.5:1 at
    31 December 20X2. Which of the following events could explain this increase?

    A   Improved inventory control
    B   The refinancing of a long-term loan
    C   A reduction in payables
    D   An increase in payables   (2 marks)

20 Which of the following represents an error of original entry?

    A   The purchase of goods for resale using cash was debited to the purchases account and credited
         to the cash book using the incorrect amount in both cases.

    B   The purchase of goods for resale using cash was debited to the motor vehicles account and
         credited to the cash book using the correct amount in both cases.

    C   The purchase of goods for resale using cash was debited to the purchases account and credited
         to the sales day book using the correct amount in both cases.

    D   The purchase of goods for resale using cash was debited to the purchases account but no credit
         entry was made.   (2 marks)

21 A machine was purchased for $100,000 on 1 January 20X1 and was expected to have a useful life of
    10 years. After 3 years, management revised their expectation of the remaining useful life to 20 years.
    The business depreciates machines using the straight line method.

    What is the carrying value of the machine at 31 December 20X5?

    $_____   (2 marks)

22 Your organisation has received a statement of account from one of its suppliers, showing an outstanding
    balance due to them of $1,350. On comparison with your ledger account, the following is determined:

    •   Your ledger account shows a credit balance of $260.
    •   The supplier has disallowed a settlement discount of $80 due to late payment of an invoice.
    •   The supplier has not yet allowed for goods returned at the end of the period of $270.
    •   Cash in transit of $830 has not been received by the supplier.

    Following consideration of these items, what is the unreconciled difference between the two records?

    A $nil
    B $10
    C $90
    D $180   (2 marks)

23 A company is preparing its statement of cash flows for the year ended 31 December 20X2. Relevant
    extracts from the accounts are as follows.

Statement of profit or loss	$	
Depreciation	15,000	
Profit on sale of non-current assets	40,000	

Statement of financial position	20X2	20X1
	$	$
Plant and machinery – cost	185,000	250,000
Plant and machinery – depreciation	45,000	50,000

    Plant and machinery additions during the year were $35,000. What is the cash flow arising from the
    sale of non-current assets?

    A $40,000
    B $100,000
    C $120,000
    D $135,000   (2 marks)

24   Which body is responsible for issuing International Financial Reporting Standards?

    A   IFRS Interpretations Committee
    B   IFRS Advisory Council
    C   International Accounting Standards Board
    D   The United Nations   **(2 marks)**

25   Teo Co acquired 95% of the ordinary share capital of Mat Co 31 December 20X0. The following information relates to Mat Co:

	20X0	20X1
	$'000	$'000
Retained earnings	700	800
Revaluation surplus	–	100
	700	900

The fair value of the non-controlling interest in Mat Co at the date of acquisition was $45,000.

What is the amount reported for non-controlling interest in the statement of financial position of the Teo Group as at 31 December 20X1?

$_____   **(2 marks)**

26   Which of the following statements is **NOT** correct?

1   AZ owns 25% of the preferred (non-voting) share capital of BX, which means that BX is an associate of AZ.

2   CW has a 10% shareholding in DY and can appoint 4 out of 6 directors to the board of DY, so DY is classified as a subsidiary of CW.

3   ES has significant influence over FT, which means that FT is an associate of ES.

4   GR owns 55% of the share capital of HU, but by agreement with the minority shareholder, does not have control or significant influence over the financial and operating policies of HU, so HU is a simple investment of GR.

        (2 marks)

27   Which, if any, of the following journal entries is correct according to their narratives?

		Debit	Credit
		$	$
1	B receivables ledger account	450	
	Irrecoverable debts account		450
	Irrecoverable balance written off		
2	Investments: Q ordinary shares	100,000	
	Share capital		100,000
	80,000 shares of 50c each issued at $1.25 in exchange for shares in Q.		
3	Suspense account	1,000	
	Motor vehicles account		1,000
	Correction of error – debit side of Motor vehicles account undercast by $1,000		

    A   None of them
    B   1 only
    C   2 only
    D   3 only   **(2 marks)**

28 Jay Co values inventories on the first in first out (FIFO) basis. Jay Co has 120 items of product A valued at $8 each in inventory at 1 October 20X9. During October 20X9, the following transactions in product A took place.

3 October	Purchases	180 items at $9 each
4 October	Sales	150 items at $12 each
8 October	Sales	80 items at $15 each
18 October	Purchases	300 items at $10 each
22 October	Sales	100 items at $15 each

What is the closing balance on the inventory account at 31 October 20X9?

$_____ **(2 marks)**

29 Fred's trial balance did not balance so he opened a suspense account with a debit balance of $346. Control accounts are maintained for receivables and payables.

Fred discovered the following:

1 The sales day book was undercast by $400.

2 Purchases of $520 from the purchases day book have only been recorded in the payables ledger control account.

3 Profit on sale of non-current assets of $670 had been recorded in the sundry income account as $760.

What is the remaining balance on Fred's suspense account after these errors have been corrected?

A $264 credit
B $136 debit
C $956 debit
D $1,266 debit **(2 marks)**

30 Charles Co entered into the following transactions:

1 He made a credit sale to Mary allowing a 5% trade discount on the list price of $640, and a further 5% discount for immediate cash payment.

2 He purchased goods with a list price of $600 and received a 10% trade discount and further 2% discount for payment within seven days. He paid three days later.

How much discount should be recorded in the Discounts Received account as a result of the above transactions?

A $10.80
B $30.40
C $62.40
D $70.80 **(2 marks)**

31 Where, in a company's financial statements complying with International Financial Reporting Standards, should you find the proceeds of non-current assets sold during the period?

A Statement of cash flows and statement of financial position
B Statement of changes in equity and statement of financial position
C Statement of profit or loss and other comprehensive income and statement of cash flows
D Statement of cash flows only **(2 marks)**

32 If the current ratio for a company is equal to its quick ratio, which of the following statements is true?

A The current ratio must be greater than one.
B The company does not carry any inventory.
C Receivables plus cash is greater than payables minus inventories.
D Working capital is positive. **(2 marks)**

33   The closing inventory of Epsilon amounted to $284,000 at 30 September 20X1, the reporting date. This total includes two inventory lines about which the inventory taker is uncertain.

  1   500 items which had cost $15 each and which were included at $7,500. These items were found to have been defective at the end of the reporting period. Remedial work after the reporting period cost $1,800 and they were then sold for $20 each. Selling expenses were $400.

  2   100 items which had cost $10 each. After the reporting period they were sold for $8 each, with selling expenses of $150.

What figure should appear in Epsilon's statement of financial position for inventory?

  A $283,650
  B $283,800
  C $284,000
  D $284,450   **(2 marks)**

34   Which **TWO** of these statements about research and development expenditure are correct?

  1   If certain conditions are satisfied, research and development expenditure must be capitalised.

  2   One of the conditions to be satisfied if development expenditure is to be capitalised is that the technical feasibility of the project is reasonably assured.

  3   The amount of capitalised development expenditure for each project should be reviewed each year. If circumstances no longer justify the capitalisation, the balance should be written off over a period not exceeding five years.

  4   Development expenditure may only be capitalised if it can be shown that adequate resources will be available to finance the completion of the project.

                                                                                                                 (2 marks)

35   A company measures the average time to collect receivables as:

[Receivables at end of financial year/Annual credit sales] × 365 days

Accounting ratios have just been calculated from the financial statements for the financial year that has just ended. These show an abnormally high average time to collect receivables, compared with ratios calculated for the previous financial year.

Which of the following may help to explain this unusually high turnover period for trade receivables?

  1   There was an unusually large sale on credit close to the end of the financial year.

  2   The company has seasonal trade, and sales in the final quarter of the year are always higher than in the other quarters.

  3   However, sales in the final quarter of the year that has just ended were lower than in the previous year.

                                                                                                                 (2 marks)

SECTION B

36　You have been given the following information relating to a limited liability company called Nobrie. This company is preparing financial statements for the year ended 31 May 20X4.

NOBRIE
STATEMENT OF PROFIT OR LOSS
FOR THE YEAR ENDED 31 MAY 20X4

	$'000
Revenue	66,600
Cost of sales	(13,785)
Gross profit	52,815
Distribution costs	(7,530)
Administrative expenses	(2,516)
Investment income	146
Finance cost	(1,177)
Profit before tax	41,738
Tax	(9,857)
Profit for the year	31,881
Retained earnings brought forward at 1 June 20X3	28,063
Retained earnings carried forward at 31 May 20X4	59,944

NOBRIE
STATEMENTS OF FINANCIAL POSITION AS AT 31 MAY

	20X4		20X3	
	$'000	$'000	$'000	$'000
Assets				
Non-current assets				
Cost		144,844		114,785
Accumulated depreciation		(27,433)		(26,319)
		117,411		88,466
Current assets				
Inventory	24,931		24,065	
Trade receivables	18,922		13,238	
Cash	3,689		2,224	
		47,542		39,527
Total assets		164,953		127,993
Equity and liabilities				
Equity				
Ordinary share capital	27,000		23,331	
Share premium	14,569		10,788	
Revaluation surplus	15,395		7,123	
Retained earnings	59,944		28,063	
		116,908		69,305
Non current liabilities				
6% loan note		17,824		24,068
Current liabilities				
Bank overdraft	5,533		6,973	
Trade payables	16,699		20,324	
Taxation	7,989		7,323	
		30,221		34,620
Total equity and liabilities		164,953		127,993

Additional information

(a)   During the year ended 31 May 20X4, the company sold a piece of equipment for $3,053,000, realising a profit of $1,540,000. There were no other disposals of non-current assets during the year.

(b)   Depreciation of $5,862,000 has been charged.

(c)   There were no amounts outstanding in respect of interest payable or receivable as at 31 May 20X3 or 20X4.

(d)   There were no dividends paid or declared during the year.

Task 1

Complete the following cash flows from operating activities section in the statement of cash flows for Nobrie for the year ended 31 May 20X4.

NOBRIE
STATEMENT OF CASH FLOWS FOR THE YEAR ENDED 30 MAY 20X4

	$'000
Cash flow from operating activities	
Net profit before tax	_____
Adjustments for	
Depreciation	_____
Profit on equipment disposal	
Investment income	_____
Interest paid	_____
Operating profit before working capital changes	
Increase in inventory	_____
Increase in receivables	
Decrease in payables	
Cash generated from operations	
Interest received	
Interest paid	_____
Tax paid	
Net cash flows from operating activities	_____

(8 marks)

Task 2

The carrying amount of property, plant and equipment disposed is $_____'000.

The purchases of property, plant and equipment for the year ended 31 May 20X4 is $_____,000.

(5 marks)

Task 3

Which **TWO** of the following increases in equity accounts are shown as cash inflows in the cash flows from financing section of the statement of cash flows:

1   Increase in share capital
2   Increase in share premium
3   Increase in revaluation reserve
4   Increase in retained earnings

(2 marks)

(Total = 15 marks)

37 The draft statements of financial position of Spyder and its subsidiary company Phly at 31 October 20X5 are as follows.

	Spyder		Phly	
	$'000	$'000	$'000	$'000
Assets				
Non-current assets				
Tangible assets				
Land and buildings		315,000		278,000
Plant		285,000		220,000
		600,000		498,000
Investment				
Shares in Phly at cost		660,000		–
Current assets				
Inventory	357,000		252,000	
Receivables	525,000		126,000	
Bank	158,000		30,000	
		1,040,000		408,000
		2,300,000		906,000
Equity and liabilities				
Equity				
$1 ordinary shares		1,500,000		600,000
Reserves		580,000		212,000
		2,080,000		812,000
Current liabilities				
Payables		220,000		94,000
Total equity and liabilities		2,300,000		906,000

The following information is also available.

(a) Spyder purchased 480 million shares in Phly some years ago, when Phly had a credit balance of $95 million in reserves. The fair value of the non-controlling interest at the date of acquisition was $165 million.

(b) At the date of acquisition the freehold land of Phly was valued at $70 million in excess of its book value. The revaluation was not recorded in the accounts of Phly.

(c) Phly's inventory includes goods purchased from Spyder at a price that includes a profit to Spyder of $12 million.

(d) At 31 October 20X5 Phly owes Spyder $25 million for goods purchased during the year.

Task 1

Calculate the total goodwill on acquisition by completing the table below.

Calculation of goodwill

	$'000
Fair value of consideration transferred	_____
Fair value of NCI at acquisition	_____
Net acquisition-date fair value of identifiable assets acquired and liabilities assumed:	_____
Goodwill	_____

(5 marks)

Task 2

Complete the following consolidated statement of financial position for Spyder as at 31 October 20X5.

SPYDER GROUP
CONSOLIDATED STATEMENT OF FINANCIAL POSITION AS AT 31 OCTOBER 20X5

	$'000
Assets	
Non-current assets	
Goodwill	
Land and buildings	_____
Plant	_____
Current assets	_____
Inventory	
Receivables	_____
Bank	_____
Total assets	_____
Equity and liabilities	_____
Equity attributable to owners of the parent	
$1 ordinary shares	
Reserves	
Non-controlling interest	_____
Current liabilities	_____
Payables	
Total equity and liabilities	_____
	_____

(10 marks)

(Total = 15 marks)

Answers to Mock Exam 2

SECTION A

1 A All three criteria must be present.

2 C The existence of a transposition error should always be revealed by a trial balance. Errors of omission and commission may or may not be revealed, depending on the nature of the error and whether the error has resulted fin a mismatch between debt and credit entries in the nominal ledger accounts. An error of omission is never revealed, because there have been no entries in the nominal ledger for the omitted item.

3 A Matic Co is a subsidiary of Nooma Co, so the results of Matic Co should be consolidated on a line by line basis with the results of Nooma Co.

4

Original cash book figure	2,490
Adjustment re charges	(50)
Adjustment re dishonoured cheque	(140)
	2,300

5 $88,000

	$
Cost of machine	80,000
Installation	5,000
Delivery	2,000
Testing	1,000
	88,000

6 C A is the definition of a liability, B is the definition of an asset and D is the definition of income according to the *Conceptual framework*.

7 A Relevance is a qualitative characteristic. The other options are accounting concepts.

8 $31,000

	Cost	Net realisable value	Lower of cost & NRV	Units	Value
	$	$	$		$
A	10	8	8	500	4,000
B	9	8	8	1,250	10,000
C	20	21	20	850	17,000
					31,000

9 B $781 profit

	$
Cost	10,000
20X1 Depreciation	2,500
	7,500
20X2 Depreciation	1,875
	5,625
20X3 Depreciation	1,406
	4,219
20X4 Part exchange	5,000
Profit	781

10 A

	$	$
Amount written off		30,000
Allowance for receivables at 31 December 20X3	29,500	
5% × $(620,000 – 30,000)		
Allowance for receivables at 1 January 20X3	35,000	
Reduction in allowance for receivables		(5,500)
Combined expense		24,500

11    $35,000

$$\text{Output tax} = \frac{235,000}{117.5} \times 17.5$$

12   A $900.   ($36,000/10) × $^3/_{12}$

13   B   This is the ratio of current assets to current liabilities. C is wrong as the five year bank loan would not normally be included with current liabilities. A is the quick ratio (excludes inventory).

14   C   It is a loan note. It is not a preference share because it is secured. An overdraft does not have a fixed return or a fixed repayment date and is not secured.

15   A

	$	$
Fair value of consideration		1,200,000
Net assets at acquisition as represented by		
Share capital	100,000	
Retained earnings	550,000	
Revaluation surplus	150,000	
Fair value adjustment	80,000	
		(880,000)
Goodwill		320,000

16   C $250,000

RECEIVABLES LEDGER CONTROL ACCOUNT

	$		$
Bal b/f	100,000	Bank	230,000
Sales (balancing figure)	250,000	Returns	12,750
		Bal c/f	107,250
	350,000		350,000

Discounts received refer to purchases and go in the payables ledger control account.

17   B   Ratios can be used to analyse financial performance, and to make comparisons of performance over time and between different businesses in the same industry, but they cannot usually provide a reliable indicator of insolvency, especially if they are prepared only once a year.

18   D $1,148,200

	$'000
Unrealised profit (15,000 × 25/125 × 60%)	1.8
Inventory (750 + 400 – 1.8)	1,148.2

19   C   Quick ratio = current assets excluding inventories / current liabilities.

The quick ratio does not include inventories or long term loans, so A and B will have no effect. An increase in payables would reduce the quick ratio.

20   A   B and C are errors of principle, D is an error of omission.

21    $63,000.

Carrying value at the end of year 3:   100,000 – (100,000 × 3/10) = $70,000

Carrying value at the end of year 5:   70,000 – (70,000 × 2/20)   = $63,000

22   C $90

	$
Ledger balance	260
Add back: disallowed discount	80
returns goods	270
cash in transit	830
Total balance	1,440
As stated by the supplier	1,350
Unreconciled difference	90

				$
23	C	$120,000		
				$
		Sale proceeds (balancing figure)		120,000
		Carrying amount (see below)		80,000
		Profit on sale		40,000
		Carrying amount at 31 December 20X1 (250,000 – 50,000)		200,000
		Additions		35,000
				235,000
		Carrying amount of disposals (balancing figure)		(80,000)
		Depreciation		(15,000)
		Carrying amount at 31 December 20X2 (185,000 – 45,000)		140,000

24 C The International Accounting Standards Board is responsible for issuing IFRSs.

		$
25		$
	Fair value of NCI at acquisition	45,000
	Plus NCI's share of post-acquisition retained earnings (and other reserves)	
	((800 – 100) × 5% + 100 × 5%)	10,000
	NCI at reporting date (31 December 20X1)	55,000

26 1 An investor must have significant influence over the investee in order for the investee to be classified as an associate, therefore (3) is correct. If the investor owns between 20% and <50% of the **ordinary shares (voting)** of the investee, significant influence can be assumed, (1) is not true as the shares held do not have voting rights. For an investee to be classified as a subsidiary, the investor must have control over the investee. Control can be demonstrated if the investor can appoint the majority of board members of the investee, so (2) is correct. (4) is also correct as despite its 55% shareholding, GR does not have control or significant influence over HU and as such is not classified as a subsidiary or as an associate, but as a simple trade investment.

27 A All three are incorrect. In (1) and (3) the debit and credit entries should be reversed and (2) should show a credit of $60,000 to the share premium account.

28 $2,700

Date		No. of items	Unit price $	Value $
1.10.X9	Balance	120	8	960
3.10.X9	Purchases	180	9	1,620
	Balance	300		2,580
4.10.X9	Sales	(120)	8	(960)
	Sales	(30)	9	(270)
	Balance	150		1,350
8.10.X9	Sales	(80)	9	(720)
	Balance	70		630
18.10.X9	Purchases	300	10	3,000
	Balance	370		3,630
22.10.X9	Sales	(70)	9	(630)
	Sales	(30)	10	(300)
	Balance	270		2,700

29 A

SUSPENSE ACCOUNT

	$		$
Bal b/f	346	Purchases (2)	520
Bal c/f	264	Sundry income (3)	90
	610		610

30 A Discounts received account for cash/settlement discounts received from suppliers on purchases. Transaction (1) relates to discounts on sales so does not impact the discounts received account. Therefore in transaction (2), purchase net of trade discount = $600 × 90% = $540 (trade discounts are not accounted for separately). Early settlement discount = 2% × $540 = $10.80.

31 D Proceeds of a sale of non-current assets will only be shown in the statement of cash flows.

32 B The company does not carry any inventory. The calculation for the quick ratio excludes inventory. So if the current ratio (including inventory) and the quick ratio (excluding inventory) are the same, this must mean that 'inventory' is zero.

33 A $283,650

	$	
	284,000	
Item 1	–	No change as NRV exceeds cost
Item 2	(350)	Reduce to NRV (1,000 – 650)
	283,650	

34 2,4 Statements (1) and (3) are incorrect.

35 1 If there has been a large credit sale near the end of the financial year, the amount owed will be included within receivables at the year end and trade receivables may be unusually high. If so, the average time for receivables to pay may be distorted, because year-end receivables are used to calculate the turnover ratio.

A large volume of sales in the final quarter of every year may explain why the measurement of the average collection period is long every year, but not why the collection period should be unusually long compared with the previous year.

Comparatively low sales in the final quarter would be more likely to result in a shorter-than-normal measurement of the average collection period.

SECTION B

36 **Task 1**

NOBRIE
STATEMENT OF CASH FLOWS FOR THE YEAR ENDED 30 MAY 20X4

	$'000	$'000
Cash flow from operating activities		
Net profit before tax	41,738	
Adjustments for		
Depreciation	5,862	
Profit on equipment disposal	(1,540)	
Investment income	(146)	
Interest paid	1,177	
Operating profit before working capital changes	47,091	
Increase in inventory	(866)	
Increase in receivables	(5,684)	
Decrease in payables	(3,625)	
Cash generated from operations	36,916	
Interest received*	146	
Interest paid*	(1,177)	
Tax paid (W1)	(9,191)	
Net cash flows from operating activities		26,694

Working for tax paid

TAXATION

	$'000		$'000
Tax paid (bal fig)	9,191	Balance b/fwd	7,323
Balance c/fwd	7,989	Statement of profit or loss	9,857
	17,180		17,180

Task 2

The carrying value of property, plant and equipment disposals is $1,513,000.

The purchases of property, plant and equipment is $28,048,000.

Workings for property, plant and equipment:

PROPERTY, PLANT AND EQUIPMENT

	$'000		$'000
Balance b/fwd (carrying value)	88,466	Disposals (carrying value) (see working below)	1,513
Revaluation (15,395 – 7,123)	8,272	Depreciation	5,862
Purchases (bal fig)	28,048	Balance c/fwd (carrying value)	117,411
	124,786		124,786

Disposals

	$'000
Proceeds	3,053
Profit	1,540
∴ Carrying value of disposals	1,513

Task 3

Answer: 1, 2

Only the increase in share capital and share premium from the cash issue of shares is shown as a cash inflow on the statement of cash flows.

The increase in the revaluation reserve is a non-cash transaction and therefore is not included in the statement of cash flows.

The increase in retained earnings is shown as profit before tax in cash flows from operating activities in the statement of cash flows.

37   **Task 1**

Calculation of goodwill

	$'000	$'000
Fair value of consideration transferred		660,000
Plus fair value of NCI at acquisition		165,000
Less net acquisition-date fair value of identifiable assets acquired and liabilities assumed:		
Share capital	600,000	
Retained earnings at acquisition	95,000	
Fair value adjustment at acquisition	70,000	
		(765,000)
Goodwill		60,000

Task 2

SPYDER GROUP
CONSOLIDATED STATEMENT OF FINANCIAL POSITION AS AT 31 OCTOBER 20X5

	$'000	$'000
Assets		
Non-current assets		
Goodwill		60,000
Land and buildings (315 + 278 + 70)		663,000
Plant (285 + 220)		505,000
		1,228,000
Current assets		
Inventory (357 + 252 – 12)	597,000	
Receivables (525 + 126 – 25)	626,000	
Bank (158 + 30)	188,000	
		1,411,000
		2,639,000
Equity and liabilities		
Equity attributable to owners of the parent		
$1 ordinary shares		1,500,000
Reserves (W2)		661,600
Non-controlling interest (W3)		188,400
		2,350,000
Current liabilities		
Payables (220 + 94 – 25)		289,000
Total equity and liabilities		2,639,000

Workings

1   *Group structure*

$$\frac{480m}{600m} = 80\%$$

2   *Retained earnings*

	Spyder $m	Phly $m
Per question	580.0	212
Adjustment (unrealised profit)	(12.0)	
Pre-acquisition retained earnings		(95)
		117
Group share of post-acq'n ret'd earnings:		
Phly (80% × 117)	93.6	
Group retained earnings	661.6	

3   *Non-controlling interest*

	$m
Fair value of NCI at acquisition	165.0
Plus NCI's share of post-acquisition retained earnings (20% × 117)	23.4
NCI at reporting date	188.4

REVIEW FORM

Name: _____   Address: _____

_____

Date: _____   _____

How have you used this Practice & Revision Kit?
(Tick one box only)

☐ On its own (book only)

☐ On a BPP in-centre course_____

☐ On a BPP online course

☐ On a course with another college

☐ Other _____

Why did you decide to purchase this Practice & Revision Kit? *(Tick one box only)*

☐ Have used complementary Interactive Text

☐ Have used BPP Texts in the past

☐ Recommendation by friend/colleague

☐ Recommendation by a lecturer at college

☐ Saw advertising

☐ Other _____

During the past six months do you recall seeing/receiving any of the following?
(Tick as many boxes as are relevant)

☐ Our advertisement in *ACCA Student Accountant*

☐ Our advertisement in *Teach Accounting*

☐ Other advertisement __

☐ Our brochure with a letter through the post

☐ ACCA E-Gain email

☐ BPP email

☐ Our website www.bpp.com

Which (if any) aspects of our advertising do you find useful?
(Tick as many boxes as are relevant)

☐ Prices and publication dates of new editions

☐ Information on Practice & Revision Kit content

☐ Facility to order books

☐ None of the above

Have you used the companion Interactive Text for this subject?   ☐ Yes   ☐ No

Your ratings, comments and suggestions would be appreciated on the following areas

	Very useful	Useful	Not useful
Introductory section (How to use this Practice & Revision Kit)	☐	☐	☐
'Do You Know' checklists	☐	☐	☐
'Did You Know' checklists	☐	☐	☐
Possible pitfalls	☐	☐	☐
Questions	☐	☐	☐
Answers	☐	☐	☐
Mock exams	☐	☐	☐
Structure & presentation	☐	☐	☐
Icons	☐	☐	☐

	Excellent	Good	Adequate	Poor
Overall opinion of this Kit	☐	☐	☐	☐

Do you intend to continue using BPP products?   ☐ Yes   ☐ No

Please note any further comments and suggestions/errors on the reverse of this page.
The author of this edition can be emailed at: accaqueries@bpp.com

REVIEW FORM (continued)

Please note any further comments and suggestions/errors below